ONE FLEW INTO THE CUCKOO'S EGG

My Autobiography

Bill Oddie

WINDSOR
PARAGON

First published 2008
by
Hodder & Stoughton
This Large Print edition published 2008
by
BBC Audiobooks Ltd
by arrangement with
Hodder & Stoughton

UK Hardcover ISBN 978 1 408 42855 9
UK Softcover   ISBN 978 1 408 42856 6

British Library Cataloguing in Publication Data

Printed and bound in Great Britain by
CPI Antony Rowe, Chippenham, Wiltshire

To my family. I love you all far too much
to get you involved in this book!

Acknowledgements

'What are acknowledgements?' I asked Helen from Hodder. She said, 'acknowledgements are whatever you like.' I thought, OK I'll go with that. So here is a list of some of the people who are responsible for 'whatever I like.' People who have enriched my life by bringing joy, excitement, inspiration, fun, support, comfort, love, companionship, and so on. Some of the names you will recognize. I like what they do. Others you won't know. I like what they are. I acknowledge them all.

Duke Ellington, Frank Sinatra, Spike Jones, Tom Lehrer, Chris Barber, Mingus, Weather Report, Keith Jarrett, Kid Creole, Randy Newman, The Band, Little Feat, Steely Dan, Joni Mitchell, Paul Simon, Shel Silverstein, Amos Garrett, Albert Lee, Dolly Parton, Michael Jackson, Prince, Djivan Gasparyan, HMV, Shirley Maclaine, Jane Fonda, Kylie. Buster Keaton, Tom and Jerry, the Simpsons. E.T. *Spinal Tap*. Bernstein, for *West Side Story*, Ashman and Menken for *Little Shop of Horrors*. Jim Henson. Stanley Matthews, Ted Dexter, Steve Ovett, John McEnroe, Christiano Ronaldo, Jeremy Guscott. Billy Bunter. Hancock. Rick Mayall, Eddie Izzard, Billy Connolly, Alan Partridge, Monty Python. *Soap*, *Six Feet Under*, *Dick Barton*, *Quatermass*. Renoir, Breugel, Bosch. Sir Peter Scott, Sir David Attenborough, Hans and Lotte, Sooty (but not Sweep). Mints, Metaza and Cox's Orange Pippins.

Mr Trott, Mr Hutton. Marian, Anastasia, Jean,

Jo, Debbie, Wiz and Flick. Eric Ennion, Richard Richardson. Tony, Richard and Robin. Andy, the late Dave Hunt. Derek. Peter Holden and Tim Appleton. Maria at Country Innovation. Mac and Tracy. Dave Lee, George Layton, Charlie Dore, Mike Gibbs. Dave and Joy McRae. Eric Idle, the other two Goodies. Jim Franklin. Uli Hintner. The Stockers, Dave Spivack. Taff and Caroline. Alice, Lin, Rutter, Gayle. Nicki and Julian. Laura's family. Rosie's friends, and the Odd Squad. Robert Greenfield. Rankin. The Marlings, the Henschels. Sheila Jordan. The Kings, the Gascoignes. Kate Smith. Chiara. Aitchenson, Watson, Gary, Mark Hitesh. Stephen. Nigel and Jackie, Nigel and Clare, Alex, Stuart, Reema, Tim, Fiona, Varley, Colin, David, Jonesy, Kate and Simon. Debs. Roger Hancock, Brian Codd. Andy and Maria. Sally, Lottie, Jelly, Helen. Pat, everyone at Polly's Hassan, everyone at the Zara. David my shrink, David my agent, and Dave. And so many more (that means you, if you feel left out!).

And myself, whithout whom this book would not have been possible.

Bill Oddie, August, 2008.

Contents

PART I

Why am I doing this?

For quite a while now people—especially publishers and my agent—have been saying, 'You ought to write your autobiography.' And I've been saying, 'No.' Why is that? Well, several reasons. The first one is meant to be positive and is appropriately delivered with an almost Wildean flourish: 'My dears,' I tell them all, 'I am far too busy living my life to write about it.' Oh, please! But it's almost true. Honest. I am ever so busy these days. It's not like they can tell me: 'You've got nothing else to do, so write!'

However, my other excuses are rather more negative. 'You ought to write your autobiography,' may seem a harmless or even flattering suggestion, but it also carries sinister implications. I can't help imagining the unspoken follow-ups to 'you ought to write your autobiography' such as 'before it's too late' . . . or 'now that your career is over' . . . or 'whilst people still know who you are.' That one really hurt, especially as it was actually said by my agent. I'm probably being paranoid, but don't you agree there is a whiff of doom about it? 'Write it now, because you never know what's going to happen next year, or next month, or tomorrow.' Am I the only one who gets the word 'autobiography' mixed up with 'obituary'? It's not just connotations. Be honest, even staring at the words right now they do look very similar. In fact I have just realised that the word 'autobiography' contains every single letter necessary to spell 'obituary'! Take the 'obituary' out of 'autobiography' and you're left with . . . a 'p', an 'h', an 'a', a 'g' and an 'o'. Rearrange those letters and you get 'hogap' or 'phoag' or . . . you have a go. I'm too scared to, in case it spells out the Swahili for 'heart attack' or something. OK, I am being frivolous. But not entirely.

The fact is that writing your 'life story'—as they used to be called—is what you were supposed to do when you retired. I am not retiring, in any sense of the word. So I'm not old enough to be doing it—or else too old, because the not entirely irrational concept of life stories being written only by people old enough to have actually *had* lives seems to have become utterly unfashionable. A glance at the bestsellers will soon tell you that. Footballers, models, pop stars, stand-up comics: they all produce autobiographies before they hit thirty. Wayne Rooney, Katie Price, Pete Doherty, Lily Allen, Russell Brand, and by the time this book is published there will be a hundred more. Now you are probably expecting me to slip into grumpy old man mode and grouch about 'flippin' kids, what do they know about life?' and so on. In fact I am personally quite a fan of autobiographies written by young people, especially if they are as eloquent as, for example, Russell Brand. There is surely also something far more valid, intriguing, immediate and possibly uplifting, or distressing, about reading a young person's account of what is actually happening to them whilst it is still happening—or was not long ago—rather than a retrospective account in an old person's memoirs. This is perhaps particularly true of authors who achieved their fame in an area of 'youth activity'— sports personalities, pop singers, models, stand-ups—all of whom, by the time they are thirty, may well be on the brink of retirement. Exactly when you are supposed to write your autobiography. Added to which—and this I reckon is a big advantage that young autobiographers have—there isn't so much to remember! It is almost inevitable and true that most young 'stars', in whatever field, will have tales to tell of their childhood, be it happy, dull, dodgy, insecure, traumatic, or whatever. One way or another, the chances are that those formative years will have been crucial to their achievements or failures. Broken homes, cruelty and abuse, adolescent delinquency, frustration, provocation, love, guidance or inspiration. It is surely one of the most universally accepted facts about human life that whatever happens to us during our 'upbringing' (childhood, adolescence) will affect the rest of our lives. So by all means let us hear these young folk's stories now, whilst they can still remember them!

Which brings me to the biggest problem I have had while embarking on my own story. I have been on earth for sixty-six years (shit, how I hate even typing that number!) and, during that time, I have had access to pens and paper, all manner of recording machines, from reel-to-reel, to mini discs, cameras from Brownies to digital, and home movies from Super 8 to HD. Plus I have been on the radio and the telly, done interviews with newspapers and magazines, written several books, and even made programmes which involved a certain element of 'looking back'. Nevertheless, the honest truth is that I can't remember much about it! It may indeed be that there is quite a lot that I don't *want* to remember. Stuff that I have 'blanked', as the analysts say, and believe me they've said it to me. Nevertheless, no matter how

5

much I rack my brain, there are huge chunks that I really can't account for. Bits and pieces, yes, I can picture some, but it's the longer units I have trouble with. Periods of time, phases. And feelings. I find myself envying other autobiographers who seem to be able to recall and even re-experience quite intense feelings. Phrases like, 'I shall never forget how I felt' or 'thinking about it now immediately brings back the feeling of nervousness', or fear, joy, panic, boredom, excitement . . . whatever. They feel it, but I don't. It just doesn't happen for me. I'm like that song from *A Chorus Line*. A drama student is doing 'method acting' exercises, supposedly to conjure up real emotions, but it ain't working. 'So I reached right down to the bottom of my soul . . . and I felt NOTHING!' I could have sung that line.

It's not, I hasten to add, that I don't have feelings. I am having one now, and it's rather sad. I have long accepted that, at various times of my life, I have suppressed my emotions. I've presumed so, because I can't remember them. However, I've also presumed that I did have them at the time. But maybe I didn't. Maybe I suppressed them even as they were happening. Maybe I'll realise that as I continue with this book.

*   *   *

So, what do I remember, and how?

It's not all a blank! Almost as if to compensate for my lack of emotional recall, my visual memory is very, very vivid. It's not what people refer to as a 'photographic memory'. I can't take one glance at a page from the telephone directory and then trot

6

out all the names and numbers. Not that I've tried it. Nor shall I. Time is short. But I do tend to see the past in pictures. In fact, I only have to close my eyes and I instantly see a scene, and most of the time it is an image from my past life. Not always, though. I'll try it right now. I close my eyes and I see . . . the harbourside at Cley in Norfolk, low tide, mud, boats and a few gulls. Open eyes and close again: now it's Cape Kennedy in Florida, with a big rocket on the launch pad about to take off. Open, close, next: a shaft of sunlight through autumn leaves of red and gold. Very pretty. I like that one. Every time it is a different picture. Not stills, moving. And in colour, but with no sound. Very entertaining but utterly random images. I am not aware of any link or connection from one to another. If you can spot one, please let me know!

These pictures in my mind's eye just pop up willy-nilly with no conscious mental process. However, rather more specifically—and perhaps 'usefully'—if I consciously throw my thoughts back to a particular day, situation or event, if I close my eyes, I can almost instantly see it. I first realised how efficiently this one worked when I was browsing through my bird notebooks, though I'm not sure exactly when this was. I have been keeping bird notebooks—sort of birdy diaries—for over fifty years, so it was ages ago. One of the joys—and points?—of diary keeping is that, every now and then, you reread what you wrote long ago. Whenever I reread my bird notes, I do the old close-my-eyes trick, and I visually relive the experiences of seeing those birds. I'll do it now. Trust me. I am now looking at the very first page in the earliest notebook I still have. There were

7

others before this, but as far as my documented birding history is concerned it began on 28 August 1956 (when I was fifteen) on a golf course alongside the Exe estuary at Dawlish Warren in Devon. The text tells the tale of a 'possible Richard's Pipit'. A dull but rather rare bird that bears some resemblance to a skylark (which is not a rare bird). I tried very hard to convince myself that the bird was indeed the aforesaid rare pipit, but I know it wasn't. And how can I be so sure? Because I can still see it. Now. I only have to close my eyes, and I can see the Exe mudflats, and the golf course, and a bunker, and some 'rough', and the bird scuttling though the long grass, and . . . it is definitely and undeniably a skylark!

Such is my recall of over fifty years' worth of notebooks. Any time I want a rerun, all I have to do is choose a page, pick a bird or a day out, close my eyes, and I see it all, in full action and glorious colour. One leading question strikes me, and it's asked with regret: why the hell did I only keep a bird diary? Imagine if I'd kept a real diary, featuring all my finest sporting and sexual exploits! And any time I became aware of the wearisome deterioration of my physical faculties—which is more or less all the time—all I'd have to do is flick back through my diary to some good bits, close my eyes and . . . Oh, I can dream!

Seriously though, my memory has limitations, especially when it comes to conjuring up pictures from my childhood. The formative years. Baby, toddler, infant, little lad, bigger lad, schoolboy, early teenager. Several years' worth, various phases, adding up to my youth, the time I find so hard to remember with any great clarity or coherence. Visually, emotionally, even emotive aspects like smells and sounds. All very hazy. I should stress that I am talking about my family life. School, sports events, playing out, the local country side—I remember quite a bit about those. It is home life that is almost entirely missing. I have a few images I can see, but they are nothing like as clear as those vividly remembered birds from my notebooks. A limited, sporadic and apparently random little gallery is the nearest I have to a family album. No such thing existed in our house. No leather-bound book with hundreds of black and white snapshots, and—sadder still— no sepia-tinted portraits in oval frames. Surely there must have been wedding photos on our mantelpiece? Were there no christenings? No Christmas gatherings of distant relations? Not even pictures of me as a baby? I have since managed to track down a few, but for the life of me I have no memory of them being on display. Maybe they never were. Maybe there were reasons for that. Maybe they will become clearer as I tell this story.

Meanwhile, what do I remember of my early childhood? I was asked this question relatively recently for a TV programme. I managed to conjure up half a dozen pictures but soon ground to a halt. I then came out with a phrase which I still think sums it up pretty well: 'It's as if my memories of childhood are short excerpts, like a trailer for a film I never saw!'

But one thing is for sure—whether I can see it or not—I was in it.

It is, I know, customary to start an autobiography with a date of birth. I intend to begin when I was

9

six. Continuing the cinematic metaphor, I will be flashing back and cutting ahead. In other words, events will not be in a strict chronological order, but rather in the order I feel best makes sense of my life as I rerun it. To make sure this won't be confusing—to you or me—I shall head each section with the time and location, just like a film script.

Time: spring (probably late May) 1947
Location: Rochdale, Lancashire.
Set: much the same as for the Hovis ads that came out twenty years later

The main street is a steep hill. It is cobbled. At the bottom of the hill is a cotton mill with steam—or is it smoke?—coming out of the chimneys. There are people hurrying to work. The men are wearing flat caps and smoking Woodbines. The women have headscarves. One of them is pushing a pram. It does not contain a baby. It is full of coke (a cheap post-war coal substitute, not to be confused with either Coca-Cola or cocaine!). The main noise is the clattering of clogs. The soundtrack is the distant strains of a brass band. Suddenly a siren wails. Several people stop, cower, and then collapse into giggling. One woman bursts into tears, and is comforted by a friend. It is not long ago that the sound of the siren would have been a warning of an impending German air-raid. Now it is telling them it's time they were inside the factory and attending their looms. The women hurry on inside, chatting cheerily. Except the one who is still crying. She probably lost a husband or maybe a son, or both, in the war. It's only two years since it ended. Maybe her house was bombed in the blitz and all her family were killed. Every work day the siren reminds her.

This street is called Sparthbottom's Road. Go on, say it out loud with a Lancashire accent: 'Sparthbottom's Road'. You can't write 'em like that! Running parallel to Sparthbottom's Road is St Alban's Terrace. The 'St Alban's' bit refers to the black brick church at the top of the hill. The houses in the terrace are narrow, two storeys high, and glued together in a long line. Each house has a small bay window, and a front door opening straight out on to a concrete path that runs the length of the terrace. On the other side of the path is an equally long dense privet hedge, about four foot high and maybe the same depth, and beyond that, a row of iron railings. These are a safety barrier, below which a stone wall drops down to the main street. Sparthbottom's Road.

I have described the front aspect of St Alban's Terrace, so now I'll describe the back. The space behind the houses was a vast sports complex, with an adjacent adventure playground and overlooking a wildlife sanctuary. Well, it was to me and the local kids. It was also a very big area. To me. At the time. In fact, I revisited Rochdale in my early twenties and it turned out that the area at the back of St Alban's Terrace was not huge at all. Not in 1962 anyway. It was still the same size in 2004, when I filmed there, and presumably it wouldn't have been any different back in 1947. It had just seemed huge to a small child—everything does—but the space was brilliantly suited to our various childish leisure activities. The first section, the sports complex, could I suppose be called the 'road' behind the terrace, but it was more of a track, as it wasn't surfaced with tarmac. It was dust or mud, depending on the weather, or deep snow during the legendary hard winter of 1947, which I remember very well. A harsh time for Britain, but a white wonderland for kids! We built snowmen so huge they have probably only recently started melting. 'Ah yes, now that's a definite sign of global warming—the Rochdale snowmen have gone all drippy.' The second bit, the adventure playground, was a huge grassy bank, enclosed by railings. Beyond which was dense woodland—the forest!

The muddy track had a dual function. It was our cricket pitch, with a milk crate for wickets, and a boundary so short that a straight hit would almost always go for a six. I seem to recall that if the ball went over a wall into a back garden it was 'six and out'. A fair punishment, since someone was going to have to endure the 'please can we have our ball back?' torture. Out of summer the cricket pitch became a football stadium (yes, jumpers for goalposts, and all that). It also doubled up as a battlefield for the not infrequent gang warfare. I know it's hard to believe, but it's true. The kids (well, the boys anyway) in each street (or terrace) referred to themselves as a 'gang'. There was a cheery and sociable side to this, 'our gang' meaning just a bunch of lads having smashing fun and spiffing adventures, so that was rather nice and healthy. What wasn't quite so cute was that every now and then there would be a gang fight. This involved two packs of schoolkids (mainly boys, but girls were involved too, I'm sure) standing not many yards apart and hurling stones at one another! Yep, stones! Possibly even the occasional house brick, and maybe a tin or bottle or two. It wasn't a game. It hurt!

And what were these fights about? The only reason I can recall was that some other street's gang had come and tried to raid our bonfire, or had already nicked some of our wood. Either way it meant battle. The bonfire? So presumably these fights only occurred just before Guy Fawkes night? Well, not as I recall. Maybe my memory is really warped, but I could swear that there was a bonfire being built at the back of our houses more or less all year round! I do remember the actual fires, especially the morning after bonfire night, 6 November, I presume (some things never change). My habit was to rush out at dawn, collect up what appeared to be spent fireworks, and chuck them on to the still burning embers. Wasn't that a daft and dangerous thing to do? Of course.

But not half as dangerous as being pelted with bottles and stones. Looking back now, I suspect we wilfully provoked these battles by starting to build next year's bonfire when the ashes of this year's had barely cooled! The custom was that anything flammable would be chucked on to the pyre at the back of the terrace, so that it grew at a pretty rapid pace until it became the envy of all the other streets in Rochdale. Envy grew into resentment, and resentment into raids. 'We'll put those St Alban's kids in their place! We'll go and nick that broken chair they've put on their bonfire. And what's that on the top? A wooden hat stand! Right, they're getting too cocky by half. We'll have that. And those old drawers, and the privet

13

cuttings. And . . . look out, they've seen us!' At which point, our gang leapt out and pelted their gang, and vice versa. And so it went on. All year round, I'll swear, probably peaking in the late autumn. Was it just in the Sparthbottom's Road area? Or were there Bonfire Wars going on all over Rochdale back then? Maybe all over England? I dunno.

Now let's return to our opening scene in St Alban's Terrace. The front door of one of the houses opens. A little lad comes out. He's off to school. That was me.

I was five years old at the time, but having been born on 7 July 1941, and this being late May 1947, I was nearly six. My school uniform was standard 1940s: grey shirt, pullover, shorts and socks, with black shoes that gave me blisters when they were new. My cap was also grey. I am assuming this is how I was dressed, because the fact is I have no actual visual memory of me or my schoolmates, and no school photos from the time. The school I went to was St Alban's Primary—I think! What do I remember of that school? Very little. I am not implying that I 'blanked' my early schooldays, and I am certainly not suggesting for one minute that they were so horrendous that I need to, but the few memories I do have are, to say the least, a bit random. The least pleasurable but almost inevitably the most vivid is of a 'weird' bloke who used to lurk around by the big iron school gates. He was probably harmless, but he might not have been. I do remember we kids were all scared of him. He had 'funny eyes'. Squinty or bulging perhaps, but definitely a bit 'wild'. I dare say we referred to him as the school 'loony', and no doubt

14

every primary school had one. The 'bogeyman' figure. This was no doubt utterly unwarranted. Or was it?

My one totally visual recall is of the day it was my turn to take the dinner money to the post office. It was a routine that these days simply wouldn't be allowed. It's pretty amazing that it was then! A small child—possibly accompanied by a second small child, though I don't remember one—clutching a little tin box full of coins, crossing a couple of main roads (long before zebra crossings or lollipop ladies), delivering the loot to the local post office, and receiving a couple of sweeties as a reward, and then making his way back to school equally unsupervised. Many set out on that journey—I imagine it was regarded as an honour to be chosen—and, as far as I know, all returned safely and with no tales to tell. Until me!

I have a tale. I can close my eyes now and see the scene. I come out of the post office, unwrapping my toffee as I cross the road. I come round the corner dribbling. Not with caramel drool, but with an old tennis ball, which to a six-year-old—and a small one at that—was about the right size to double up as a football. No one had real footballs in those days. I remember tapping the ball ahead of me, and as I ran to catch it up . . . there he was. I said I don't recall feelings very graphically, but I think I can safely say I was totally terrified. Even more so, as the ball trundled across the pavement and came to rest . . . right at his feet. Then it got worse. Instead of tapping it back to me, he picked it up. Now OK, I concede that not even the most amiable, avuncular adult alive could have resisted teasing a small schoolboy under such

15

circumstances. Such phrases as 'Do you want your ball back?' or 'Come and get it', said in a cheerful, Father-Christmassy sort of way, would simply be an utterly innocuous invitation to play ball. But said to me by a loony, with peculiar eyes, with a reputation for lurking outside the school gates, his voice took on all the perverted menace of the Child Catcher from *Chitty Chitty Bang Bang* (a movie yet to be made in 1947). Go on, try it in that sinister voice: 'Little boy-eee! Come and get your ba-awl!' Followed by the least assuring promise in the history of child molestation: 'It's all right, little boy. I won't hurt you.'

And he didn't. I was far too quick for him. He did lunge at me as I scuttled past him, and he actually got a bony hand on my shoulder, but I hurled myself so hard at the gate that it swung open and I was through it and slamming it shut before he was able to get a grip. What happened next I am purely guessing. I remember reporting it to teacher, and I don't remember seeing the strange man again. Was he warned off? Was he locked up? I don't know. One thing I do know though: I got my ball back.

I know that because that afternoon—or maybe it was another afternoon shortly afterwards—I was wandering home from school, and as I crossed over at the top of Sparthbottom's Road I was again, as ever, dribbling my ball along. Maybe I had acquired another tennis ball. It doesn't matter. What does matter is that the rest of that afternoon constitutes by far the longest clear memory of my time in Rochdale. Indeed, the events encapsulated many ingredients that I now know have been integral to the rest of my life.

As I approached the top end of Sparthbottom's Road I quickened my pace, as I always did whenever I had to pass close by the graveyard of St Alban's Church. I don't suppose it was intrinsically any spookier than any other graveyard, and in fact it constituted the nearest open space playground. Local kids used to play Cowboys and Indians in there. (Children don't play that any more. If they did, it would presumably be retitled 'Gays and Native Americans'.) Looking back, there is a slightly sinister irony in playing a game in a cemetery which involved pretending to kill one another, but I suppose to a kid there's nothing very disturbing about pretend death. Gravestones doubled up as cacti and canyons to six-year-old Cowboys and Indians, and the St Alban churchyard was particularly well suited to games which entailed hiding, since quite a few of the graves were open! I don't mean there were body snatchers abroad, but several of what on the face of it appeared to be concrete tombs had missing lids or collapsed sides, so kid logic told you that there ought to be a dead body in there, and if there wasn't it had either been stolen or had transformed into a zombie.

Inevitably, kids spooked themselves and one another by daring to peer inside. It was also unthinkable that any new kid on the block would not have been told tales of skulls, skeletons, ghosts and ghouls. Since I wasn't actually born in St Alban's Terrace, I myself must have been the victim of such teasing when I'd first gone out to play with the locals at the age of—what was I?—I presume four or five. It certainly worked! If I do my close-my-eyes trick and think back, I can see the cold, grey churchyard, and the equally cold, grey tombs, one of which has the lid half missing. I am alone, as if abandoned. As if my mates have suddenly left me. Maybe we were playing 'hide and seek' and I was 'it'. I had closed my eyes and counted to fifty, opened them and could see no one. Not in itself sinister. That was the idea of the game. I don't know if I searched far or for how long. All I remember—and I can see it now—is that my attention was drawn to the presence of 'something' in that slightly open stone tomb. And then suddenly, as I stared, a hand emerged, then an arm—bare, white, disembodied, surely dead, and yet undead. And no sooner had I seen it, than it had gone and I was left trembling and terrified. If I said I recall what happened next I'd be lying. Did I carry on playing hide and seek? I doubt it. Did my friends eventually reappear? I expect so. Did anyone else claim to have seen a spooky white hand? Probably. Did anyone own up that it was them playing an obviously pretty effective jape? Of course not. All I do recall is that from that day on, as I went to and from school, I hurried past the St Alban's churchyard as quickly as possible, and I didn't look up. I literally kept my eye on the ball. The tennis ball that I was tapping ever closer to the sanctuary of my home.

Except that on this particular afternoon my ball control let me down and the ball skittered away and rebounded off my very own front doorstep and rolled under the privet hedge that skirted the length of St Alban's Terrace. Have you ever tried finding a dingy old tennis ball that has disappeared into the gloomy featureless abyss that is the 'inside' of a thick privet hedge? It ain't easy,

18

especially if you didn't see exactly the point of entry. Anyone who has thrashed a volley over the fence at the tennis court will know this all too well: you think you've noted exactly where it plopped down behind the bushes, but tennis balls can not only bounce and roll, once they are out of sight of their 'owners' they are capable of scuttling and hiding entirely of their own accord. You may even be certain you know where it landed, and you may be right, but in the time it takes to get out of the court, tiptoe over the nettles, and slide past the brambles, not only will your pinpointing be less valid, the ball itself will have had plenty of time to relocate itself miles away from where you expect it. Such rules apply not only to the snootiest tennis club, but also to the privet hedges of Rochdale in the 1940s.

So there I was, on my hands and knees, crawling literally inside the hedge where the bushes fuse into one big scratchy, twiggy tangle, that is almost as impenetrable as the Vietnam jungle, or a roll of barbed wire, and just as painful as either. Ants bit my hands, and twigs lacerated my legs, as I groped around in the layer of dead leaves and detritus that is the carpet beneath any privets. Not only do tennis balls scuttle and hide, they can also bury themselves, so I had no choice but to search by feeling around, which meant that my fingers more than once got gashed by discarded tin cans and bits of broken glass. I hasten to add that all this torture is something that I and every schoolboy then and since suffers any time they play ball anywhere near a hedge. It's what you put up with if you want to get your ball back. And of course that is one of the major credos in a schoolboy's code of honour: you

19

must always get your ball back. One of the very first sentences a schoolboy learns is, 'Please can we have our ball back?' Having to ask someone really scary and angry is the worst thing, but no matter if it plops down a drain, drops on to live railway lines, lands in a Rottweiler's food bowl, or indeed, rolls under a privet hedge, it must be retrieved. But this time, honour was not going to be satisfied. I felt around for a long time, but I simply couldn't find that ball. But what I did find was much more intriguing.

As I lay crouched inside the hedge in a position that was near foetal and near tears, I became aware that I was being watched by two beady little eyes. Barely a foot above my head was a bird's-nest. Small, neat and woven snugly into the black, bare branches. The outside of a privet may be ever green, but the inside is ever dark. At first glance, the nest appeared equally sombre, but as I stared at it my eyes became aware that it was in fact more a soft greeny grey, the colour of moss, because that is what it was made of. It was a small nest—much the same size as my lost ball in fact and not dissimilar in texture. There's a nice whimsical notion: that lost tennis balls turn into bird's-nests! (Actually, conservationists do make artificial harvest mouse nests from old tennis balls . . . but I didn't know that in 1947.) Neither did I know what bird the nest belonged to, even though it was sitting there watching me. All I could see were its twinkly little eyes. If I could have seen the whole bird I still wouldn't have known what it was. At that stage in life I was not a birdwatcher. I was not even aware of such an activity. I had not heard of birdwatchers. None of my friends were birdwatchers. But I was curious. I actually do remember feeling a frisson of guilt when I 'accidentally on purpose' let my hand grope forwards just a little too close to the nest, whereupon the bird felt threatened enough to flit away. It was, thinking about it, a pretty brave little crittur to have sat there for so long, until almost touched by enormous fingers on a hand that to it must have looked as giant as King Kong's!

Those fingers were now trembling as I felt around inside the nest and immediately traced the shape of those tempting jewels that no schoolboy of the time could resist. Eggs. Birds' eggs. Although I had no friends who were birdwatchers, I had several who were egg collectors. Most schoolboys of that era collected birds' eggs, but not me. Until then. The hedge was so dense that I literally couldn't get off my knees and see into the nest. So I let my fingers do the exploring. One . . . two . . . three . . . four eggs . . . no, five! Was my touch deceiving me, or were there four little ones, and one that felt a bit bigger? I took one of the 'small' ones between finger and thumb and took it out of the nest so I could look at it. Tiny. Exquisite. Deep blue. No spots. I reached up and replaced that one, and took another little 'un. Same size, same colour. I popped that one back and had another feel. Four the same, surely. But what about the fifth? Finger and thumb, let's have a look at that one. 'Wow! That's weird.' This egg was a little bigger. And a little rounder. And it was a completely different colour. Not blue. Whitish. And covered in dark spots and freckles. I had no idea what it was, and I have no idea what the reasoning was that led me to replace the 'odd' egg, and take one of the little blue ones. Maybe I just thought they looked prettier! Alas, I do mean take. I clutched the egg in my hand, scrunching up my fingers to make a sort of a cradle. I had quite a gentle touch for a small boy! I very carefully crawled backwards out from inside and under the hedge, and back on to the path that ran along in front of the houses of St Alban's Terrace.

My own front door wasn't far away, but that wasn't the official way in. Actually, that's another thing that's just struck me. I do not remember ever going into the house though the front door. Maybe it didn't open. Maybe I'd lost the key. Surely it can't have been some kind of house rule? My dad hadn't banned me from going in the front in case the neighbours would have disapproved. Would I have brought the tone of the neighbourhood down? I think not. Come on, we're talking flat caps and cobblestones round there. It's more likely that I was—as most of us were—a latchkey kid. What does that mean? I suppose the 'latch' was an old-fashioned word for lock. If the door is left 'off the latch' it is left unlocked. So 'on the latch' is locked. In which case, you need to unlock it with a key. A latchkey. Anyway . . . whether or not I had a key to it, the latch in question must have belonged to the back door, because that was the way I went into our house. Always. Every time.

So it was towards the back door I was heading that afternoon. It's fair to assume I was in a state of joy and jubilation. OK, I had lost my ball, but I knew it was still under there somewhere, so I could try again, and what a consolation I had, clutched in my hot little hand. My short journey took me scuttling along the track behind St Alban's Terrace

22

and past the bonfire which was already looking quite majestic at the foot of what I then thought of as our huge green grassy bank, which on re-inspection twenty years later turned out to be barely the size of a tennis court. My memory had exaggerated its size in the same way that it had exaggerated the length of the whole terrace—as a kid it seemed to stretch off into infinity—and the denseness of the forest beyond the railings at the far end. As a child, I thought of it as being a strictly no-go area. I simply never even considered wandering into the woods, especially as I had been told it was the lair of 'lions and tigers and bears'. And I believed it. OK, I have borrowed my words from a famous fable, but the fact is somebody— probably the same little scamp who'd given me a wave from the grave?—had convinced me that if I ventured beyond the fence and into the woods, I would not escape alive or at least un-gnawed by ferocious wild beasts!

Clearly I considered my environment in Rochdale to be fraught with violence and danger, but I dare say all little kids of that era and area probably felt much the same. After all, for most of our lives till then we really had been under constant threat of a fate far worse than being chased by bogeymen, spooked by ghosts, or attacked by lions. Being pelted with stones by a rival gang was far preferable to being bombed. We had survived the war. And so had our parents. Well, mine had. Some kids had lost members of their families. I still had mine. A dad, a mum, and a granny—Dad's mum. On the face of it, things seemed OK. But they weren't.

Still clutching my egg in one hand, I opened the

23

back gate with the other. This brought me into our garden. Who am I kidding? It was not a garden, but maybe it was a bit more than a backyard. On one side there was a coal shed where we kept a supply of coke and something even less burnable called 'nutty slack', which I imagine was the coalmine equivalent of tobacco sweepings off a cigarette factory floor. And probably even more toxic. Alongside the coal shed was another bricked space with bits of junk—a bike? a pram?—and it was also where I had kept a box with straw and a couple of pet white mice in it. They didn't last long, as I kept forgetting to feed them, but I think on this particular afternoon they were still alive. On the right was what I remember as an old sink or horse trough with some mud in it, but which was I suspect meant to be a flower-bed. I'm sure there were no flowers. There was a back room window, through which a passer-by might have caught a glimpse of me being soaped down in a tin bath on the kitchen table, something I probably hadn't realised at the time. On this occasion there was no bath on the table (and of course no me), but there did seem to be lots of plates. But they were not laid out neatly for tea. In fact they seemed in some disarray. Scattered rather than laid. And some were broken.

I turned the key in the back door latch, or maybe it was already open. I went in and was confronted by a scene that has stayed with me for life. There are details missing, and out-of-focus edges, but the essence is perfectly clear. The whole room was strewn with broken crockery. White crockery. Plates, cups, saucers. On the table, on the dressing table, on the chairs, all over the floor. All over the

24

place. All broken. Smashed. In pieces. Some rounded, some jagged. All bright, shiny and white. Except for the blood. Specks and speckles of red. Spatters on the wall. Smears on the lino. But most vivid of all on the crockery. A room full of broken crockery, sparkling white speckled with crimson. If I close my eyes now I can see it today as I saw it then. It's a clear and strangely clean image. Even though everything was shattered, it wasn't a mess. And that colour scheme. Classic. Red and white. White and red. What on earth had happened?

Who could I ask? 'Dad? Dad?' No reply. Rather less confidently: 'Mum?' No reply. 'Gran?' I don't honestly know if my granny had been upstairs, in the front room, hiding under the table, or standing there all along. I can't even be confident that it was she who explained the situation to me, but who else? I certainly don't remember if it was a long or short explanation. Probably short. All I remember is this: 'Your mother was here. She attacked your dad. He's all right, but he's at the hospital. Your mother's gone.' It's all I knew then, and it's all I know now.

I can only presume that Dad came back fairly soon and no doubt told me that everything was fine. He presumably also reassured me that Mum would not be returning imminently. Yes, that's right, my dad reassured me that my mum would not be coming back. Something wrong there, isn't there? Mums are supposed to come back. They are not actually supposed to go away. They are supposed to be there all the time. In those days, more than dads. Dads went off to war, dads went to work. Mums stayed at home and looked after the children.

'Your mum is not coming back.' These are not normally words of comfort to a kid. But they were to me. I may have been scared of bogeymen, and ghosts, and wild animals, but most of all I was scared of my mum. Not that she had ever harmed or threatened me. Not that I had ever witnessed her harm my dad. Not that I had even seen any evidence of such a thing. Not until now, and even now I still only had my granny's word for it. 'She attacked your dad.' Never for one moment did I think . . . why? Maybe Dad had attacked her. I had heard them rowing at night. Shouting, yelling, but no screams of pain. At least, I don't think so. I used to get under the blankets to cut out the shouting, and eventually my dad would come in and reassure me. 'It's OK. It's nothing, just words. Bit of a row. It's fine now.' And it would usually go quiet and I'd go to sleep. It didn't even happen very often. Because Mum wasn't there very often. When Dad said to me that day, 'She won't be back', I don't know how long she had been away. I wasn't aware of missing her, because I hadn't got used to her. Here is a fact. I cannot remember any time whatsoever in my childhood—or beyond— when Mum was actually living with us. As a mother, as a wife. Mum and Dad as parents. I don't remember her playing with me, or taking me to school, or giving me a bath, or reading to me, or us going on holiday. I don't remember her cuddling me, and I don't remember wanting a cuddle. I don't remember wanting anything from her. Except for her to stay away. Because I was scared of her. But she did stay away, and so I wasn't scared very often. I am not saying that there weren't times when Mum and Dad were together

26

with me as their one and only child. A small but happy family. I'm not saying Mum didn't cuddle me or that I didn't cling to her. I'm not saying that she didn't play with me, or read to me, sing to me or bath me. I am saying that if these things did happen, I don't remember them.

In fact, I only have about half a dozen clear visual memories of moments with Mum. The extracts that make up the trailer to the film I will never see. As I said before, that afternoon in 1947 is arguably my most vivid recollection, and looking back at it now it seems almost beyond coincidence how many elements of my then future life were in there somewhere. Some of my abiding passions. Birds and wildlife (the nest and eggs); sport (football, tennis, cricket already going strong); music and the radio were represented (whatever was on the wireless at the time); and it's even struck me since that the broken crockery looked like the aftermath of Greek dancing! (Pity about the blood, mind you.) As for the effect my family situation must have had on me as a child, and how it would affect my character and experiences as an adult . . . well, it doesn't need a shrink to point out that there were bound to be consequences. Except that as a matter of fact it did—take a shrink, that is—and it didn't happen for a long, long time.

Meanwhile, I can't take you away from Sparthbottom's Road in 1947 without sorting out the identification issues of my first true ornithological experience. The nest in the privet hedge belonged to a Dunnock or Hedge Sparrow, the eggs of which are a deep unspotted ultramarine. The mystery fifth egg—slightly larger and rounder, and pale and spotted—was that of a cuckoo. The egg I took started off my egg collection and it has since struck me that if I had taken the cuckoo's egg instead, I would have saved the lives of the little hedge sparrows it would eventually have turfed out. That's what cuckoos do. It is certainly a fact that that is the one and only cuckoo's egg I have ever found.

It also strikes me that this could have been nature indulging in a little bit of ironic wordplay which I have only just figured out. 'Cuckoo' . . . as in 'crazy', 'mad', 'doolally', 'nuts'.

Time: sometime in 2000 and something
Location: a small studio at a local radio station

I was there to be interviewed, but I can't recall what about. Probably *Springwatch*, or maybe *How to Watch Wildlife*. I was chatting with the interviewer, but it was either before or after the actual broadcast. In other words, we were not 'on air'. I'd probably been reminiscing about early birding exploits, and perhaps boasting about how I like to feel I sort of discovered a place called Upton Warren, which is now a nationally famous nature reserve, but when I first went there as a teenager was just a few flood pools and a gravel pit. The truth is, I didn't discover it, but perhaps I did help to 'put it on the map' as it were.

'Did you live near there then?' asked the interviewer.

'Not really,' I told him. 'We lived in Quinton, on the edge of Birmingham', which is where we'd moved to when we left Rochdale in about 1948. I must have been seventeen when I first 'found'

Upton, because I used to drive there at weekends, so it must have been when I had just passed my test, and Dad used to let me borrow his car. I often wonder if he checked the milometer, because I used to tell him I was just nipping down the road to a reservoir barely a couple of miles from home, but in fact I often did a huge circuit of all the decent bird spots of the West Midlands, which must surely have clocked up 100 miles or more. I was just about to launch into a convoluted—and only arguably interesting—explanation of reservoir birdwatching during the late 1950s, when the interviewer mercifully (for both of us) cut me off:

'Only, you see, I know Upton,' he said, 'because it's near Bromsgrove, and I was brought up there. Did you ever visit Bromsgrove?'

'I certainly did,' I replied. 'Bromsgrove School were our big rugby rivals when I went to King Edward's, Birmingham. The big game of the year was KES v Bromsgrove. We used to play for something called the Siviter Smith Cup, and we'd won it for several years. Till 1959, when I was captain of rugby and . . . we lost!' I wished I'd never started that one. Bad memory. But it wasn't as bad as the memory the interviewer's next remark triggered off.

'Didn't I read somewhere that your mother used to live near Bromsgrove?'

I was quite taken aback. 'Well, yes, she didn't really live there. She was in a hospital there.'

'Barnsley Hall?'

'Yes, Barnsley Hall. It was a psychiatric hospital.'

'Of course we used to call it Barmy Hall.'

'Yeah, of course you did.'

'We used to go on school outings there.'

29

'I'm sorry?' I couldn't quite believe what he'd just said! 'You went on school outings to Barnsley Hall? Was it still a . . .' I hesitated.

'Yeah, a . . . well, in those days they called them . . .'

I provided the words: 'Lunatic asylums.'

'Yes. Nowadays, it'd be a psychiatric hospital, or just a hospital, not even a mental hospital, that's gone out, but when I was a kid . . .'

'And me,' I added and continued, 'it would've been a loony bin, or a madhouse . . . and the patients . . . loonies, nutters, madmen, and madwomen.'

'And your mother was there?' It wasn't an insensitive question, it was fine, sympathetic even, he didn't need to apologise, but he did. 'I'm sorry'.

'It's OK, I don't mind talking about it.' So we did.

'How long was she was there?'

'I don't know. I never knew her at home. So all the time I lived in Birmingham, she must have been in . . . Barmy Hall.'

'I am sorry,' he repeated. He was probably wishing he had never started it, but I was glad he had. I had a question for him. 'Can we just go back a minute? What you said . . . when you were at school near Bromsgrove . . . you used to go on outings—to the local mental hospital?'

At this point, you will appreciate that, though quite a few of my childhood recollections sadden me, I am—I'm happy to say—totally incapable of resisting anything with comic possibilities, no matter how 'distasteful', and this was—is—surely a beauty! I mean, most schools have class trips to the local nature reserve, or the zoo, or a museum, possibly even a factory, or a police station, and it's certainly not uncommon, and in fact highly laudable, for kids to visit a hospital, or an old folk's home. But this was a first. And I dare say a last. A school trip to a loony bin! Under what heading? was it 'careers', or 'history', or even 'wildlife'? Or was it a warning? 'If you lot don't do your homework you'll end up in here.'

I felt the need to know more. 'How old were your class? Sixth formers?'

'No, no, year ones and twos. About ten or eleven.'

'OK. And did you, er . . . what did you actually do?'

'We had talks from nurses and doctors'.

'Did you talk to the loonies . . . the patients?'

'Well, not really. I don't think a lot of them knew what was going on.'

Maybe they were just totally gobsmacked. Couldn't believe their eyes. 'I could swear I've just seen a bunch of schoolkids arrive on a charabanc, but surely not? I think I really am going barmy!'

I couldn't resist asking the next question: 'So, did you get to sort of join in? You know, try on the straitjackets? Test the handcuffs? And what about ECT?'

'Oh yes, they showed us the electric shock machines.'

'Did they let you have a go? "OK, children, now who'd like to have a shock? And who wants to press the button?" "Oh, me, Miss, please, Miss, me, me!" "I want to do it, Miss!" "Oh it's not fair, Miss, Jimmy got to give the tranquilliser jabs." "OK, OK, you can all have a few volts. Now form a queue. And stop arguing, or I'll have you all

31

thrown in a padded cell.'"

I didn't wait for an answer. I was on a roll. 'And when you got back to school, did you have to sort of act it out? Like "OK . . . this side of the class are the nurses and doctors, and the rest of you are the nutters. So who wants to be Napoleon? And who's good at banging their head against the wall? And who can rock backwards and forwards and talk to themselves at the same time?"'

The mind boggles! School trips to a loony bin! I had to ask: 'Did you enjoy going to Barnsley Hall?' The interviewer seemed suitably embarrassed: 'Well, it was a laugh. We used to just find it funny.'

'And do you feel you learnt anything about mental illnesses?'

'Well, no, not really.'

'Well, you know why that is?' I suddenly went serious. 'Because, in those days, they didn't know very much.' And ain't that the truth.

And that included me. When I was a schoolkid, I didn't know very much. I didn't know when my mother had been taken into 'hospital'. Or what kind of hospital it was. Or what was wrong with her. Or even where the hospital was. I can only repeat what I have already said: my childhood memories regarding my mum are very few and very random. The broken plates scene is the only one from Rochdale. The family—Dad, Gran and me—moved to Birmingham in 1948.

I remember a bit about the move. There was no trepidation or sadness, and no feeling of disorientation, as I recall, or if there was it was instantly obliterated when I saw kids perched on and behind garden walls playing Cowboys and Indians. I didn't instantly ask to join in, I simply

32

noted their presence, and felt sure that I'd be fine. I knew this culture, albeit the setting was a little more genteel than Rochdale. Quinton was rather greener and more sedate than Sparthbottom's Road, and with delightful appropriateness our new address reflected the improvement. We now lived in Oak Tree Crescent.

To make me feel even more at home, there was a splendid cricket ground right in front of our semi-detached home, in the form of a 'turning circle' at the end of the cul-de-sac. Instead of a milk crate, the wickets were chalked on to a wall, which you bowled at from by the lamppost. The track was probably a little less than the statutory twenty-two yards, but perfect for kids. The boundaries were a little further than at the St Alban's ground, and I think the 'lost ball' rule was less stringent. If you hit it into a garden you could run six, but no more. Then we all went and searched for the ball, having got permission from the house owners, so we didn't have to keep asking, 'Please can we have our ball back?' Inevitably there was one house owner that didn't like balls, kids, cricket or possibly anything except his beloved border plants, but this only added a bit of spice to the game, and may well have improved the accuracy of our shot placing. Many's the fine innings I played on the Oval (well, the circle). My record score—as I recall—being slightly over 400! No insidious comparisons between the merits or demerits of Rochdale and Birmingham at the time, but clearly Dad considered the move down from the north to the midlands to be a move up the social ladder, and it clearly was. Quinton, Birmingham 32. In those days I suppose it was quintessential middle-class suburbia, and it probably still is.

Having arrived at the age of seven, I lived there until I went off to university in 1960, when I was nineteen. Formative years indeed. I have many, many memories (mostly pretty happy ones) of schooldays and nights, weekends developing my birdwatching persona, and trips beginning to explore Britain, and—for better or worse—becoming me. I have a vivid visual recall of the neighbourhood around Quinton. I have been back a few times in recent years and have found my way around with an efficiency that even impressed me. Walks, cycle routes, short cuts, landmarks and open spaces that still exist, and the sites of those that have disappeared under development. My head is home to albums full of clear and detailed pictures. And there is a considerable cast of people too. Other kids who lived in the street and nearby, mates from the three schools I attended: Lapal Primary, Halesowen Grammar and King Edward's School, Birmingham. I remember music I heard, games I played, matches I went to, girls I had crushes on, boys I considered my best friends, the lot. We were not poor. Dad exuded a certain modest affluence. He wore nice suits, played bowls and won cups for it and spent an hour or two every evening at the local, the Stag, where he also played darts, and won more cups. His accountancy work earned him 'a decent screw', as they say up north! Certainly, I wanted for nothing. In no way was I a deprived child. Except I didn't have a mum.

I must stress right now that this was not something I even thought about at the time, nor for a very long time after. It is a rather stark illustration of that old adage: 'What you haven't had, you don't miss.' I have no recall of Mum living with us in Rochdale, and it's the same in Birmingham. I don't know where she was when we moved to Quinton. I have a very vague recollection of being told that she'd be coming down later or something, and presumably she did indeed move to the midlands, but she didnmove in with us, or if she did it wasn't for long. I have seen one black and white snapshot of Mum in a deckchair in the garden, but I don't remember the actual occasion, nor can I now find the photo.

In fact, I have only three memory pictures of my mother in Oak Tree Crescent. Two of them are rather scary. The first one shouldn't have been, but it was. I came home from school, went upstairs to go to the loo, and found the bathroom—and more specifically the bath—occupied by a frankly pretty large naked lady, not entirely covered by frothy suds and brandishing a loofah. The door had not been locked, and I didn't expect anyone, let alone Mum, to be in there. She smiled cheerily, and I think requested a hug, which I declined, or made very cursory—in the first place because hugging large naked slippery women isn't actually very easy (like trying to cuddle a giant bar of soap), and secondly because I wasn't entirely sure that it *was* my mum! That's honestly true. I assume I hadn't seen her for a while, not that I had seen much of her at any time. Now I was seeing rather too much! Looking back, I'm not surprised I was a bit freaked out. Whatever age I was—and I suspect it was only nine or ten—I wasn't used to fleshly close encounters with naked women of any kind—it was definitely a first!—and the fact that she was nonchalantly assuming that I would call her

35

'Mummy' was pretty bizarre. As ever in my young life, I never got a clear explanation of where she had come from, or where she went. I didn't actually see her get out of the bath—fortunately—but next time I went to the loo, she'd gone.

The second graphic memory was rather less traumatic. I and a couple of friends were watching our impressive new telly—four foot high with a nine-inch screen, black and white of course—and there was a puppet show on, *Muffin the Mule*. Muffin was a wooden horsy thing with Dalmatian-type black and white spots (no point in wasting colour in those days). Maybe he was a hybrid! He was on strings operated from above, and he mainly clattered about on the closed piano lid of a posh lady called Annette Mills. The puppeteer, or marionette operator, never did master his art sufficiently to keep Muffin's hooves in natural-looking contact with the floor (or piano lid). This meant that Muffin didn't really trot, gallop or even walk so much as float. In fact, whenever his feet did touch the ground, he tended to crumple up completely, and Ms Mills would say something like: 'Oopsa daisy, Muffin, oh you are wobbly today!' Me and my chums were understandably totally engrossed by this high-quality entertainment. Mind you, the telly itself was such a novelty that they could have shown a blank card and we would have been riveted. (In fact, they often did show a card, which said: 'Normal service will be resumed as soon as possible.') Anyway, that afternoon I was so captivated by Muffin's antics, that I didn't realise that a portly woman had crept into the room behind me. Suddenly she chuckled (no one could resist Muffin), and I whipped round and recognised her: Mum with clothes on! And that's about the extent of that memory, except that I also have a very vivid recall of the next act on Muffin's show, which was—I kid you not—simply a little bit of rag which dangled around above the piano lid on a string that was probably meant to be invisible, but wasn't. Maybe it was meant to be a butterfly. Special effects budgets were no doubt very tight just after the war. Or maybe it was a new character called 'Raggy'. All I know is—and I really do remember this very clearly—I didn't like it. But Mum thought it was hilarious. At least, she kept laughing out loud and then looking at me as if to say, 'Isn't this fun?' But it wasn't.

However, the Muffin and Raggy show was like a trip to paradise compared with my third memory of Mum at Oak Tree Crescent. This one really is unadulteratedly horrible, and very sad. I don't know how I actually felt about it at the time, but it can't have done me much good. For Mum—and Dad—it must have been horrific. I feel I should describe it in the present tense, the way we often relate our dreams, but this was indeed a nightmare.

It is outside our house in Oak Tree Crescent. It is a sunny day. I am 'playing out' in the cricket circle with a few friends. Nearby is a van. It looks like an ambulance, but it is black. Suddenly we are all distracted by the sound of screaming and scuffling. It is coming from our house. The front door crashes open, and there is my mother, yelling, scratching, crying and lashing out at the people who are trying to restrain her. Are they doctors or policemen? My dad is involved, being lashed at by Mum, and at the same time trying to placate her.

37

My granny is in the background, in the house, still in the hall. I don't know if Mum screams out names . . . maybe mine. I and my friends simply stay frozen to the spot, as Mum is bundled, still thrashing and screaming, into the van. Doors slam. The van drives away. Did Dad go too? I don't know. I feel almost sure that he didn't. I am pretty certain that he watched the van disappear, then came over to me and my mates and reassured us: 'It's OK. It's OK. It's fine.' But it very obviously wasn't.

Writing this now, I can hardly believe I wasn't given any clear explanation or information. Reading this now, you may be thinking much the same thing. 'Surely he must have asked? Surely someone must have told him?' Well, if I did ask, I didn't get an answer. As regards whatever was wrong with Mum, all I was ever told was something like 'She has trouble with her nerves'. I presume 'nerves' had a different connotation in those days. We think of it as in 'nervous', but then it was more 'nerves' as in 'frayed nerves'. As in extreme stress or trauma. As in mental problems. As in a 'nervous breakdown'. Those have gone out of fashion too, haven't they? But it is only words that change. The illnesses stay the same. Yesterday's nervous breakdown is today's 'clinical depression', or 'bipolar disorder', or 'psychosis', or 'addiction', or 'schizophrenia', or 'post-natal trauma', and there are more. These days there are so many ways of being 'barmy'. Which is a very good sign. It means that it is now acknow ledged that mental problems can come in all sorts of infinite varieties, and require a highly flexible attitude to causes and treatments. It is now widely recognised that they are very, very complex. But it is not that long ago that it was all too simple.

Back to the 1950s . . .

Time: mid-1950s
Location: near Bromsgrove

I too visited Barmy Hall when I was a schoolboy. But it wasn't a class outing. I wasn't with a bunch of my mates, and I wasn't supervised by a teacher. There was just me and my dad. I have no record of the exact date or even the year. I think I was about fourteen or fifteen, which means it was 1955 or '56. I suspect it was during the winter, or at least not high summer. If I do my close-my-eyes routine now, the hospital grounds do not look very verdant. On the other hand, they are pretty impressive. More like a deer park surrounding a stately home. But the trees are black and leafless, and there are certainly no deer grazing in the meadows either side of us as we drive slowly up the private road in Dad's strangely racy little car. A 1950s style MG, no less. It was a present to himself for passing his test so relatively late in life. He would have been in his mid forties then. Heaven knows, for a man I never recall behaving any way other than restrained, and whose working image was dapper and besuited, with leisure wear never more flamboyant than a smart pullover, nice slacks and casual shoes, buying a little 'brum brum' sports car was either a gesture of defiance, or a total aberration. He certainly didn't drive fast. And he didn't keep the car very long. At least it didn't have bodywork in racing green, or alarming

39

scarlet. It was shiny black. It must have looked like a small hearse creeping up to the grim edifice that was Barnsley Hall.

It sounds like a mansion and it certainly looked like one. Memory is a notorious exaggerator of size, but I feel safe in saying Barnsley Hall was big. Such words as 'towering', 'sprawling' and 'impressive' come to mind—perhaps even 'intimidating' or 'forbidding'. The adjectives were probably dictated by such factors as the weather, or whether or not you knew it was an asylum. We parked, got out, locked the MG and scrunched towards the front door. Such places always have gravel paths. Great footsteps effect on the soundtrack. And what a fantastic location too.

OK, let me set something up here. This occurred in the mid 1950s. Long, long before *One Flew Over the Cuckoo's Nest*. I dare say you are willing to agree that it is one of the great movies, and certainly I have been riveted by it several times over the years. It is possible that my visual recall of my visit to Barmy Hall has been influenced by seeing *Cuckoo's Nest* (as they probably call it in the moving picture industry) but I don't think so. I think it's reasonable to suppose that what happened that day was something I would either have blanked entirely or remembered for ever. I don't believe that my brain has done a remake. The scene I remember is as it really was. It is just that when I saw the film I felt something close to déjà vu. OK, the young (then very young!) Jack Nicholson wasn't in the habit of popping over to Bromsgrove in the 1950s, and there weren't any enormous Red Indians in Worcestershire as far as I know. Nor did your average midlander talk with

40

an American accent. But otherwise . . . boy, did they get it right.

What I remember most vividly is the corridor. I assume we'd been met by a doctor or nurse, and Dad would, I am sure, have asked whether or not he should remain with me, and I am equally sure that he was told 'no'. Not only would that not have been a very good idea (whatever state my mother was in, I doubted that she would have been pleased to see him) but also it wasn't the point. The point was—I presume I was told—to see if my mother would recognise me! Which in itself clearly implies that she was by no means *compos mentis*. 'Not all there', as they used to say in those days. Whether I was nervous, or scared, or excited, or bewildered, or curious I just don't know. All I know is that I and a nurse (she was female, I know that much) set off down a long corridor which, had it been in a movie, would have required every filmic trick in the book to do it justice. A long tracking shot, a slow zoom, perfect timing, hours and hours of subtle lighting to create just enough shafts and shadows to highlight the carefully positioned extras'. And extras there were indeed. The inmates, patients—I'm not sure what I thought of them as. They were mostly quite subdued. Not ranting and raving. Not rattling doors or groping through grilled windows. Nor was there a huge number of them, but each one was registered by me, though not focused on or stared at as we walked slowly and silently down the corridor. Quite subtle performances. One man simply stood and gazed into the distance. A woman in a dressing gown talked to herself. Another woman sang, quite loudly, but oblivious

41

to anyone but herself. The nurse smiled at her, and at me, and I no doubt smiled back, but the woman didn't. Another woman sat in a static wheelchair and rocked gently. Another one slept. I may be embellishing the soundtrack, but I am pretty sure there was a distant piano playing, and now and then there'd be a moan or a laugh. It wasn't scary, and it certainly wasn't bedlam. In fact, it was quite calm. Peaceful. Tranquil. No, that's not quite the right word. Tranquill-ised. Of course.

Eventually we reached the end of the never-ending corridor and turned right. We seemed to be now proceeding down a cul-de-sac, which was closed off not by a solid wall but by French windows. The glass let in a soft glow and, as the sun broke through the clouds outside, a spotlight of sunshine. This cast a shadow across a set of 'screens'. The sort of screens you expect to appear in a hospital when the doctor calls out, 'Nurse, the screens.' They were on little casters, so that they could be trundled around. They appeared to be screening the window, cutting out the glare, but presumably there was someone behind them. 'Lilian is just enjoying the sun,' whispered the nurse. Maybe she sensed my momentary puzzlement. 'Lilian. Your mum.'

Blimey. The last time I had seen her she was being carted off by an ambulance—or was it a Black Maria?—four or five years ago. Not only had I not seen her since then, nor heard from her, I hadn't really heard anything *about* her! I presume my dad had been visiting her in the hospital. Or had he? Maybe he had been told not to. Maybe she didn't want him to. How about my granny? But she was Dad's mum. I'd never heard her even mention Lilian. Or how about Lilian's mum? My other granny. I had no idea. I had never met her. At least not that I remembered. There was also Lilian's sister, my Auntie Margery. I now know that Margery did visit Barnsley Hall, and indeed was considerably concerned and involved, but I didn't know that then. In fact, I didn't know her either.

Neither did I know what to expect as I and the nurse approached the screens. The nurse spoke cheerily: 'Lilian. You have a visitor. Look, Lilian, it's Bill. Your son. Bill.' The woman who sat there didn't seem to recognise the nurse, let alone me. The truth is, I didn't recognise her. I had no memory of her sitting in a chair. In the bath, yes. Being dragged away, yes. On neither occasion had I really and truly looked at her. I simply did not have a clear picture from years ago with which to compare this woman, and I certainly didn't have a vision of a slim lively woman who cuddled me, and bathed me, and played with me, and was always there to pack me off to school, and had my tea ready when I got back. I couldn't at that moment have felt surprise or sadness at how she looked now compared with 'then'. As a matter of fact, compared with a wild harridan, screaming, scratching and kicking, or indeed smashing white plates on my dad's head till they were splattered with blood, this lady was a considerable improvement! She was plump, she was quiet, and she seemed utterly harmless. But was she really my mum?

I think the nurse left us alone together, but I presume she didn't go very far. I don't remember if I tried to have a conversation. I don't remember if there was any physical contact. I don't think it lasted very long. I think the nurse returned and probably asked: 'How did it go?' To which I no doubt looked a bit helpless and hopeless and said: 'She doesn't seem to recognise me at all.' By way of an explan ation the nurse said: 'She is on quite heavy medication.' Yeah, well, I guess it would have to be pretty heavy to entirely obliterate a mother's knowledge of her own son. 'OK, Lilian,' the nurse told her gently, 'Bill's got to go now.' (Meaning Bill wants to go? Or what's the point in Bill staying? Or indeed what was the point of him coming in the first place?) 'Do you want to say goodbye?' I didn't get the impression that Mum wanted to say anything, but she did. She came out with one of the greatest non sequiturs I have ever heard. A line that was so utterly irrelevant to the situation that it has remained completely unforgettable. Mother's pronouncement was not directed at me, or the nurse, or indeed at anyone else. It was a statement of fact, a revelation, maybe even a dire warning. 'Television,' she said, 'is dead bodies and cardboard!'

A memorable line indeed, and the title of an autobiography if ever I heard one, but my publisher reckoned it was a bit too doomy. Fair enough. And, in any case, it obviously doesn't mean anything. *Or does it?*

Music link: 'Waah wah waaaah.'

Fade to black. Cut to the next scene.

Time: the early 1960s
Locations: various

I never went to visit my mum again, and her illness or the prognosis for her future were never subjects which came up in conversation with my dad or granny. As it happens, there weren't a lot of family conversations about anything, but more of that later. Sometime in what I have worked out was 1960 I heard mention of a 'new law' (the Mental Health Act of 1959), which allowed close family to insist that mental patients were released—no, discharged—from hospital, if they were no longer considered dangerous. Apparently my mother, benefiting from advances in medication and judged to be now 'no risk', had therefore left Barnsley Hall, and gone back to live in Rochdale, probably with her mother, my 'other granny', whom I had never met.

By this time I was at Cambridge University and spending most of the year there. During the holidays I was almost invariably somewhere on the British coast or a remote island, watching birds. Very occasionally I went back to Birmingham and stayed at Dad's new and very comfortable flat in the then rural village of Hagley, which is some little way beyond the outskirts of Birmingham and most definitely in the Worcestershire countryside. I remember Dad asking me if my mother had tried to contact me since she had been back in Rochdale, and he seemed relieved when I said that I had heard nothing from or about her. He added what seemed to amount to a warning that she 'might try and get in touch'. I dare say I attempted to get more information out of him, maybe even talk in more detail about his earlier life. Or their earlier life together. How did he meet Mum? How long were they courting before they got married? When, how, and even why did things start to go wrong? But clearly Dad wasn't telling me anything. I assumed—no doubt rightly—that it was all very painful, and he didn't want to talk about it. Such words as 'denial' or 'guilt' simply weren't in the vocabulary in those days.

It was around then that I recall theorising about why Mum and Dad didn't get on. I knew Dad was a highly intelligent person, albeit that he had left school at the age of fourteen, in order to take up an apprenticeship as an accountant, I think in a light bulb factory. During my lifetime, he had risen to the rank of assistant chief accountant at the Midlands Electricity Board, thus maintaining a link with light bulbs! I had no way of knowing, but I sort of assumed that my mother had not been as intelligent as he was and I remember formulating a rather pompous hypothesis that it was never a good idea for a married couple to be intellectually mismatched. In other words: 'Gentlemen, don't marry a bimbo! Ladies, don't marry a twerp!' As it happens, it is a maxim I have followed in the rest of my life and I don't think it is an entirely bad one, but I am utterly embarrassed to admit that I was capable of such pontification by my late teens. But that's what a good education does to a simple lad from Lancashire.

Another theory was that perhaps my mother was a sensual—nay, sexual—person, but my dad was less passionate. Or maybe vice versa, but I doubted that, since I myself can vouch for the fact that he was not a very tactile person. So, I surmised, maybe there was a sexual incompatibility. To which the appropriate response must be: 'How the fuck would you know?!' Anyone less qualified to delve into such matters than myself at the age of eighteen, I cannot imagine. I was still a virgin.

My third theory was that perhaps my mother had always been 'unstable', but that—rather than being put off by that—my dad would have considered it a challenge. I don't mean that in any perverse or arrogant way. It's just that one of the things I was most certain of about my dad was that his sense of responsibility was rigorous to the point of masochism. The fact that he had looked after my granny until she died in 1958 at the age of ninety-something was surely proof of that. She wasn't easy to live with!

Of course, I kept my theories to myself. I now regret it. Maybe Dad would have welcomed a confessional 'heart to heart', but the evidence suggests otherwise. I am pretty sure he would have 'clammed up', if only for my sake. That is surely the key to why so little was told and so much withheld regarding what had happened to Mum, and indeed Dad. He was protecting me. But from what exactly? The truth? The emotions? Protection from feelings? In recent years, I have come to realise that that kind of protection can be downright dangerous. But in those days, it was what people generally did, especially when children were involved.

However, by the early 1960s, my 'childhood' was surely over, and my little family were distributed in a completely different way. Granny was in the ground. Mum was in a flat in Rochdale. I was at university, and Dad was 'free' of all three of us. Except he was still worrying about me. He was clearly concerned that my mother might try to contact me. Eventually she did. Or maybe someone else did, on her behalf. I can't remember exactly, but I was now faced with the fact that my mother was presumably relatively sane, safe and 'available'. Did she want to see me? Did I want to see her? Would it be advisable? I needed advice. But from whom?

I didn't discuss it with Dad. Neither did I tell him that I had decided to ring Barnsley Hall and talk to a doctor. This was the first time that I stood a chance of getting a proper medical diagnosis. All I had ever heard up to this point was: 'Your mother had trouble with her nerves.' We wouldn't accept that kind of waffle these days, would we? We are all familiar with the available ailments now, aren't we? Even if we aren't exactly certain what they mean. We certainly don't expect or accept a generalisation that amounts to: 'We're not really sure what's wrong!' We want to know. Is it clinical depression? Bipolar disorder? Trauma? Anxiety? Can I have something more specific than 'dodgy nerves', please, Doctor?

The doctor gave me something more specific. 'Your mother was schizophrenic,' he told me.

'What, dual personalities?'

'Yes, exactly. And unfortunately one of them was quite violent.' It made as much sense as anything. At least from now on if people asked me: 'Why was your mother sent to a mental home?' I could tell them she was 'dangerously schizophrenic'. That certainly sounded reason enough. And what

Sefton council

Y A WARMING CAPPUCCINO FROM
OUR NEW COFFEE MACHINE

Borrowed Items 25/06/2018 15:16
XXXXXX941X

Title	Due Date
teresting, very interesting	16/07/2018
he flew into the cuckoo's	16/07/2018

dicates items borrowed today

nk you for using this service
son Greeting from Formby Library
ne: 01704 874177

little of her behaviour I had witnessed first hand seemed to fit pretty well. 'Jolly mother' laughs at a bit of rag dangling on a string. 'Dodgy mother' breaks plates on Dad's head. I know which is pref erable, but, to be honest, I hadn't liked either of them very much. They had both freaked me out, and even as I was speaking to the doctor on the phone, I could feel the potential for being freaked out beginning to re-emerge. 'So,' I asked the doctor, 'is she all right now?' The answer was something like 'She'll never be completely as she used to be'—a meaningless statement to me, since I had no idea how she'd been—'but, she's no longer dangerous. Were you thinking of visiting her?' This certainly begged the next question and, to be honest, when I asked it, I knew what answer I was hoping to get.

'Do you think I should see her?' It was like the final of a game show with Chris Tarrant or Ant and Dec spinning out the answer . . . 'Yes or no? Which is it to be? It's all down to the doctor. So, Bill Oddie, aged twenty and a bit, the answer to the final question—should you or should you not go and visit your mother?—is . . . No.' The audience in my brain and chest leapt to their feet and whooped with delight. There was more. A reason for the doctor's decision: 'On balance I don't think you should make direct contact with her. It could set her back.' The audience applauded and sighed with relief. I am not proud to say that, but at the same time if I try to stand back and be dispassionate, I think it's not an entirely indefensible reaction. 'Do you want to go and begin a relationship with a woman who didn't recognise you last time you saw her and may have

49

tried to kill your dad and lives miles away in a town which you have no wish to revisit and could still be mentally unstable?' I don't think 'no' is an entirely callous answer. And just in case I was wavering, the doctor had given me that little bonus, an excuse. 'It could set her back.'

So that was it. I would not be making contact with my mother. For her own good.

Time: the swinging 1960s
Location: all over the place!

Oh, to be young in the Swinging Sixties! I was. It's one of the few consolations for now being in my own rather less swinging sixties. I mean, come on, what a decade! Especially if you were into comedy and music. And I was into both, as audience and participant. I may even have made a few contributions to some of the iconic happenings of the 1960s, but I'll let history—who the dickens *is* history?—be the judge of that. If you wish to do a bit of judging yourself, I'll refer you to the second half of this book. But not yet. Meanwhile, as regards my relationship with what little was left of my family, the 1960s in essence took me away from all that.

Even if the doctor's advice not to *risk* meeting up with my mother had not been what I wanted to hear, it would have been almost a physical impossibility to contradict it. She was living in Rochdale. I spent term-times at Cambridge, and holidays on far-flung, bird-infested and almost inaccessible islands, or doing 'vac jobs', which included van driving and scaffolding. Also there

50

were various sporting activities, the most bizarre of which involved a rugby tour to Barcelona where our college team beat the whole of Spain, and I was dubbed *'El Pape'* (the Pope!) by the local press because, at the time, I sported a neat round bald patch like a tonsure. This was not a current hair fashion. It had been created by my nervous habit of pulling out strands of hair. Some people suck their thumbs or bite their nails, I literally tore my hair out! I didn't think much of it at the time. I didn't feel frustrated or stressed. The hair pulling thing was something I did absent-mindedly and was surely of no psychological significance? Any more than were my other little habits of being sick almost every day, whilst also suffering from frequent nosebleeds and excessively sweaty palms. These days, such activities might be interpreted as clear indications of a certain amount of repressed emotions, or sublimated anger, but we didn't have that sort of thing back in the 1960s.

Besides which, my life was becoming a wondrous rollercoaster of new experiences, worldwide travel, and not inconsiderable success.

The circumstances by which I found myself in the entertainment business are for a later chapter. For the time being, all I want to point out is that for most of the 1960s my mother was even less in my life or mind than she had been when she was incarcerated in Barnsley Hall. Let's face it, I had quite a lot to distract me! In 1963, the end-of-term Cambridge Footlights show—with a cast including John Cleese, Tim Brooke-Taylor and Graham Chapman—transferred to London and ran for ages in the West End. With Cambridge now behind us, we toured New Zealand for a couple of

51

months; and in the autumn of 1964 we became part of the so-called 'British Invasion' of America. We played on and off Broadway to rave reviews, and then, along with Tim, Willie Rushton and Jean Hart—my wife to be, a singer I had been introduced to by my flatmate Stephen Frears (the movie director) at Soho's famous Establishment Club, in the company of such as Peter Cook and Dudley Moore—we toured the whole of America with a stage version of *That Was the Week That Was* (starring David Frost). Returning to London, Jean and I lived in a house owned by revered composer Richard Rodney Bennett, who often had jazz musicians such as Annie Ross or Oscar Peterson play in his front room. I was involved in BBC Radio's *I'm Sorry I'll Read That Again* (for younger readers, that's *I'm Sorry I Haven't a Clue* with proper scripts! Oooh, bitchy!), and I also worked as a scriptwriter for such diverse talents as Tommy Cooper, Ronnie Barker and Lulu. Not to mention making a couple of pop records produced by George Martin (the Beatles' producer) with a band that included Rick Wakeman (eventually of Yes), John Paul Jones (Led Zeppelin) and Mitch Mitchell (Jimi Hendrix); as well as scripting lots of episodes of *Doctor in the House* with Graeme Garden, with whom I also did a weird late-night TV series called *Twice a Fortnight*, which featured Germaine Greer (then an actress), and Mike Palin and Terry Jones (eventual Pythons), and with guest bands that included the Moody Blues and Cream! Enough name-dropping for you? If not, there's more later in the book.

Meanwhile, I'm sure my point is clearly made. It's a long, long way from the bright lights of showbizville to a high-rise flat in Rochdale. Frankly, it is unlikely that during this time I ever even thought about Mum. It is also possible that she didn't think much about me either! I may have been doing well, but I wasn't exactly a household name or face. It wasn't on the telly much, and, even if I was, I doubt the smartarse, Oxbridge type, wacky, zany, clever-clever, off-beat comedy shows I was involved in, were favourite viewing in t'industrial north. I suppose what I and my cohorts were doing was the 'alternative comedy' of its day. ('Yeah. Alternative to funny!' as many of the old-school comedians inevitably quipped whenever they got a chance.) So, I was very, very busy, but not terribly visible, and it may indeed be that—especially after years of 'treatment' to her brain—my mother thought as little of me during the 1960s as I did of her. Of course I still had my dad. Then, in 1969, he died.

I know a little bit more about Dad now than I was aware of when he was alive, but not a lot. I don't believe there are any great secrets that are yet to be revealed, or that will remain for ever hidden. Dad was not a mysterious man. I believe he was honest, honourable, and—above everything else—immensely conscientious. I have always felt that whatever he did, he did 'for the best'. He must have had flaws and weaknesses, but I really don't want to hear about them. Why would I? Let's face it, especially when we are young, we tend to have a somewhat simplistic take on our parents. Love or hate. Often directed at the same parent or parents in a short space of time! 'I love you.' 'I hate you.' 'You don't understand me.' 'Help! I need you.' If, as in my case, one of your parents disappears from your life for unknown reasons, at worst you despise and dismiss them, at best you become indifferent. I suppose a child can't afford to do anything else. It's not that I blamed my mother for her illness and absence, but in a sense I did 'demonise' her. Conversely, I sort of 'canonised' my dad. That word 'saintly' mainly implies someone who never seems affected by negative emotions or motives. Who doesn't get angry, or envious, or resentful, or weepy, or pathetic. Somebody strong, competent, reliable, with a clear vision and a confident sense of purpose and direction. A protector and a guide. Someone who doesn't panic. That was my dad. Well, he was to me.

He not only made absolutely certain that I had all the educational opportunities that he didn't have, he also unfailingly encouraged me to achieve the things which he either had no chance to achieve, or that he felt were worth achieving. Fortunately, I suppose with me he was working with a blank canvas! We certainly had no great expectations in the Oddie dynasty. I didn't come from a long line of achievers. In fact, as I eventually discovered, I came from a long line of mill workers. I have always liked to picture Dad shocking his parents by announcing: 'Father, Mother, I have something to tell you. I know you'll not be happy about this but . . . I am not going to work in t'mill! I am going to be . . . an accountant!' 'Eeee, lad, you've brought shame on t'family.' My father the rebel!

I benefited from his determination. Just as he was determined to better himself, he was determined that I would too. Ironically, I suppose

Mum's absence made things even more straightforward. I got Dad's full support and attention. Neither did I have any siblings to compete with or be intimidated by. Nor was I burdened with great awareness of what was possible, available or desirable. I only became conscious of the nightmare of infinite choices when I had children of my own, as my daughters were subjected to all the confusing alternatives of life as a middle-class teenager in London. Not just drugs, sex and rock and roll. Fashion, style, consumer pressure, politics, and—worst of all—an avalanche of information technology, constantly evolving, ever proliferating, mind-bogglingly ingenious and deceptively enabling. Take a photo, shoot a movie, listen to music, write a song, play a game, text America, talk to Australia, find friends, make a date, meet a stranger . . . pay the bills. Anything is possible, and all on a mobile phone. I'm not knocking it, but my God it's overwhelming. So much information. So much awareness. So many choices. Choices. Choices. I didn't have choices when I were a lad. And I were lucky! I really mean this. My life was not complicated.

Once we'd moved to Birmingham, Dad guided me. He sussed out a good local school, Lapal Primary. Then, when they asked parents if they wanted their kids to be 'guinea pigs' and take the 11-plus early, Dad volunteered me. I passed. Though that is no doubt a comment on the exam rather than my precociousness. Thus I went off to Halesowen Grammar School, where I was nearly a year and a half below the average age. Academically I managed fine, but my age and diminutive stature were a bit of a disadvantage when it came to sports. At that stage in life one and half years' age difference translates into several inches and a couple of stone! I tried hard, but I really didn't stand a chance. I am not sure whether Dad's motivation for the next move was so that I experienced equality on the rugby pitch; more likely he was already looking way ahead to university, and had researched the school most likely to get me there. Thus he signed me up to take the entrance exam for King Edward's School, Birmingham. There are lots of King Edward's schools all round Birmingham and beyond, but this was *the* King Edward's. Not in those days a full-blown public school, but above a grammar school. It had its own entrance exam and the academic standard was very high. KES boys were expected to go on to university, and each year quite a few of them got to Oxford and Cambridge.

I suspect it was my ever-escalating obsession with birds that contributed to my unquestioning acceptance of Dad's educational strategies. As long as I could walk to the woods or cycle off to the local reservoir, I really didn't think of much else. I didn't regard Dad's plans and suggestions as choices. I just did as I was told—or maybe that should be as I was asked. I am aware, looking back, and I think I even was at the time, that to some extent Dad was living vicariously through me. It's neither illogical nor surprising, I guess. His marriage had disintegrated under particularly harrowing circumstances. The whole business with Mum must have been distressing, exhausting and bewildering. He had lost a woman he loved. His wife. And their only child had lost his mother.

Ironically, Dad's own mother was an added responsibility. She wasn't infirm, but she was getting on a bit. She was eighty-odd when we moved to Birmingham. Under such circumstances, it wasn't exactly likely that Dad would be able to incorporate much adventure or variety into his life. It was absolutely imperative that he remained stable, reliable, solvent, totally in control, and there. He simply couldn't and didn't ever go away.

He did have a few leisure pursuits but they were all pretty close to home. Popping down the Stag, playing darts, cards and bowls, watching the local football team, West Bromwich Albion, and having the occasional flutter on the horses. My hobbies required more specialised equipment and greater mobility. Dad provided both. He made sure I had whatever I needed. Bird books, binoculars and telescope, and transport to and from the reservoir—my 'local'! He would drop me off and pick me up. He even organised a couple of short holidays to Norfolk—my choice—where he would ferry me around. This was particularly generous, since birdwatching was certainly not his thing. However, sport was. He paid for running spikes and new rugby boots, cricket bats and tennis rackets. We went to all West Brom's home matches together, and he got us tickets for one of the very first 'foreign' club encounters, Wolves v Honved (the champions of Hungary, which then had the best national team in the world—the magical Magyars). Even better, we were at Wembley in 1953 for the legendary 'Matthews Cup Final' when Blackpool were losing 3–1 to Bolton Wanderers with five minutes to go and came back to win 4–3! Stanley Matthews, old twinkletoes, the Cristiano

Ronaldo of his day. Except he was a thirty-eight-year-old, nearly bald Lancastrian!

Dad also contributed to my third great obsession, music. Although he himself had little interest beyond a couple of Bing Crosby albums, I'm sure it was Dad rather than my pocket money that provided a Dansette record player, a Bill Haley LP, a more or less constant supply of trad jazz records, and even a washboard for my school skiffle group!

Despite his overseeing and even organisation of my life, I never once felt that Dad was trying to push me in any particular direction, except up! The only time he tried was when he persuaded me to go into the science stream at school because, he said, 'That's where the jobs are.' Nowadays I suppose it would be computer programming. However, he was humble and wise enough to respond to my English teacher pointing out in my school report that my marks and behaviour in science classes were appalling, whilst those in English and history were rather good. 'Are you sure,' Mr Hutton wrote, 'he would not be happier studying the arts?' I was. Despite the fact that Dad must have been convinced I'd never be able to get a proper job. The splendid truth is, of course, that I never did!

I am sure it wasn't in a field that Dad had in mind, but he was able to enjoy some of my success. One of my happiest memories of him is when he came over to America in 1964 to watch me appearing on Broadway in *Cambridge Circus* (in a cast including Tim Brooke-Taylor, Graham Chapman and John Cleese). It was the first—and I think only—time that Dad ever went abroad! I am also glad that on another occasion he was able to meet my first daughter, Kate, albeit that she was a very new little baby at the time when we stayed with him in Hagley. Mind you, there was a slightly sad and perhaps significant aspect to that visit, as my first wife Jean reminded me not that long ago. 'Do you remember?' she said. 'We weren't allowed to share a bed.' Surely Dad didn't literally forbid it? But he must have made it clear that it wasn't acceptable, or that it would make him feel uncomfortable or something. 'The other thing I remember,' said Jean, 'was that I never, ever saw him touch you. Not even a pat, let alone a hug.'

In 1983 I wrote a page about Dad in my book *Gone Birding*. I have just reread it, and I see no reason to change or qualify what I said and thought then.

As long as I remember, Dad had suffered from bronchial asthma. For years he had made relatively light of it, referring to the little inhaler he had to use as his 'puffer'. Whilst I lived at home he never seemed to take his illness too seriously, and consequently neither did I. I remember he used to be gripped by awful coughing fits and wheezy breathlessness, but a couple of puffs seemed to put him right; though forty cigarettes a day soon put him wrong again. I don't think he wanted me to know how ill he was. He was extremely self-conscious about the idea of his becoming a burden to me, and he was determined that I would never have to look after him. I felt this was as a result of his having chosen to care for his mother, my granny. He had allowed her to dominate his life and suppress his

59

social life completely. When she died, frankly, it must have been a relief to him. In a way it gave him his freedom, but it was too late. During those years he had got out of the habit of really being able to enjoy himself. The presence of his mother barely allowed him to. I think he knew it, and he had unselfishly resolved that I would not be inhibited in the same way as him. In fact, he took the greatest pleasure in my achievements, many of which he engineered. He may have lived vicariously through me, but I regarded it as support and encouragement, not as a burden. I was and am delighted that I fulfilled his hopes (or were they expectations?), albeit no doubt not in an area he'd ever even thought about. My son the satirist!

Dad was intelligent, modest, conscientious and above all unselfish. I wish for his sake he hadn't been. Once I'd left home and moved to London, he seemed to lose much of his optimism and enthusiasm. I shall never forget suddenly realising that, only a year or two after leaving university, I was actually earning more than my dad. It must have seemed strange to him too. As much as Dad took pride and joy in my success, it must also have drained him. It was as if his work was at an end. The bronchial asthma took over, almost as if he could now let it. He refused to come to London and live with me. In 1968 he moved, alone, into a small house and was forced to retire from his job. In the summer of 1969, he went into hospital, and in the autumn he died.

He was fifty-eight. Nine years younger than I am now.

Thus ended the 1960s. The Beatles had come and gone, skirts had got shorter, England had won the World Cup (and I was there!), and my never large family had got even smaller. If anyone, by way of conversation, asked me about my parents, I took to simply saying, 'I don't have any.' To which the enquirer usually responded with an 'Oh, I'm sorry.' This gave me the options of either maintaining an 'I'd rather not talk about it' silence or embarking on the long and—let's face it—fairly dramatic tale of my mother's illness and my deprived childhood. Either way, I was likely to get a bit of sympathy, and I can't believe I didn't use it on occasions in the hope of earning a little feminine physical TLC. But hey, I needed it! Still do.

There was, however, an irony to be dealt with in 1969. As my dad disappeared, my mum reappeared. The two were not unconnected. In his will, my dad left me everything, which wasn't very much. Basically, it amounted to the value of his little house which, as I recall, eventually fetched about £10,000. I don't know if solicitors keep in touch with each other, or whether a code of conduct dictates that news of anyone's death and subsequent inheritance is distributed amongst all living relatives. It wasn't as if Mum was an official bereaved spouse, given that Dad had actually got a divorce at some stage, presumably on the grounds of 'irretrievable breakdown'. My mum's, as it happens. Presumably, Dad had been paying her some kind of alimony, and maybe the will did not include a continuation of this arrangement. In any event, I got a letter from a Lancastrian law firm contesting the will, and claiming that Mum should

61

be a beneficiary. I had no inclination to argue. I don't recall if I split the bounty, or sent her the lot. Either way, it was a practical and totally dispassionate decision, intended to maintain the status quo of the past ten years. Mother in Rochdale. Me and new family in London. No contact.

Time: the 1970s
Location: mainly in London, England

The Beatles may have split by this time, but their wisdom lived on: 'Can't buy me love' . . . so . . . 'Just give me money!'

It was in 1970 that *The Goodies* first appeared on the nation's TV screens, and it was in 1970 that I got my first handwritten letter from my mother telling me she was having trouble paying her bills. No coincidence, I'm sure. It may seem callous that I didn't respond instantly with a concerned reply, possibly even a visit to Rochdale to make sure she was OK—or at least a cheque—but I felt I needed advice. More than one person asked me: 'Are you sure it's really your mother?' That may seem extraordinarily mistrustful, but it is a fact that anyone who appears on the telly is likely to get letters asking for money. 'Begging letters', they call them. And I suppose that's what they are. Is a begging letter easier to resist than a begging hand, backed up by real human eyes, and an audible human voice? Perhaps, but when the 'beggar' is in the street in front of you, at least you can see who you are being asked to give to. You know what they look and sound like, and you just might feel you can judge whether your donation will be going on food, booze or drugs. Maybe I am gullible, but I don't think I have ever felt that I am being 'conned' by anyone claiming homelessness or hunger. Whatever the truth of their circumstances, they are pretty certainly a human being in a mess. But a begging letter could have been written by anyone, even if it is signed 'Mother'.

What to do? I was doing very well in my work. I could afford a contribution. It wasn't losing the lolly I was afraid of, it was contact. And I did need to be certain it really was Mum asking for help. I can't recall if I wrote to a solicitor or to her, but a correspondence began, which continued in much the same form for the next ten years. Basically, my mother wrote and asked for money. I sent her money. Then she asked for more. And more, and more. Again and again and again. I tried to keep things impersonal, first of all by sending a relatively large cheque to cover, say, the next six months or even a year. It wasn't enough, or maybe she couldn't resist spending it all at once. So, I set up a regular banker's order. Still not enough. I tried getting her to send me the actual electricity, gas or rent bills, and I paid them directly. But she still asked for more. No matter what I tried, I got letters which always told of some kind of impending disaster, which only I—or my money—could avert. 'My heating will be cut off', 'The phone will be disconnected', 'I will be evicted', etc etc etc. The few people who were aware of what was happening often advised me to stop sending money, or to stop corresponding at all. They said that what I was being subjected to was 'emotional blackmail'. It was, and it was working, and yes, I resented it.

Despite this, I didn't totally blame my mother. I felt pretty sure that she was to an extent being 'put up to it'. I could easily imagine her in the pub in Rochdale being wound up by a 'friend'. 'I saw your son on telly last night. He must be a millionaire, him. All them people on telly are millionaires. And he was on *Top of the Pops*. Them pop stars are all millionaires too. So he must be a millionaire twice. He should be looking after you he should.' To which, I would like to think my mum said, 'Well, he is actually.' Maybe she did. But I don't suppose that relieved the pressure. 'What's he pay for then? Just your gas and electric, and TV, and phone, and rent, and cigarettes and food and drink and stuff? Pah! He should've bought you a house in the West Indies. And a car, and a private jet! By the way, can you lend me a fiver?'

Pardon my slightly jaundiced view of the warm-hearted, down-to-earth, speak-as-I-find, common-as-muck but salt-of-the-earth, lovable, I-belong-in-Coronation Street northerner, but it's not my favourite stereotype. I have always claimed that I am allowed to slag off t'north, because I'm from there. As it happens, I have never much enjoyed soap operas or comedies about dysfunctional northern families, any more than I feel a warm glow about jolly cockneys or Eastenders. Quite where, when or how I developed this attitude of blatant intellectual snobbery, I do not know. Maybe it's because I was brought up with it when I was a little kid, even if I don't remember the details! I do remember pontificating in a school debate: 'If I wanted to watch a soap opera, I could bash a hole in the wall and listen to the next-door neighbours.' I can't remember if the motion was carried or not, or indeed what it was. Perhaps something like 'This house is not common.'

I do, however, remember the tone of my mum's letters. They usually began with a straight-to-the-point statement. 'Dear Bill, I am going to be thrown out if I do not pay the rent. I can't afford it. I had to pay for some new glasses too. I enclose the receipt.' She may or may not have asked nicely! I don't remember a lot of 'please' or 'thank you', which suggested to me that she was being told that it was her 'right' rather than a request. There wasn't much, if any, reference to whatever I was doing on the telly to earn my millions. There were, however, frequent references to church, the Lord, Jesus and praying, and occasional comments on new neighbours. I particularly remember the final sentence of one of her letters: 'The pakis have moved in next door, but I put my faith in the Lord!' To do what? Smite the pakis, and the blackies, and indeed anyone who wasn't from Lancashire, and white? Being myself a survivor of the 'summer of love', and more than a little aware of apartheid in South Africa and race riots in America, I found this combination of religion and racism just about as unendearing as it got. Call me picky, but it wasn't what I looked for in a mother!

As you are no doubt deducing from my ever more abrasive tone, this 1970s situation was something I consciously and considerably resented. Bitter? Undoubtedly. As it happens, the mid-seventies was also the time when my first marriage was going wrong, bringing a deal of pain and confusion to my whole family. No one is unaffected at such times, and it hit us all: Jean, me, and my gorgeous daughters Kate and Bonnie. No blame, no details and no stories, though. Suffice it to say that there was a fair bit of anger around, and I suppose it would have been good to be able to call on a little parental solace and even advice. But there was none to be had. Jean had no available mum or dad either. Which meant that my daughters had no cheery grandparents they could escape to now and then. As for me, I had a racist Christian fundamentalist with a history of mental instability, who might well be capable of violence, and whose only interest in me was my bank account. Or so it seemed.

And so passed the 1970s.

Fame, fortune, and fucking around. The latter quite literally for the second half of the decade, when I took full advantage of the Goodies' near rock and roll status, and applied myself to—and largely succeeded in—making up for the lack of a 'wild oats' period, which I should have had back in the sixties when, let's face it, there was a lot of it about! To borrow from Dickens, the seventies were for me 'the best of times and the worst of times', when many aspects of my life were almost constantly changing. But as the next decade dawned, some things remained the same. Mum was still asking for money, and I still hadn't met her.

Then I heard from Auntie Margery.

Time: 1980-ish
Location: Hampstead, London

Margery was Mum's younger sister, which of course made her my auntie. But Margery hadn't been the sort of auntie you went to visit when you were a little lad, who gave you buns and lemonade, and took you on outings to the zoo, and who sometimes had you to stay over in a little bedroom kept specially for you. Nor was she the wild, embarrassing kind of auntie who wears bizarre clothes and plays musical instruments and sings very loudly and may be a bit mad. Then again, maybe Margery *was* a bit like that last one. After all, how would I know? I had never met her! At least not as far as I knew, or that I could remember. I had occasionally heard her referred to by my dad or granny, but when they spoke of her or 'that side of the family', their voices dropped to a whisper and took on a tone that was sombre, secretive and even a wee bit sinister. My gran would come out with expressions such as 'She were a bad 'un.' There were also dark references to my 'other granny', Mum and Margery's mother. She was another one I had never consciously met, but whom I did remember from a sepia photo in which she resembled a cross between Queen Mary (the monarch, not the ship) and a giant. How I knew she was enormous from a little snapshot I don't know, but I do know I felt no more affection for this particular granny than I did for Queen Mary herself. So, like so many other things and people in the Oddie household, Margery was someone we didn't talk about. If I ever enquired— and I'm not sure that I did—I would no doubt

67

have been told it was 'best I didn't know'. And I didn't!

In fact, Auntie Margery had tried to make contact with me once during the mid-seventies, by turning up in the audience for a Goodies recording. I think a floor manager told me she was there—which no doubt ruined my performance!—and after the recording she was waiting by the door to say hello. Which was about all I let her say. I recall I was stressed, fearful and angry. She was probably totally terrified, but I didn't consider that for one moment. I told her to go, and to leave me alone. Which she did. Until she sent the letter.

The tone of it was actually very sympathetic. She wasn't having a go at me for neglecting my mother. She expressed understanding of how I felt about being constantly asked for money by a woman whom, in essence, I didn't know, and had only pretty horrible memories of. But Margery was writing to say she had a plan, advice, a theory, call it what you will. 'I think that if you actually go and see your mum, she will stop the emotional blackmail letters.' Margery even offered to arrange the reunion. She would have known that I was at the time working at least one day a week for BBC Manchester, presenting a new general interest and entertainment show called *Fax*. (It was actually rather good, and ran for three series, got a big audience and proved to the BBC that 5 p.m. was a very popular slot. So they gave it to *EastEnders*!) Anyway, so I was in Manchester, and Mum was in Rochdale. They are only a few miles apart. In fact there was nothing except a bus ride stopping Mum turning up in the studio audience as Margery had done, but I dare say that was—rightly—judged to be not a very good idea. No, Margery would go and get Mum, and drive her into Manchester. Margery, it was turning out, was one of those aunts who drove both a car and a motorbike, read widely, had travelled the world, and had an absolutely fascinating tale to tell. Not a 'bad 'un' at all. More of this later.

Meanwhile, the date was set.

Time: 15 April 1984
Location: the dining room of a very large hotel in Manchester

I am sitting at a table with a lovely lady called Laura. Aha, a new character! Indeed, and a very significant one. Having emerged from my promiscuous, no-strings-attached phase, I had now begun a rather more significant relationship with Laura. We were married in 1983, and we still are. So, that was no lady, that was my wife. She had offered to give me moral and any other support I needed on 'meet your mother' day. It can't have been easy, and must have taken a deal of nerve. After all, Laura knew even less about my mum than I did, and what little she did know I had told her, and what I'd told her was unusual to say the least, if not downright scary. So, as she sat with me waiting, she had no idea what to expect. Neither did I.

So what were my feelings? Excitement? Not really. Trepidation? Definitely. Curiosity? Maybe a bit. Nervous? You bet. Normally these 'meet the parents' moments represent a big hurdle for only one half of a couple. This one was a bit novel.

Neither of us knew the woman we were about to meet. I dare say I ran through the facts for Laura, and indeed for myself . . .

It was nearly thirty years since I had last seen my mother face to face, at Barnsley Hall, when she hadn't known who I was. The last time we had been together when we did at least recognise one another was nearer forty years ago. Before that, my memories of her were limited to half a dozen generally disturbing images. What little I knew of her beliefs and tastes, I disliked intensely. I did not know her voice. I did not know what she looked like.

'This is definitely weird,' I thought out loud. 'I am going to meet my mother.'

*   *   *

I think it's fair to say I would not have recognised her. I did recognise Auntie Margery, following our brief and uncomfortable encounter at the BBC studio. So I presumed the woman that Margery was gently directing towards our table was . . .

'Lilian,' announced Margery, 'this is Bill.' So at least we now knew who we were. I assume she recognised me from off the telly. Laura was also duly named: 'This is Laura, Bill's young lady'.

'My wife,' I added. Laura smiled her 'hello', and her presence most certainly added a cheery aura, which was and still is one of her great talents. She is quite simply one of the most likeable and sociable people I have ever known. I, however, am not, especially when being introduced to a total stranger who I am told gave me life! I would be lying if I claimed to remember a single word that was spoken. I know what wasn't said. There were no great outpourings of emotions. No 'Oh my God's. Not even significant speechlessness. No one was simply lost for words. *This Is Your Life* or *Surprise Surprise* it was not. Laura has since confirmed the unmemorableness of the conversation by admitting that she too remembers precisely nothing!

Typically, with my photographic recall, I can remember what my mum looked like. Height wise she was smaller than I expected, width wise she was bigger. She was plump, round in body and in face. Bowling-pin legs clad in dense brown, almost surgical stocking material. Hair fairly short and a bit curly—not a 'perm'—and greying. Glasses. And a hat. The truth is, I couldn't swear she actually was wearing a hat but that's how I picture her. A little round hat. And even as I write this description, I recognise it. But not as my mum. It's the identikit cliché little old lady. The Granny in the Giles cartoons, *Monty Python*'s Pepper Pots, Tim Brooke-Taylor in drag in *The Goodies*! There are whole packs of them in any northern drama on the telly. This isn't a description of a person. It's a caricature. Maybe that's why that reunion didn't affect me emotionally. It wasn't real.

*   *   *

And after that? That perception of my mother never really changed. Whilst I was still working in Manchester I visited her at her flat on the outskirts of Rochdale. The first time Margery wasn't there, but again Laura came with me and we all went out to lunch at a local eatery. Laura remembers more than I do, or at least she remembers how she felt. 'Uneasy' is the word she uses. She remembers my mother as being rather glazed, 'not quite there', not silent, but not very communicative. Laura also recalls thinking: 'She seems like a perfectly harmless old lady, but might she suddenly turn violent? She's been in a mental home. She attacked Bill's dad, she's clearly had a lot of treatment and medication, she seems slightly sedated now, in fact. Will it wear off? Is it safe?' Frankly and sadly, I am sure I speak for both Laura and myself when I say that our main feeling when the visit was over was one of relief.

Laura actually expressed concern that I intended to go to Mum's flat again early in 1985. As it turned out, it was to be my last visit, and it was my decision not to return. It was a short and extremely uncomfortable experience. I could barely see across the room for the dense pall of cigarette smoke, and although I mentioned that I didn't smoke myself, and clearly could barely breathe without coughing, she lit up several more times. Meanwhile she almost completely ignored my attempts at conversation, which was almost impossible anyway because she had the television on at a volume that was literally distorting the sound. It wasn't long before I'd had enough. I gave her money and I gave up. If Mum was trying to punish me or put me off, she did a great job. Maybe she was just admitting that we had nothing in common, nor any emotional ties, and that it was actually a better deal to have a famous son on the telly whom she could be proud of at the pub, and who sent her enough cash to be able to buy everyone a round. I am not being self-consciously cynical or sarcastic; it's the very least she deserved. It's probably all that was possible.

By the end of 1985, Laura and I had a new Oddie to distract us: Rosie was born on the night before Hallowe'en, and thus completed my trio of fabulous daughters who collectively represent my greatest achievement in life. OK, they've got pretty special mothers too, but I am going to claim some credit! My own mother didn't get the chance to be special for herself, or for her child. The irony does not escape me that having been deprived of female presence in my younger years, I have more than made up for it, I am happy to say, in the rest of my life!

Mum/Lilian/Mother was able to at least have some access to or awareness of my growing family. Around 1987 Margery really 'took over'. She arranged for her sister to move south and live with her in Brighton. I visited there a few times, and on at least one occasion Margery brought Mum up to London, where she met the trio of Kate, Bonnie and baby Rosie. Laura reckons there is a photo somewhere of Mum in our garden, but I can't find it. The sad truth is that nothing really seemed to make much impression. My—and Laura's— memory of my mum during the late 1980s is of a person who was 'amiably detached'. That seems a fair expression. She smoked constantly. She was also 'getting on a bit', as they say in t'north. Margery got her admitted to a 'rest home', though I dare say that rest was one of the things she'd had rather a surfeit of in her life! During 1989, her health began to deteriorate and the next year she was taken into hospital. She died on 13 June 1990, aged seventy-six. I paid for the funeral and a headstone, but I didn't go.

*   *   *

As I am writing this a pattern is beginning to emerge. God knows I don't believe in fate, destiny, numerology or astrology, and I don't believe in God either, so I am going to have to put this one down to coincidence. Ten-year cycles. Decades. History—especially popular culture—is divided up into them. So, it seems, is my life! I suppose the fact that I was born in 1941 sort of invites that way of looking at things, but there have been quite a number of rather neat ten-year phases.

- At the end of the 1940s we moved to Birmingham.
- In 1950 Mum was admitted to Barnsley Hall, and remained there for ten years.
- In 1960, after ten years of secondary school education, I moved on to Cambridge. I didn't stay there for ten years, but, let's face it, the sixties were ten years that were worth being involved in by anybody's standards! Added to which, Dad sustained the pattern by lasting ten years after I'd left home, until he died in 1969.
- The 1970s are easy. *The Goodies* ran for exactly ten years.
- And the 1980s got off to a good start when I met Laura. They were also my mother's final ten years. She died in 1990. I was parentless.
- The 1990s could be designated the decade I found a new direction work-wise, as the 'ex-Goody and comedian' morphed into 'Britain's best-known birdwatcher' (an accolade which I

74

tend to ungraciously counter by asking: 'Can you name any other celebrity birdwatcher?'). But here the ten-year pattern begins to falter, since my wildlife presenter persona has lasted for fifteen years, with hopefully a few more still to come.

But there's more to life than work and catchphrase identities. What about me as a person? Did anything happen in 2000? Did any significant personal developments occur to mark the new millennium and set the tone for the current decade? You bet.

Frankly, throughout 2000 I knew it was coming. Or at least I would have done if I'd been aware of the symptoms, and even considered for one moment that I could be susceptible to such a thing. OK, my mother had been locked up in an asylum for ten years, I knew that, but it had never once been put to me that her mental problems could be hereditary. After all, as far as I knew, there was no history of such a thing in our family, and in any case if there was a genetic weakness, it was surely only on my mother's side. My father was about as stable (as un-unstable) as a human being could be. Never once had I seen him even cry, express anguish, or appear to be anything other than totally under control. Yes, yes, I now know that that in itself should have worried me, but it didn't then. As far as I was concerned, Dad was sanity personified, and since Dad was the only parent I had really had, it's not surprising that I considered myself to belong 'on his side' as it were.

All my life I had prided myself on being as 'normal' as my dad. I was not impulsive or disorganised, and I liked to think I was reliable and conscientious. I had never followed the fashionable crowd of the time. I was not a teddy boy, nor a mod or a rocker, and even though my long hair and beads may have looked like the uniform of a hippie, I wasn't the real thing. It was a sartorial decision. I just hated wearing suits and ties. I still do. I never fell apart under stress, and I'd never taken solace in drink or drugs, which, let's face it, is quite an achievement for someone who had been been immersed in the Swinging Sixties! I will now make one of the few shocking confessions in this book: I admit that, despite mingling with all sorts of musos and thespians for many years, I didn't once smoke a joint. Indeed, if I said that my abstinence was a factor in the break-up of my first marriage, there would be a tiny element of truth in it. But I am not going to elaborate, because I don't go in for elaboration much either. Well, I used not to.

Nowadays, I can't get enough of it. There are few things I like better than elaborating on and analysing the mysteries of human beings, especially myself! And I have no objection to other people having a go at sorting me out either. But I didn't have that attitude back in the twentieth century, i.e. most of my life! I didn't actually suppress and withhold emotions and information, as my dad had done for so long—protecting your child from the truth was what a responsible parent did in those days, and he was nothing if not responsible—but I wasn't very sympathetic to reasons why people behaved badly. Ever since I was a student I'd had little truck with the 'they are insecure' excuse. This always seemed to be the explanation that let perpetrators of the most appalling behaviour off the hook. 'Why does he get so embarrassingly pissed every Friday?' Because he's in secure. 'Why does he go around nicking everyone's girlfriends?' Because he's insecure. 'Why can't he be faithful?' Because he's insecure. 'Why is he such a show-off?' Insecure. 'A liar?' Insecure. 'A bully, an oaf, a cheat? A total dickhead?' Insecure. I suppose it was insecurity that made Hitler invade Poland, and provides the excuse for just about everything George W. Bush has said and done. Mind you, if he isn't insecure, he bloody well should be.

Notice how all my examples are masculine? It's funny how my harshest criticism, intolerance even, was invariably directed at men. Towards women, I was—and still am—far more understanding and forgiving. Now could that be because I don't want to insult or antagonise them, for fear that they might bugger off and leave me? In other words, because I myself am . . . insecure! Mm. I think that's what they call being 'hoist with your own petard'. All these years I didn't realise I had one!

I will unhesistatingly and willingly accept and admit my own insecurities now, but if you had called me 'insecure' at any time during the first sixty years of my life, I would have biffed you on the nose. 'Why is he so aggressive?' Insecure. As a few people told me at the time, and many have reminded me since, I had quite a bad reputation for being belligerent, argumentative, unsociable, moody and harsh. As my best mate put it at my fiftieth birthday party: 'What I really, really admire about Bill is that he is the grumpiest person I know, but he gets away with it.' Another close friend used to call me 'Grumpibollocks'. Presumably for a reason.

But the present decade has witnessed quite a change. By the year 2000 I was becoming increasingly aware that I wasn't entirely 'getting away with it'. I started writing cryptic little notes in my appointments diary alongside the details of whatever I was doing that day, be it a voice-over, a meeting, filming, whatever. I was very busy, but clearly not entirely happy. Against the 14 May 2000 entry I had scribbled: 'Stress, panic, and suppressed anger.' Not, I imagine, themes for my next birdwatching programme! A few months later I wrote: 'Aware of anxiety, hyperventilation etc.' And, as absolute proof that I was indeed becoming more concerned about such things, there are appointments with my GP, an acupuncturist, even a cranial massage therapist. Believe me, when a lad from Rochdale starts turning to that sort of namby-pamby, New Age, so-called 'alternative' mumbo-jumbo, there is definitely summat wrong wi' him! Grief, I even started going along to Laura's yoga class.

As the year went on, I frequently complained of what I called 'skullcap head', a sort of woozy feeling, a bit like jet lag, or as if I'd been wearing a rather over-tight crash helmet. It wasn't truly painful, but it bothered me in that I felt as if I was becoming a little bit removed from reality. I don't mean that psychologically. The sensation was physical. I wasn't getting mentally confused. Or maybe I was.

Early in 2000, I had a rather unnerving experience of momentary memory loss. I had a very busy day. In the morning I was incarcerated in the tiny tomb that is a sound recording studio, adding a commentary to a film about ducks. Unfortunately, I had to break off before I had finished, literally run to the carpark, and drive to south London for a meeting with my accountant, who burbled on for an hour without me understanding a single word. Nothing unusual about that, mind you. Then it was back in the car, drive back to Soho, and park again. As I scurried along, it struck me that I hadn't had time to eat, so I leapt into a takeaway and rapidly purchased some sushi, which I was still failing to digest when I resumed my position at the microphone. I carried on the commentary where I'd left off, and after another hour or so I was finished.

As is often the case, the producer suggested we just check back the beginning of the film to make sure the voice delivery was consistent. No sooner did the opening titles appear on the screen than I proclaimed: 'I don't recognise this.' As the film began, the engineer was still fiddling with knobs and faders in order to bring up my voice. He was having a little trouble finding it instantly, which is often the way. However, I knew exactly why he couldn't find my first bit of commentary. He couldn't find it because I hadn't done it. Which is what I assertively announced to the others.

'I didn't do this bit.'

'Yes you did,' the producer assured me.

But I was adamant. 'I didn't. I have never seen those ducks before!'

By now, I suspect, the producer and the engineer were thinking, 'He's been overdoing it. He needs to go home and rest.' So they kindly told me, 'It was fine. So let's leave it at that.'

But it wasn't fine by me! I was convinced that they were making a ridiculous mistake by sending me home when I had not done the first few minutes of the voice-over.

'I didn't do it,' I insisted.

'You did,' they chorused.

'OK, then,' I demanded, 'play it to me.'

At which moment the engineer found the right fader and, sure enough, there was my voice, loud and confident, fitting the pictures exactly. In fact, rather a good job. But I still couldn't remember doing it.

The truth is that I am sure many readers will have had similar experiences when the workload has got too heavy, and intrinsically there was nothing particularly sinister about it. But it bothered me, because nothing like that had ever happened before. It bothered me even more when, a few months later, a similar sort of thing happened again, at the end of a day which turned out to be the trigger for what was undoubtedly the scariest thing I have ever experienced in the whole of my life.

Time: 26 September 2000
Location: Newquay, Cornwall, via the M4

It is a long drive from Hampstead to Newquay, but it was better than going by train because I had a certain amount of heavy, awkward gear to take and it was easier to shove it in the boot of my car. This included a slide projector and a couple of carousels of slides, plus a pair of large leather gauntlets, a bright orange fright wig, and a life-size cuddly toy puffin. These were the essentials I required to deliver my two-hour one-man show *Follow That Bird—An Evening with Bill Oddie*, an entertainment in which I asked myself the sort of questions that would trigger off tales, anecdotes and interesting facts, all illustrated with my own slides, and involving 'demonstrations' with informative intent, but performed in a humorous and actually quite exhausting manner! My TV wildlife programmes at the time were gentle and ruminative, but my stage act was little short of hyperactive. The gloves and puffin were integral to my acting out what it was like to catch and ring seabirds. It involved ventriloquism—the puffin spoke—and some manic contortions and bird wrestling that Rod Hull and Emu would have beeen proud of. The orange fright wig was the stunning climax of a sequence in which I impersonated the mating display of a New Guinea bower bird! Honestly. This involved a lot of bouncing up and down in ever decreasing circles, and finally flashing my fiery crest. In other words, suddenly slapping on the wig which had hitherto been cunningly secreted behind a chair. The effect was as if my head had suddenly burst into flames and was so convincing—or so daft—that it invariably received a round of applause, as indeed the actual bower bird had got from me when I saw it do the same thing in the depths of a dark New Guinea rainforest some twenty years ago. I also impersonated various duck calls and the mating strut of the Blue-footed Booby, which bore a striking resemblance to one of John Cleese's silly walks. I have always thought that the connection between wildlife and comedy is much closer than people realise, and I suppose my stage show was designed to prove just that, albeit that there was a serious message behind it all. Nature is entertaining in all sorts of ways— visually, aurally, dramatically, romantically, spiritually even. That's what nature is. It is life.

Anyway, back to that night's performance in Newquay. I wasn't nervous. I never do get nervous before wildlife shows, whether on stage or on telly. Maybe because I enjoy them so much. But I was feeling a wee bit disorientated. It wasn't entirely illogical. I was used to doing shows in theatres, concert halls, lecture rooms and so on, but I had never done one in a tent! It turned out that my appearance was part of a general 'festival of the outdoors'. It was a good job they hadn't extended the theme to outdoor slide shows, because it was bucketing down that evening and had been for several days, so that the festival site now looked like a small-scale Glastonbury in one of its muddiest years. There were literally pools and puddles everywhere, and wooden 'duckboards' had had to be put down so people could actually get to the tents without sinking in the quagmire. So, looking back now, no wonder I felt a bit disorientated. I said I didn't get nervous, but I did like to have half an hour's 'quiet time' in a dressing room just to check my slides and gather my thoughts. In fact, I also often used to do a short meditation routine for which I borrowed the standard Buddhist chant 'nam myoho renge keo', which my daughter Bonnie had taught me. (I crave the forgiveness of her and all Buddhists if I have spelt it wrong.) It also appealed to me that I had read in a magazine that several of my favourite

82

jazz musicians prepared for concerts in the same way. I like to think of myself as the Herbie Hancock of wildlife slide shows! But that night in Newquay there was no time for all that calm and 'control'. When I eventually sloshed my way into the back entrance of the tent—well, marquee, I suppose—I discovered that my audience must have known a better route because they were all in there ready and waiting. No chance of meditating in the dressing room. There wasn't one. No time to check the slide projector, or the sound system, or the lighting either. I had hardly said hello to the organisers before my carousels had been whipped out of my hands, the house lights dimmed, and someone was on the mike introducing me. And I was on.

My first words were something like 'Oh, bloody hell!'—which is not how I normally started a slide show. 'OK, OK, I'll talk!' I said in the manner of a prisoner being interrogated and having a blinding table lamp directed at his face, because that is more or less what had happened. Only it wasn't a table lamp, it was a couple of spotlights. They were aimed straight at me and were incredibly strong. So strong that I was temporarily blinded. Having milked the situation for comedy value, I asked quite seriously if there was any chance of dimming or turning off the spotlights. A disembodied voice from the dark told me that there wasn't. The brighter the light in your eyes, the less you can see out front, so I launched into the show unable to actually see if there was anyone out there listening or watching me. As it happens, that's normally fine by me. In many performance situations, I prefer not to be able to see the audience. If I am acting or singing, I sort of retreat into a private world in which I can be totally uninhibited. Being made aware that there are people watching me can be quite embarrassing!

But doing my 'bird show' required much more intimate contact with the audience. I wanted them to get involved and join in when I asked them to. I really needed to be able to see them, but with two blinding spotlights in my eyes, I couldn't. Which added to the feeling of being strangely disembodied. Nevertheless, there was nothing really weird happening yet. Until half-time.

It was only during the interval that I realised that I was not just feeling a bit distant from the proceedings, I wasn't actually sure that I had done the first half properly at all. I found myself trying to go through it in my head. I remembered the bright lights. I was sure I had done the first bit about 'how I began birdwatching'; and told the story of trying to blow a pheasant's egg when I was a kid, but finding it had gone so bad and gooey that I'd had to suck it instead, which inevitably led to me throwing up over my whole collection. Aversion therapy that made me give up egg collecting and become a proper birdwatcher! I was certain I had told that story. But after that bit, I simply couldn't remember anything else until a few minutes ago, when I'd said 'OK, I am going to take a short break now, and in the second half I'll take you travelling.' I meant I would go on to my adventures abroad, featuring my hilarious orange wig and the booby's funny walk. That was still to come, but what I was more concerned about was what had already gone. Or not!

I began to seek circumstantial evidence. Had I

done the puffin-ringing routine? My puffin was no longer in the shoulder bag I carried my props in, so presumably I had. Did it go well? I couldn't remember. I ran through the various sections of the first half, and became convinced that I must have 'dried', as they say in the theatre, i.e. stopped because I had forgotten my lines. I felt sure I had then left out a whole chunk, and picked it up again for the last bit. Had the audience noticed, I wondered? They seemed happy enough. I could hear them chuntering away in the bar at the other end of the tent. They sounded contented. They hadn't booed me off. Neither had anyone backstage asked me if I was OK. So presumably I seemed normal! Then it struck me there was one way that I could check whether or not things had gone awry. My act involved a large number of slides, arranged in a very specific order. I operated the changer myself with a small remote control, and the timing was absolutely crucial. The simple and indisputable fact was that, if I had indeed forgotten my lines, and missed out sequences, then in no time at all the slides would have have been completely 'out of sync' and made no sense whatsoever. I know that I hadn't been able to see the audience, but I knew they were there—a couple of hundred of them– and I couldn't believe that they would have been polite enough to sit through a complete shambles without at least a fidget of embarrassment, or even a little helpful comment, or indeed a barrage of barracking and a walk-out! With some small trepidation, I looked at the slide still on the screen. It was the last one in the first half carousel. Just as it should be. I must have done the show on 'automatic pilot', as it were. Almost an hour, but just like those few minutes of duck commentary, I couldn't remember a thing about it.

Once again I consoled myself that there were extenuating circumstances, and indeed there were. The stress of rushing, no time to do checks, a strange venue and two viciously bright lights in my eyes. Indeed there was some consolation in the fact that I was obviously so practised in my routine that I could achieve a passable performance even under conditions that were little short of torture! What a trouper!

The interval was long enough for me to 'get myself together', as it were, and the second half went fine, and I was as totally aware of my performance and of the audience reaction as was my wont. Awareness—of the performance and how it's going, not the audience—is something I pride myself on, which is probably why the incident worried me, as well it might. For several reasons. It was the second time this memory loss thing had happened. Was I overdoing it? I was finding this belting up and down the country doing slide shows quite a stressful schedule. It was also a rather lonely activity. Staying in hotels. Having breakfast by myself. And the long drives. Ah yes, the driving. As it happens, the Newquay trip hadn't been arduous so much as tedious. Motorway—the M4—most of the way there and back. Maybe two or three tapes' worth each way. I was in those days in the habit of rating journeys by the number of ninety-minute cassettes I would get through. I had made hundreds of compilations featuring favourite tracks and artists, different styles and new releases. Listening to the music was the major, and arguably the only, consolation for having to do a long drive. 'Oh well, at least I can listen to the new Prince triple album.' I like to think that Prince only recorded so profusely on my account. Why else release a triple album?

So I returned to London on the morning of 27 September, safe and sound, but having had a rather strange experience. But wait, you may well be thinking, he said something happened on that trip that led to the worst moment of his life. Indeed it had. But I didn't realise it at the time. In fact, I remained totally oblivious of it till about two months later!

Time: November 2000
Location: home

In mid November, I received a summons for speeding. I was surprised, to say the least, and for two reasons. In the first place I generally don't speed. Honest, guv. Secondly, I certainly hadn't been pulled over and booked in recent memory. In fact, I never had. So I perused the document in puzzlement. It actually took me a while to realise that it was a 'caught on camera' job. That was also a first for me. And what was the specific offence? Doing—and I honestly don't have a record of the exact figure—just over 80mph in a 50mph zone. What? 30mph over the limit?! I simply knew that I never had done that, and never would do it. Honest again, guv. Truly and genuinely honest. I have already pleaded that I pride myself on being responsible and so on (thanks, Dad!) and I simply haven't got it in me to go around breaking the law.

Well, not knowingly anyway. As I stared disbelievingly at the summons, a few other key words and numbers came into focus. Firstly, the date: 26 September. Where had I been then? The next detail told me: 'the M4, just outside Bristol.' On my way to Newquay.

My brain began to protest at what was clearly an unjust accusation. The M4 is a full-blown motorway. It has a 70mph speed limit, but who amongst us hasn't strayed up to 80 on a clear uncongested downhill stretch, before realising and dropping back? Am I being far too trusting of traffic control police in always having assumed that you wouldn't get clobbered unless you were up toward the nineties and beyond? Which, as I recall, plenty of cars were doing as they overtook me on that stretch of road that very day. In which case, presumably a whole avalanche of summonses must have been sent out, because it was then that I registered the exact wording of the offence: travelling at 80-ish 'in a *temporary* 50mph zone'. Temporary? Bleeding fictional, I'd say.

I have already alluded to my visual memory, and the picture I reran in my head of that stretch of the M4 was pretty vivid. Go west from London, go round Bristol, and then there is a long stretch, mostly downhill, as you head off towards Devon and Cornwall. I could remember it clearly. At that stage on 26 September, the weather had been quite pleasant (the deluges were further west), and I even recalled seeing a temporary 50mph sign and thinking, 'Why is that there?' There were no roadworks, no dodgy road conditions, no cones, nothing that would justify a temporary speed restriction. Nevertheless, I and most other drivers slowed down. After a considerable time and distance, though, and in the absence of any more 50mph signs, the traffic—and there wasn't much—began to speed up, and I began to go with the flow. I was thinking, as I dare say all the other drivers were, 'Surely it's not still fifty?' There were certainly no signs telling us that it still was. Nor, I admit, had I been aware of a sign saying that we were out of the temporary restriction and back to seventy. Maybe there had been, but I hadn't noticed it? Everyone else seemed to have gone back to seventy or, in the case of various Mercedes and BMWs, a lot more. And so I, in my little Renault, followed in their wake. I even remembered noticing my speedometer creeping up to eighty, and taking my foot off the accelerator. And thus I had carried on innocently and legally down to Newquay.

On the return journey, I presumably dropped down to fifty when requested, and may or may not have thought, 'I still can't see why the restriction, when there are no roadworks or any other apparent reason.' How naive am I? When have logical reasons ever been necessary to justify enforcing illogical traffic restrictions?

So what am I saying? That getting a speeding summons is the worst thing that has ever happened to me? Of course not. On the other hand, it began to seem so. As the year 2000 trundled inexorably towards Christmas, I became more and more obsessed with the summons. My first reaction of surprise was so genuine that I simply thought: 'This is clearly ridiculous. All I have to do is explain the circumstances, and I will get a polite letter back saying: "We quite understand. We really must do better with our temporary road signs. Sorry we upset you. Yours truly, the Bristol Constabulary".' And I would be let off, and acknowledged as the highly responsible driver I was, and still am. Yes, I was naive. Of course I got a reply which in effect said: 'Do you live in cloud cuckoo land or what? You're nicked, mate.' Moreover, it also set the date of a court hearing, for which I would have to traipse all the way down to the Bristol suburb near where the crime had occurred. I was still clinging on to some daft notion of British justice, but it was beginning to slip from my grasp, and so was my ability to stop thinking about it, day and night.

I began to drive everyone around me crazy by going on and on about it. I was desperately seeking support, from anyone within earshot. 'Surely I won't be convicted, and get a driving ban? I've had a clean licence for over forty years! Does that count for nothing?' No doubt my friends and family were trying to comfort me, or were they perhaps trying to get me to shut up? I am sure I was getting sympathy, but I was also getting more and more annoying, and more and more distraught. And I am sure my family were getting more and more concerned for me.

I was getting concerned for myself. It was against the stoical Oddie nature to have truck with such 'weaknesses', but I began to accept that over the past weeks, OK months, OK years, OK maybe all my life, I had shown many classic symptoms of stress, anxiety, and suppressed anger. 'The grumpiest person I know and he gets away with it.' Oh, no he doesn't! I had even begun to investigate some of the common syndromes and the appropriate jargon. I went to the doctor, who diagnosed that I was habitually hyperventilating, and I accepted this and practised the breathing exercises he gave me. I also accepted that the fuzzy headaches and stomach twinges that I'd had for ages, but were getting worse, were surely stress-related. Someone recommended an acupuncturist, and I went several times but with variable results. The one thing I had to concede was that the needles certainly did have an effect. Sometimes I came out feeling more relaxed, but on another occasion I felt much, much worse, and I was rather alarmed when the acupuncturist herself seemed panicked, as if one of the needles had triggered off a response she really hadn't intended. She said something like: 'It's a thin line between a good effect and a bad. Acupuncture is very powerful.' I believe that. I didn't go there again.

I did have to go to court.

Time: 4 January 2001
Location: somewhere near Bristol

I had just begun my sixtieth year. It's never too late to have new experiences! Laura drove me down to some utterly anonymous suburb of Bristol. Presumably we drove down the fateful M4, and no doubt I muttered darkly and bitterly if we passed through any temporary 50mph areas. It was a dreary, damp and gloomy day in early January, the gloomiest month. The time of the court case had inevitably been postponed, so we had to go and 'waste' an hour, which we did in a desperately doomy little café, in the sort of shopping mall that, if it had been created as an art installation and labelled 'Soul-less', would win a Turner Prize. By the time we got back to the courthouse, or municipal buildings or whatever they were, there were a few more delinquents awaiting their sentences, sorry I mean 'hearings'. A word which implied someone might listen, but I doubted it.

Amongst the sinners was a sweet old lady to whom Laura and I felt strangely drawn. It was as if we had something in common. Indeed we did. She too had been caught on camera speeding in a temporary 50mph area on the M4 in late September. 'Just outside Bristol?' 'Yes.' 'On that long downhill bit?' 'Yes'. 'Did you see any fifty signs?' 'No.' We bonded as fellow criminals. It takes one to know one. I asked her what wicked, perverted assignment she had been recklessly racing towards. 'I was going down to see my sister in Cornwall. I hadn't visited her for ages. We had such a nice day. And then this happens.' I don't know how much that lady was fined, but I am sure she couldn't afford it.

I pleaded guilty, as technically I clearly was. However, I wasn't banned. I had got my producer to write a letter explaining how important it was for me to be seen driving to watch wildlife on the telly, which may have helped. What presumably didn't help was being a so called 'celebrity', since that meant I clearly needed to be made an example of. I got a £600 fine (nothing to a millionaire such as I, of course) and six points on my licence. I was relieved, and yet incensed. 'But let's face it,' Laura pointed out—with indisputable yet slightly irritating truth—'you were guilty. At least you didn't get banned.'

I got something far, far worse, which—ironically—kept me off the road for several months.

Time: 8 January 2001
Location: the edge of Hampstead Heath

I had told Laura I was going for a walk, but I could barely move. My hands were shaking and my legs were wobbly. Laura came with me. We had only just barely crossed the road to the Heath when I stopped, burst into tears and announced: 'I think I'm having some kind of breakdown.'

Well, I was right about that. Later that day Laura took me to see my GP and he confirmed my diagnosis. 'You are suffering from clinical depression.' So how did he work that one out? Probably from the fact that I had shuffled into the surgery at a speed that would have embarrassed a sloth. From the fact that I slumped into a chair and sat there staring at the floor. From the fact that my eyes kept closing. From the fact that I could barely talk. From the fact that if I tried to speak, I kept bursting into tears. 'In fact,' added the doctor, 'this is as bad as I have ever seen.'

He prescribed an antidepressant and arranged for a specialist to come and see me. I spent the rest of that week in bed. Sometimes sleeping, sometimes weeping. Often tossing and turning, and wailing such things as 'It's gone. It's all gone.' What had gone? Feelings. All feelings gone, except the one that told me exactly that. A feeling of emptiness. Of total utter complete despair and negativity.

Laura tried to console me. All my family did, but I simply couldn't respond. What about them? What about my wife? My daughters? My grandson? 'What about us?' asked Laura.

My response was the most hurtful thing I have ever said, and the most shocking thing to me is that I meant it: 'I don't care.'

That's how bad it is. If you asked me now what is the most joyous aspect of my life, I would unhesitatingly say that it is my family. All my gorgeous girls and my beautiful boy. It follows that, to me, the most precious commodity is life itself. Theirs and mine. I am alive, and I want to remain so as long as possible, so that I can enjoy my family. And therein lies the horror of clinical depression. You are reduced to a state where you totally deny and destroy the things you hold most dear. Its most extreme expression is of course suicide. When the specialist came to see me, she asked the big question by which the seriousness of a depression is judged: 'Do you have suicidal feelings?' I am sure my lack of response was answer enough. I think my eventual words were something like: 'I think about it, but I don't think I'd do it.' That was quite enough. It was decided that I should go into hospital. Not sectioned, nor committed. Voluntarily. I do recall a certain sense of relief at making the decision to be shut away from the outside world. I am sure my family were also relieved. Not because I would be out of the way, but because I would be in proper care. They must also have been very scared for me.

I am not sure when the irony struck me, but if you have read this far I am sure it is striking you right now! I was about to become an inmate of

94

Barmy Hall. Like mother, like son.

Indeed the first hospital I went to was all too reminiscent of my mother's former residence. It too was a sort of Gothic mansion with grounds like a deer park. It wasn't in Worcestershire, it was in north London, but I am sure the connotations of the architecture alone were enough to induce the sheer terror that engulfed me the minute I was led into a small room that I remember now only as a cell. I cowered in a corner in the traditional manner of a drug addict in a biopic movie—think Diana Ross as Billie Holiday in *Lady Sings the Blues*, for example—but I was not acting. Neither was I on drugs, except the antidepressant, and maybe a mild tranquilliser. I pleaded with Laura not to leave me there. What a conflict of emotions she must have felt. It is appalling and frightening enough to witness a person you know and love transformed into a whimpering wreck, let alone be faced with making decisions that may scare them or even turn them against you, even though it is for their own good. But I really didn't want to be left in that place. I kept apologising to Laura—'I'm sorry, I'm sorry.' And she kept assuring me, 'It's not your fault.' It wasn't. I was ill. I knew it. I also knew I needed 'professional help', but not there.

As it happens, the hospital made the decision for us. First of all by simply leaving us in that room for an hour and offering no acknowledgement of my presence apart from asking me to fill in a form. No welcome, no sympathy, no notice. Then the phone rang. It turned out to be reception wanting to know if they could put a call through from a journalist. So much for privacy and protection! We left immediately.

95

Later in the day I checked into a distinctly more homely establishment, right in the middle of London, in a bunch of terraced houses that you would assume were private residences or some kind of offices, unless you happened to notice the discreet brass plate by the door, and possibly the fact that most of the windows had bars across them. But then so do most buildings in cities. It's just security. The difference is that the bars are usually meant to keep people out, whereas these were to keep them in. Nevertheless, let's just say it was a far cry from Barmy Hall, and the clientele, far from being disorientated or almost terminally sedated, were actually a pretty lively and fascinating cross-section of twenty-first-century London society, suffering from a variety of now widely recognised 'mental illnesses', each one with a specific name. Not that you need to know exactly what's wrong with you before booking a room in such a place. There is only one qualification necessary, one question that needs answering: can you—or your insurance company—pay the bill?

In case you are wondering, I paid for myself and, yes, it was extremely expensive. Was it worth it? For the time being I will simply say 'Yes'.

Time: early February 2008
Location: my office

I now have a decision to make. I could write pages and pages about my experiences of depression, both personal and in general. I could tell you what happened to me, what helped and what didn't. I could say what I think of the treatments available.

I could be critical, and I could be contentious. In fact I could write a whole book about it. But I am not going to. One reason is that there are already many, many books on the subject. Some written by people who have suffered far more than I have. Others by experts who have studied every aspect of mental health, and know much more than I do.

Neither do I wish to become—how can I put this without offending a few people?—I don't want to be best known as a 'celebrity depressive'. Let's face it, it's a slightly oversubscribed market anyway! I sometimes think celebrity illnesses are about to take over from house makeovers, cooking programmes and so-called reality shows. I am certainly not belittling or doubting the mental problems of fellow 'celebs', and neither do I doubt that hearing about the troubles of a 'personality' can be something of a comfort to 'normal' people. It helps destigmatise the whole area of mental illness and—perhaps even more valuable—makes people realise that it can happen to us all. If a cheery little chap like Bill Oddie can have a breakdown, then surely so can anyone? If that's a consolation, that's fine by me!

I will just say a couple of things though about the celebrity mental patient syndrome. Firstly, we so-called celebrities are not by the very nature of our fame entirely 'normal'. Some bits of us—mental and physical—are normal, but other bits are exclusive to the extremely abnormal state of being a 'celebrity'. Secondly, we can probably afford to have our own room in a private hospital. It's bloody expensive, but it gives us a sporting chance!

There is one more reason I am restricting information about my experiences of depression. I really don't want to go there again. In fact, I *have* quite literally been there again. Twice. After recovering (remember that word—it's important) from the first collapse, I suffered a relapse late in 2002, and recovered (there's that word again). Then, in December 2005, I had another, less protracted hospitalisation, which wasn't the best way to spend Christmas, but fortunately it passed through like a fast-moving area of low pressure. That's a meteorological pun, by the way. Another kind of 'depression'! Mind you, it is not a bad parallel, and leads me neatly to the only 'message' I have to offer. Whether they are in your head or in the atmosphere, depressions can and do pass through. Recovery happens.

However, I can only speak for myself. The one absolute conclusion I have come to is that it's not possible to be totally dogmatic about mental illnesses. There are, I am sure, certain syndromes and generally accepted truths and tendencies, but like so many things in life, very little is proven or certain. It may seem self-centred or even selfish, but all I can offer is my own experience. Here is a simple fact. In the middle of a depression, I have never felt worse. Nowadays, I have never felt better. I don't mean manic. I am not bipolar. Just better! I hope that that in itself is encouraging to anyone reading this book who does or might suffer from depression. Recovery happens.

The only bit of practical advice I feel justified in giving—because I believe it truly is important—is to find out as much as you possibly can about what is happening, or has happened. Knowledge is power. I know it sounds like some kind of political or even military manifesto, but if the enemy or opposition is depression, I believe it is true. Don't be afraid of the truth. Don't be scared to find out. Talk and listen.

At the start of the new millennium this was a lesson I was only just beginning to learn for myself. And I was learning it the hard way! Stress, anxiety, a breakdown, a depression, a spell in hospital, a recovery, a relapse, another spell in hospital, affecting me and my family. Things changing, so far for the worse. Now they needed to change for the better. What more appropriate time to quote a wise little mantra that hangs on the wall of many a recovery venue and should be in every house. It may well have started as a prayer but it is the beginning of self-help.

> Grant me the serenity to accept the things I
>   cannot change,
> The courage to change the things I can,
> And the wisdom to know the difference.

The first thing I needed to change was my attitude to and my perception of the past, and the effect it might or might not have had on me. It may be hard to believe that I had never even thought about it before, but I truly hadn't. Now, however, I was being forced to consider, explore and maybe accept the possibility that my problems just might—and almost certainly did—have something to do with my mum. Had I, albeit belatedly, inherited a family flaw? Was there a history of mental instability in the Oddie family genes? Had the signs been there in my own personality all along, and had I failed to recognise or acknowledge them? Could I, should I, have seen this coming? Had other people in my own family seen the signs? Either of my two very special wives? Any of my three fabulous daughters? I have now figured out answers to a lot—though not all—of those questions. But then I only started asking them a few years ago. Only after my sixtieth birthday was I inclined—perhaps compelled—to think about what I knew and didn't know. Only after my sixty-first did I really learn to talk and listen.

Time: December 2002
Location: a psychiatrist's couch, Swiss Cottage, London

'I'm surprised it hasn't happened before . . . you've done well to get this far.' The words were said by a therapist, a psychoanalyst, a shrink. I was on the couch. I had been talking to him, he had been listening. Now he was talking and I was listening. I had been telling him all I knew about my family history, myself, my dad, my gran and, of course, my mum. Looking back now—and it's not long ago, so I can remember it pretty clearly—I can only presume his analytic heart must have palpitated with anticipation as he listened to my response to that most fundamental of requests posed to anyone who finds themselves on the couch. 'So, tell me about your mother.'

Even what was, on the face of it, a negative reply must have whetted his appetite. I told him: 'I wasn't brought up by my mother. I only have very few memories of her. Most of my childhood, she was in a mental home.'

100

'Blimey,' he must have been thinking, 'I've really hit the jackpot here!'

He went on to ask me: 'Have you any brothers or sisters?'

'No, I am an only child,' I replied, expecting that to get an enigmatic sort of 'yes, I thought so' type response. Instead, there was a short silence, until I added, 'Actually, I believe I may have had a sister . . . born before me. But she died after a few days. I can't even remember who told me that. Nobody ever talked about it.'

To which my therapist did indeed give a sort of knowing 'Mmm', as if to say, 'That's what happened in those days.'

Quite so, I thought. On two accounts. There was greater infant mortality. And people didn't talk about things.

But my therapist was obviously thinking more deeply than that. He came out with a line that had a strange echo of the words my mother had said to me when I went to see her in Barnsley Hall: 'Television is dead bodies and cardboard.' Now the therapist said: 'There's usually a dead baby involved somewhere.'

'What do you mean?' I asked.

'Your mother had what they used to call a nervous breakdown.'

Ah, yes. *Trouble with her nerves.* I remembered that expression. Nerves as in nervous breakdown.

'Nowadays, it would be called a depression,' he went on. 'She had a severe depression. Now you've had a depression.'

'Does that mean it is hereditary?'

'Maybe, but I don't believe it is necessarily,' he replied.

101

I wasn't sure where this was going, but it was reminding me just how little I knew. Nothing new there, though. All my life I had been aware that there was all sorts of stuff that I hadn't been told, or couldn't remember, or simply did not know. And all my life I really hadn't *wanted* to know. Why should I? What good would it do? I didn't feel deprived. I didn't feel damaged. As far as I knew, I had never shown any signs of what one might call mental frailty. 'I was grumpy. But I got away with it.' But now, only now, at the age of sixty, I was being forced to face the fact that I hadn't got away with it at all. So that had changed. Something else had changed too. After a lifetime of not wanting to know, now I did. It wasn't just curiosity, this could well be self-preservation. I didn't just *want* to know. I *needed* to know. But how was I going to find out?

Time: March 2003
Location: a cosy room in a 'rest home' in Sussex, near the sea

I drove down to the south coast to see Auntie Margery. It was the first time I had risked a long drive since the Newquay incident. I could say that I was ultra-cautious now that I had six points on my licence, but I didn't have to be. In case there are any Bristol police reading this, I would like to reiterate that I am and always have been a very careful driver. Oh Bill, let it go. OK. Anyway, I had arranged to meet Auntie Margery. We met. We hugged. And we talked. Or rather, I interviewed her! I asked question after question about Mum,

Dad, Gran, herself and the family histories of the Oddies (Dad's side) and the Cleggs (Mum's and Margery's). Margery told me everything she could remember. She protested that her memory was not what it used to be, but it seemed pretty good to me. What's more, she was sometimes able to illustrate her answers with photos from scrapbooks she had kept during a time when she had done a fair amount of travelling, including a period working in the Middle East. There were also a number of shots of her in a chorus line, singing and dancing in frilly costumes, and—by way of a contrast—in full leathers leaning skittishly on her motorbike! The truth was that—as she herself conceded—Margery had spent so much of her life 'following her muse' that there had been long periods where she had lost touch with what was happening to the rest of her family. Even, she admitted, her own offspring. Perhaps it was this cavalier neglect that had qualified Margery for my granny's judgement of her as 'a bad 'un', but I couldn't help thinking that it might also have been an envious euphemism for a free-spirited woman who was intent on living life to the full and as her own person, rather than stay closeted and clinging to her son like a leech to a leg.

Is that a harsh simile? Did my granny suck the life blood out of my dad? I thought so. Margery thought so too. '*And* your mother,' she added. Really? This was a new one on me! As Margery continued, her tone became slightly angry. Or was it bitter? Or sad? 'Oh yes,' she said, 'I'm afraid your granny had a lot to answer for. She did a lot of damage.' Blimey. This clearly was stuff I knew nothing about at all. I asked questions. Margery talked. I listened.

I also taped. Three cassettes' worth. It was not, I assure you, intended as early research for this book. This was for me. It was as if I needed to try and replace 'characters' from my unseen movie with real people. Margery had already undergone a transformation. She was not just a bad 'un. Or if she had been—and I suspect she'd say she was!—she was a very interesting one. In fact, she was fascinating.

As I drove back to London—sedately and safely, of course—part of me was quite cross. Damn, damn, damn! All these years I had had a motorbiking, theatrical, adventurer auntie, and I didn't know. Or had I not allowed myself to find out? Damn, damn, damn! At least I know now. I visit Margery now and then (not often enough), have phone chats, send her books (she is a voracious reader), and I have told her that if she wakes up one morning and fancies jetting off to India or Africa, I would be delighted to send her there—and bring her back!

But I dare say you are wondering about the details of what I learnt from Margery about my family history? Three cassettes' worth. Forgive me if I withhold the information a wee while. It is just that over the following months I discovered more and more. Thanks to the BBC!

Time: later in 2003
Location: Rochdale and Birmingham

That year I was asked if I would care to be a 'subject' on a new series called *Who Do You Think*

104

You Are? about—would you believe?—tracing family histories. The production company, Wall to Wall, may have seen the series as a way to popularise genealogy. I saw it as an irresistible opportunity to get the BBC to organise and finance my research! During the making of the programme I went back to Rochdale, where I revisited Sparthbottom's Road, and talked to an erstwhile member of our gang, who confirmed my stories of stone-throwing battles. He even told me that he remembered my dad and my granny, but not my mum. So I hadn't 'blanked' or 'reconstructed' those early years. (I was becoming familiar with such terms from therapy.) Mum really *hadn't* been there!

We also went to Oak Tree Crescent in Birmingham, and I chatted to Trevor, the lad who'd lived next door back in the 1950s. He did remember Mum, but it was the same memory as mine, of her being carted off by an ambulance or police car, screaming and kicking. I remember it happening just the once. Trevor told me it happened several times. He had since worked out a theory, that my mother was in Barnsley Hall but was allowed back home for weekends. She was no doubt heavily sedated, but by Sunday afternoon the medication had begun to wear off, and that's when trouble ensued. He may well be right.

I also revisited Barmy Hall, but found it converted into some kind of office complex, for insurance or something. There were still a few long corridors, but the lighting was terribly unsubtle. *One Flew Over the Cuckoo's Nest* just wouldn't work with energy-saving light bulbs. The only reference to the building's previous use was a large photo and a sort of architectural plan of the layout from when it was a hospital. I can't believe that the current office workers haven't been tempted to risk adding a little graffiti: 'You don't have to be mad to live here . . . oh, you do actually!' I bet nary a day goes by without the office joker referring to straitjackets and nutters. David Brent would have a field day.

Going back there didn't upset me or anything, but I did shed a little tear or two when I talked to several elderly ladies who had been nurses at the Hall and actually remembered my mum. What they remembered was surprising, comforting and, ultimately, sad. 'Oh, Lilian was lovely. She was always singing. And playing the piano!' Playing the piano?! Trevor had also said something about that. I had protested that we didn't have a piano. Why would I blank a piano? But Margery had said the same thing, and these ladies insisted. They also spoke of working at Barnsley Hall as if it were more like a holiday camp than a lunatic asylum, as they told me tales of Christmas concerts and New Year's balls! The producer of *Who Do You Think You Are?* had tried to find my mother's medical records, but had been told that they no longer existed. Apparently the official policy is that they only keep one in three sets of records from the old days, and that the choice is totally random. This was disappointing, as I was anxious to discover more specific ally what Mum had been suffering from, rather than the waffly 'trouble with her nerves' or even the doctor's dramatic 'violent schizophrenia'. I asked the nurses, and one of them was perfectly specific. 'We really didn't know much about mental health in those days, but looking back, I'd definitely say that your mother had what we would now call "bipolar disorder".' Manic depressive. Maybe. Frankly, in my own experience of myself and other people, it is rarely possible to pronounce an absolutely indisputable straightforward diagnosis when the patient is alive and available, let alone when they are long gone! I know the manic bit can take the form of violence, but all these tales of my mother singing and boogieing at the old joanna didn't sound terribly typical of a depressive side. Then again, that might have been the 'normal phase', when she was neither manic nor depressed. Like I said, I am not sure there are many rules. But maybe there is one.

As my journey to discover 'who did I think I was' took me deeper and more facts emerged, my therapist's comment began to make sense and ring true. 'There's usually a dead baby involved.' In my mother's case, I discovered that there was, in fact, not just one dead baby but two. Margery told me this, and a copy of the death certificate confirmed it.

Time for another of my statements. In the process of talking to Margery, and thanks to the sensitive and meticulous research of *Who Do You think You Are?*, I discovered many, many things about the history of the Oddie family and the times they lived through. I can't pretend that ultimately I wasn't a little disappointed not to discover that one of my forefathers had been a highwayman or a pirate. Or even a burglar or a pickpocket. I never really expected to uncover royal or even aristocratic lineage, but surely there must have been somebody who had achieved something notable? Alas, no. Not even the slightest notoriety. Nor were there any heroes, great sportsmen, travellers or pioneers of even the most obscure activities. Certainly no comedy writers or birdwatchers. The inescapable truth is that generations of Oddies—men and women— had worked in t'mills. It were tough, and many of them had died prematurely of the consequences of hard labour in appalling conditions.

At least two of the deaths had made the newspapers. My great-grandfather worked as a nightwatchman at a chemicals factory. He fell into a vat of 'boiling vitriol' whilst on the nightshift. I dare say that wasn't all he was on!

My grandfather—it had never even struck me that my granny must once have had a husband— developed throat cancer after a lifetime of being a power loom 'overlooker'. This was an impeccable job description. He overlooked (checked out, maintained etc) the looms. This entailed a practice known as 'kissing the shuttle', which involved drawing the cotton thread into the wooden shuttle by mouth, with a sharp intake of breath. It was long suspected and eventually proved that this often caused severe breathing problems and even throat cancer, but factory doctors were under orders to deny this, to avoid workers taking legal action against their employers. My grandad was taken into hospital for an operation, but suffered heart failure when the surgeon refused to use ether as the anaesthetic, because there was a danger of him exploding! My grandfather, I mean. Honestly, this is what it said in the *Rochdale Observer* in 1927: 'The procedure was such that a powerful electric spark was introduced into the patient's mouth. If ether had been used there

108

would have been a grave risk of an explosion.' So chloroform was used instead, despite the equally grave risk of a heart attack. I agree the surgeon had an un enviable choice. I suppose he took the less messy option, but—no disrespect to his memory—I must admit I wouldn't have minded having an exploding grandad.

Most of the information the research turned up concerned my father's side of the family. One of the flaws of this genealogy business is that it tends to be a bit sexist!

But the truth about what had happened to my mother in the two years before I was born overshadowed everything else. My father and mother—Harry and Lilian—had got married in 1937. The following year, Lilian became pregnant. Early in 1939, she had a miscarriage, very, very late, at seven months. Indeed, was it a miscarriage or a stillborn baby? But it wasn't long before Lilian was pregnant again. On 16 January 1940, she gave birth to a girl. She was christened Margaret Jean. On the 21st, the baby died. The death certificate records: 'Age: five days. Cause of death: Inanition'—which is defined as 'exhaustion or weakness, as from lack of food'. Two years. Two dead babies. But by the end of 1940, Lilian was pregnant again. On 7 July 1941, Lilian gave birth to a boy. William Edgar Oddie. Me. I survived. The miscarriage and the baby girl's birth and death had all happened at Lilian and Harry's home, probably with no nurse or midwife in attendance. I was born in the local hospital, which may well be why I am here.

The Second World War was raging. There were food shortages. Medical care was scarce.

109

Counselling and therapy were non-existent. Although it is likely that my mother cared for me for a year, maybe two, it seems that her mental health began to deteriorate by the time I was a toddler. Perhaps I was becoming too much for her. Maybe she couldn't cope. How could she have done? Trauma, bereavement, grief, no time to mourn, probably leading to chronic post-natal depression. But it wouldn't have been recognised as that then. Whatever it was called, it was reason enough in those days for a woman to be incarcerated in a mental hospital. You didn't have to be mad to live there, just heartbroken.

Time: early in 2004
Location: therapist's consulting room, Hampstead

'So how do you feel about your mother now? Now that you know what you know?'

'Sad, obviously, but mainly it has . . .' I chose my words carefully '. . . undemonised her. Is that it?' There was quite a long silence. Therapists don't fill those. 'I must have been angry. I hated her. I used to actually say that—I hate her. But not really her. "Resent" would have been a better word, I suppose. I have always envied people who have mothers they get on with, or, even if they don't, at least they can communicate with. At least speak the same language, you know. And I envy blokes who have a sister, too. So I suppose I resented that. Which is awful. As if I was thinking, Mother, you let my sister die. I mean I know that's a really horrible way to put it. But maybe it has all been in there all this time, and now . . . it . . .' I was about

110

to say, 'It all has to come out', but the therapist cut me off in the time-honoured way: 'I'm afraid time's up. That's it for today.'

The fact is that it has all been continuing to come out for the past seven years. I am tempted to quip: 'Better out than in!' But it's not a joke, I mean that. It has taken time, and it is still work in progress. Except that it doesn't feel like work now. I believe it is good for me, and for all the people around me. I hope they agree. But of course there is one person it is too late to be good for. My mum. It would be ridiculous to say that I now love her, or indeed even like her. The fact is, I didn't know her. Nothing can change that. But at least now I can understand what happened. I can sympathise, though that is far too weak a word. And at least, thanks to my 'research', I now have a more accurate picture of what happened. And I also now know that her later life had . . . would you call them consolations? I don't know. You judge.

The nurses' memories of Mum at Barnsley Hall are not of a miserable person. Indeed one might well assume that she was happy there. Moreover, after the showing of *Who Do You Think You Are?* I got several letters from people who had met Mum in Rochdale in the years after she left hospital. Typically they told of her starting a conversation in the pub or in the park, guiding it on to the subject of TV, and eventually slipping in somewhere that I was in *The Goodies*. The writer would invariably say that 'she was obviously very proud'. They usually also added 'she loved you', which I am sure was meant reassuringly, as the programme had obviously implied that I had been deprived of

111

mother love. It was better than 'she hated you' , but I hope it doesn't seem callous if I say it sort of didn't mean anything to me. But thanks for letting me know.

By far the most pleasing letter came from— here's some kind of poetic symmetry—a psychotherapist! She was also a mother, and she wrote to me from Cheshire. 'Your mother, Mrs Oddie, was an important figure in our lives between 1970 and 1977.' She then went on to explain how, when she and her husband had moved up to Rochdale from London, she needed to find a childminder for their youngest son so that she could continue her studies. She found my mother's name on a list of vetted childminders and interviewed her.

She was extremely open and honest about her psychiatric history and felt confident that continuing her medication she remained emotionally stable. I don't know if we were naive, but in all the time that I knew her, your mother was never violent or bad-tempered. She was sunny in temperament, rather an innocent abroad, and could easily be exploited by others.

Reading that sentence made me think back to Mum's letters from the 1970s—the 'emotional blackmail years', as I called them—when she was constantly asking for money. I had always felt that she was 'put up to that'. But certainly not by this lady. The next paragraph in her letter says so much, so clearly, that I hope she won't mind my quoting it all.

When I first introduced her to Adrian (the baby), she was so full of joy, warm and welcoming, and I quickly felt that my mothering instinct was right; that she and Adrian would be good together; a good fit. He loved her from the beginning, and she adored him. I think that my baby became a surrogate replacement for the little girl she had lost so tragically and later for you, the son she yearned to be near and loved so constantly. She quickly became a member of the family and could be relied on to help us out if we were in difficulty. Once he could talk and walk, Adrian—who couldn't quite get his tongue round Mrs Oddie and called her Soddie, not through any disrespect you understand, but because that was the best he could manage at the time—and she would play so well together. She would laugh and hold his hand and come in and see what new delights he wanted to show her. At some stage during this time she thanked me; I remember her saying to me that she was so grateful that I had trusted her enough to let her look after my children (there was an older boy as well) and that by this good faith in her she had regained some self-respect.

And there's more. The lady then goes on to tell me what Adrian told her after he saw the *Who Do You Think You Are?* programme in 2004:

Adrian remembers how she always willingly shared in his little world. She would watch him creating his fantasy dramas with his small toys, they would have lunch and watch *Rainbow* together, with him sitting next to her holding his hand. She took him out for walks in the park. She

113

would patiently sit with him drawing pictures and colouring in his colouring books. She would read to him. He remembers that in her flat she collected all the memorabilia she could about you. She had all the Goodies Annuals, photographs, and newspaper cuttings. He remembers how, as the boys got older, she and they would watch *The Goodies* on television. His impression was that whilst she was hungry for know ledge of you, and was able through your public persona to metaphorically touch you, she knew that anything more tangible would never be permitted. Adrian believes that she loved you constantly and from a distance.

Reading that for the first time I didn't know whether to laugh or cry. I settled on laughing. The only thing I didn't envy Adrian was that he had to watch *The Goodies*—but, let's face it, I am even joking about that. All I'd ever watched with mother was bloody *Muffin the Mule*, and that stupid piece of rag on a string! The final irony is that apparently Adrian went on to work at the BBC as a director with children's television. If he brings back the Muffin and Raggy show I will know my mum really did influence him! I will leave the final statement to Adrian's mum: 'I want you to know that your mother, far from being the picture of a madwoman that I guess you came to believe, was a most loving, simple soul.'

Yes. I can believe that. Now.

*　　　*　　　*

There is one person I have mentioned fairly often

and yet said very little about. My granny. I can't say I ever felt very fondly towards her. Indeed, even though she was my father's mother, I never really felt that he was very close to her either. And yet she lived with us. Always. What's more, when I discovered more from Margery and the programme research, it seems that she had lived with Dad for almost the whole of his life. Dad's brother Edgar—my uncle Edgar—was born in 1908. Dad was born three years later. Their dad, my grandfather, was called Wilkinson Oddie, which I dare say wasn't such a posh name then as it would be now! My gran was called Emily.

The family survived the First World War, but in 1927 Wilkinson died on the operating table whilst being treated—or not—for lung cancer. Edgar was nineteen, Harry sixteen and, as was inevitable in those days, both would have left school at fourteen and both were in regular employment. It was only natural that their mum would continue to live with them—or vice versa—and that they would look after her. What was slightly less natural, though not that unusual then, was that when Dad and Mum got married ten years later, they had Emily living with them too.

Apparently, there was supposed to be an arrangement that she would alternate between her two sons' homes, but Edgar's new wife Marion wouldn't have it. Lilian probably had no choice. It seems that with Harry it was always a case of 'And my mother came too'—which, as it happens, was a popular music hall song of the day! I presume not literally inspired by my dad and gran. It need not have been a disastrous arrangement, but the more I learnt about it, the more I was beginning to

115

realise that it was far from ideal. The first indication I had was Margery's comment that my gran 'had a lot to answer for'. I pushed her to tell me more, and she did. Apparently Emily had always been rather domineering, especially on matters relating to motherhood. After all, she had raised two sons. It was easy to imagine her bossing my mother around when she was pregnant for the first time. She was presumably in the house when the first late miscarriage occurred, though there is no reason to believe that she was involved in any way. On the other hand, it does seem likely that she did not call for any kind of help, because a year later a worryingly similar thing occurred.

Margery had already told me of occasions when baby Margaret Jean had been constantly crying in her cot, but my granny had prevented Lilian from going to tend to her. Presumably it was an assertion of the hard school of mothering. 'Let them cry, it's good for them' . . . 'They've got to learn', and so on. But this baby was only a day or two old, and quite likely had been born under stress, and was already weak. I was horrified when Margery told me this, but also couldn't help wondering how she could be so sure. I was pretty certain that Margery had not been in Rochdale at the time. I wondered if her recollection was over-critical for a reason. Clearly she didn't like Gran.

She wasn't the only one. As it turned out, I received confirm ation of the distressing circumstances of the baby's death in another of the letters I got after *Who Do You Think You Are?* was screened. This one came from a lady whose family had lived next door to my mum, dad and gran at the end of the 1930s, and she would have been a little girl of six or seven at the time. She wrote to say how well she remembered her mother and my mum being friends, and how she herself would go next door if no one was home at her house, 'where Mrs Oddie would greet me with such a warm smile. I can see her now, in a wrap-around patterned apron, buttering malt bread. I was very fond of her, and I am sure that children are a shrewd judge of adults.'

As if to back up that claim, she went on to say how much she and her mum had disliked my gran. The next paragraph was quite chilling.

> There was some sort of upset when my mother was eager to call the midwife to your mother in prolonged labour—and your grandmother refused. I was invited to see the baby girl when your grandmother was out. Sitting rigid, I looked down at the little face with black hair, feeling so proud, but concerned that her little foot had been trapped in childbirth. A few days later came the sad news that the baby had died. My mother sat with Lilian whilst the baby was taken away. I watched in horror from the bushes between the houses and the road. It was one of the most traumatic memories of my early life.

The letter ended with kind and understanding words about Mum, and not so kind words about Gran. 'Your mother was a lovely person. She must have suffered postnatal depression. No wonder with a mother-in-law like that!' I had other letters referring to Gran as an 'unpleasant lady', and an 'unlikeable woman', and Margery went so far as to imply that my mother being prevented from going to her crying baby or calling for help may have hastened the death. Imagine that. Continuing to live in the same house with a person who was instrumental in the death of your child. Imagine the resentment. Imagine the guilt. Imagine what it might do to your mind. To your sanity. Mum really *didn't* stand a chance.

Gran wasn't coming out of this too well. And neither was Dad. Why did he let his mother rule and perhaps ruin his life, and his wife's? A misplaced sense of 'duty'? But what were the choices? Was Marion at fault for refusing to have the old lady at Uncle Edgar's? Or was that self-preservation? How 'difficult' or domineering was Gran? Was she hard-hearted, or just misguided? There must have been reasons why they all made the decisions they did. Indeed, there must have been reasons for Gran's unlovable and unloving behaviour. Looking back and trying to understand it all—which of course I never will—there is one ingredient that seems to have been in short supply in our family at that time, and possibly for some time before that: love. Simple, warm, cuddly, affectionate love. Margery told me that her (and Lilian's) mother was a 'cold person', and she describes their father as 'distant.' What an irony, then, that the one person who was probably truly and naturally affectionate was my mum. Even more ironic that the only time I remember her hugging me, I froze with fear.

*   *   *

Right then, that's enough of that! It is time to bring on the song titles. 'Accentuate the positive, eliminate the negative'. 'All you need is love'. 'Put on a happy face'. 'Always look on the bright side of life'. And to commandeer and misquote another Monty Python catchphrase: 'I were lucky!' It is true, I have been.

Quite apart from the emotional aspect of *Who Do You Think You Are?*, the totally unbroadcastable and utterly immodest conclusion I came to after my search back through the Oddie family history was that frankly, so far, I am by far the most interesting and successful one! No point in being coy, it's undeniable. A scholarship to Cambridge, followed by forty-odd years of fame and a certain amount of fortune. Unarguable. I've done well for myself. With a lot of help from my friends. As it happens, a great deal of my 'public' history has already been made available on radio, telly, and in many books, some of them written by me. There is even a certain amount of relevant biographical stuff in various tomes about the 'history of British comedy' and the like. So, really and truly, are there any questions left to ask? Well, actually, yes there are. I am going to ask them. I shall also answer them. I should perhaps remind myself here that I can be a harsh interviewer.

PART II

The interview

1

I ask myself . . .

Bill, you are a man of many talents . . .
. . . But master of none, that's what you were going to
say, isn't it?
Is that what you think?
What do you mean? Is that what I think you were
going to say? Or is that what I think about myself?
Whichever.
OK, I think that's what a lot of people think.
Including me?
Probably, yes.
And you?
I think I am pretty good at some things. Quite a lot of
things, actually.
Cocky little bugger, aren't you?
Maybe sometimes. Or maybe I just have confidence in
my own abilities. Oh, I don't know. I'm getting confused
already. I'm not sure about this asking myself questions
business. Which is me ? The one asking, or the one
answering?
Both.
But they are completely different.
**Maybe you are schizophrenic. Maybe you
inherited that from your mother.**
She wasn't schizophrenic. She was bipolar.
So is that what you inherited?
No. I didn't inherit anything!
**Nothing? Are you telling me—telling yourself—
that you are so bloody unique and so cocky that
you feel confident in rejecting the whole concept
of genetics?**

123

No. Of course not. Obviously I must have inherited some things. But can we just stick to the positive things, please?

That's what I am trying to do. As you would realise, if you'd let me finish.

OK. Sorry. Go on, then.

As I was saying, Bill, you are a man of many talents. You have written for and appeared on stage, radio and television, in shows that were very popular. You have written and sung songs that got into the hit parade. You have also written quite a lot of books. You are a genuine authority on wildlife—especially birds. You can play several instruments—not brilliantly but quite well—and you used to play—past tense, I'm afraid—several sports—also not brilliantly but quite well—and you are not a bad artist. So, my question is: how much do you think you have inherited from your parents, or other members of your family?

Mmm. Good question. You see, for years I thought I really hadn't inherited anything. It wasn't arrogance, honestly. It's just that I couldn't see any connections. That's still true to a point. I have often been asked how and why did I get into birdwatching? Was someone in the family interested in nature? The answer is no. Did you live in the countryside? Definitely no. The only question that makes some sense is: did you need an excuse to get out of the house? I suppose I did. Yes! What's more, I used to stay out, some days from dawn till dusk, at a god-forsaken concrete reservoir that was often almost totally birdless, but I found being there preferable to life at Oak Tree Crescent, which, mind you, wasn't so much unpleasant as dull!

The art thing I may have got from my uncle Edgar, Dad's brother. I can't remember actually ever seeing

124

them together, but he referred to Dad as 'our kid', which is the same way that Noel Gallagher refers to Liam. There the resemblance ends. I can't imagine anyone less like the Gallagher brothers than Harry and Edgar! I never even heard either of them swear! I can imagine either of the Gallaghers doing a bit of dabbling on canvas, but I'd be surprised—and disappointed—if they weren't a bit more imaginative than Uncle Edgar. Technically, he was pretty good at drawing and watercolouring, but his subject matter was a little unadventurous. Edgar painted boats. Or rather he did watercolours of boats. Just boats. Nothing but boats. They varied in size, both the paintings and the boats. Some of them were sailing boats and some of them had funnels, and may have qualified as ships, which are surely boats by another name. They were very realistic boats. What's more, they floated on a pretty decent sea. Waves aren't easy to do. I also recall some competent clouds. There may also have been a few of those simplistic seagulls that look like Vs or Ws, but they were not so inspiring as to explain my fixation on birds. Nevertheless, I am happy to accept that my ability to draw quite well might have come from Edgar. On the other hand, he may also have been responsible for my dislike of boats.

And what did you get from your dad?
I have already written about the many ways my dad influenced my life, encouraged my interests, and I am sure contributed to various aspects of my character. He may well have passed on some of his sporting inclinations, but I am pretty sure his genes were more or less devoid of musical or theatrical ingredients. Neither my nor the BBC's excavations into my family history unearthed the slightest evidence that any Oddie had any vestige of rhythm, melody or

imagination running through their veins. Until me!

So where did you get it from?

Clearly from the Clegg family, my mother's side, but I didn't know that until a couple of years ago! Yet again I find myself amazed and not a little resentful about how much information I didn't grow up with. The Cleggs may not have been literally steeped in showbiz, but it seems they enjoyed cutting a rug, tickling the ivories, a rollicking knees-up and a good old singsong, not to mention having a flutter, and dabbling in oils. The list of interests and activities of various family members on Mum's side included concert pianist, singer, dancer, artist and gambler. Add to this, nurses' and neighbours' memories of Mum singing and playing the piano, and Margery's album of photos of her younger days in chorus lines, and straddling a Harley Davidson, and I surely have no choice but to accept that I am as much a Clegg as an Oddie—or perhaps more. Bill Clegg. William Clegg. Willie Clegg? Little Willie Clegg? Billy Clegg! That sounds like a northern comic's name if ever I heard one. OK, Mum, thanks for the genes. I wear them with pride.

What about your gran? Could you have inherited anything from her?

Oh yes, my gran, Dad's mum. So far she hasn't come out of this book too well, has she?

Not a bundle of laughs, no.

I think it is time I put that right. Even if the laughs are at her expense. I feel a bit guilty about what I'm about to tell you, but not guilty enough to desist.

I do not possess—I'm not even aware of the existence of—a single photograph of my gran. Which is pretty extraordinary, considering that she was 'the woman of the house' for seventeen years of my life. I do remember exactly what she looked like but—despite the clarity of the image—I still find it hard to think of her as a human being. In fact, I think of her more as a monkey. This is because, frankly, she did look a bit like one. Well, quite a lot actually. One of those little rhesus monkeys. For a start, she wasn't very big. Not as tiny as a rhesus monkey, of course, but only five foot or less. However, it was her face that was so undeniably primate. She wore her hair scraped back and fastened in a 'bun' at the back of her head. This had the effect of framing her features, just as a monkey's face is framed by fur. It also revealed her slightly sticky-out ears. She wore round wire glasses which accentuated her eyes, so that she had a perpetually startled expression—as monkeys often do—and, to complete the effect, her false teeth were a bit too big, which meant that they forced her lips open and set her mouth in a protruding grin which could be easily mistaken for a gnashing of teeth, which is of course what chimps do when they are cross.

It was Gran's teeth that provided my dad and me with many an evening of merriment. On the negative side, I'm afraid it has to be said that Gran's permanent presence was a factor in us having very few opportunities for 'father and son' talks. She simply would never, ever leave us alone, which was definitely inhibiting. On the other hand, there was a considerable consolation. As an evening progressed towards bedtime, instead of tactfully retiring to her room, Gran would almost defiantly stay in her armchair. Eventually, though, she would begin to nod off. At which point, her mouth would relax and slacken, and her false teeth begin to slip forward. This in itself was quite diverting, as her toothy grin became more and more gross. Dad and I, amid suppressed giggles, would bet on how long it would be before Gran's teeth finally leapt free and landed in her lap. The process was often accelerated by her flatulence. Every now and again, she would let out a little fart, and her teeth would edge ever closer to the precipice. The most satisfying and hilarious climax was when she let go a real ripsnorter, which provided the perfect sound effect as her teeth shot out as if propelled by a rocket. At this point, Gran would wake up to find herself confronted by three broad smiles, belonging to me, Dad and her own false teeth. I used to fantasise about them chattering with laughter like those clockwork yackety teeth you buy from a joke shop.

Yes, but what has that got to do with whether or not you have inherited any creative characteristics from your granny?

More than you could possibly guess. So I will tell you. Many people, when they are young, experience the comfort—or embarrassment—of genetic continuity, when it is pointed out that they have been blessed—or cursed—with certain family features. On balance, I don't think most kids feel anything but slightly ill at ease when they are told: 'Oh yes, you've definitely got your Granny's eyes'—or nose, or indeed teeth. Which in the case of *my* granny could have been literally possible. We had to make our own entertainment back in them days, so I dare say 'hiding granny's dentures' was quite a popular pastime for some kids. I hasten to say that I never stooped that low, partly because I knew my dad would kill me, and secondly because the only time I did see her without her teeth in, it totally freaked me out. It was a weird effect, as if she had swallowed her own lips. At least, she no longer had a mouth like a monkey. More like a fig. Or another part of the human anatomy normally not so visible . . . actually, I don't think I'll go there. Except I can't avoid it.

128

Good. Carry on.

OK, here goes. Second shameful admission of this book. I'd like to think you will greet it with sympathy, rather than amusement or distaste. The feature I was bequeathed by Gran was not facial, it was quite the opposite. To quote the lad who lived next door, whom I was in the habit of playing football with, on the occasion when his ear detected a fruity raspberry as I tipped a shot round the goalpost 'Blimey, you've got your granny's farts.' Which clearly indicates that she was well known for it down our street.

Surely there were small boys in Rochdale in the late 1940s who would have considered such a judgement as an accolade?

Indeed. Had I myself been witty enough, I could have claimed that it was being thus jet-propelled that had allowed me to make such a good save. Had I been confident enough, I would have relished the attention, and given a demonstration of virtuoso flatulence, as if to prove that I was totally in control of whatever trumps and squeaks I was emitting. Instead, I was deeply and humiliatingly embarrassed. My so-called friend made it worse by prancing around holding his nose and chanting, 'Pooh pooh! Somebody's let off! Who's dropped one?'—and so loudly that it was as if he was consulting the neighbours. Anyone hearing the question and peering out of a back window or over the fence and witnessing the scene would hardly have had to be Hercule Poirot to work out which of the two small boys had just involuntarily broken wind. Is it the tubby one, now rummaging in the garden shed in search of his old gas mask? Or is it the little lad who is blushing, about to burst into tears, and is now scurrying off home muttering, 'I'd better go to the lav'?

Bill, surely that incident is evidence that you were

129

a grossly oversensitive child. Arguably in denial of his own schoolboyness. A kid embarrassed to fart in front of his friends! What is that about?

I don't know, but the truth is I have still not conquered my innate fear of farting. I slightly admire—and yet despise—blokes who flaunt their flatulence. The ones who call for silence in the room, invite someone to pull their finger and then let one go. The ones who light them. The housemates on *Big Brother*—male and female—whose wind-breaking is at least more entertaining than what comes out of their mouths.

Ooops, grumpy old man bit there!

No, actually, coy little boy.

Maybe I was raised in more genteel times. Certainly hat doffing, hand shaking, holding doors open and giving up seats for ladies were standard practice. So, of course, was suppressing 'unpleasant' feelings. Maybe that included trapped wind! Grannies were presumably exempt from this rule of etiquette, as a privilege of old age. Added to which, let's face it, immediately after the war, folks could do with all the laughs they could get. However, to verge on the serious, I reckon my self-consciousness was something to do with control, or rather lack of it. I am well aware that not being in control of my feelings and faculties panics me. I don't get drunk—I get sick first! I don't do drugs. I don't do irresponsible or impulsive, and I don't do uncontrollable anger.

But you do suffer from uncontrollable flatulence!

It's not chronic, and everyone experiences it from time to time.

Has it ever happened in high-profile circumstances, such as on live telly, or while collecting your OBE from the Queen?

Thankfully, no. I can anticipate, to a point, the times I am

130

most susceptible. The goalkeeping incident was a clue to the riskiest circumstances, which are at moments of unpremeditated physical exertion. Fortunately, these don't extend to sex, though there was a well-known female TV personality who exhorted her lovers to greater endeavours by instructing them to 'fuck me till I fart!'

Call me unromantic, but I don't think I'd find that much of a turn-on! So, assuming that your little weakness in that area was inherited from your gran, how can you regard it as anything but an unwelcome affliction? How on earth have you managed to forgive rather than curse her? Or indeed—almost—thank her?

One reason is that one particular physical exertion which may be involuntarily accompanied by a little trump is laughter!

You fart when you laugh?

Not every time, but it can happen. If I am convulsed by uncontrollable merriment, I may not be able to avoid 'letting one go', as that boy next door put it. If you think I am making this up, ask Tim Brooke-Taylor or Graeme Garden about it. We got to the stage where we rated the hilariousness of lines in *The Goodies* scripts by whether or not they got an audible reaction.

And you don't mean a laugh. . .

It wasn't an infallible rule, but we began to discern a correlation between the funniness of the joke and the volume of the 'raspberry'. We christened it the 'Fartometer'. If I am absolutely honest, a teeny bit of me was still embarrassed, but I had to accept that it was as good a way as any of judging a script, and that it was an absolutely genuinely honest reaction. I wasn't able to manipulate it to the extent, for example, of rewarding my own lines with bigger trumps than

Graeme's. The Fartometer does not lie.

So thanks, Gran. How could I possibly resent the gift of laughter? Or the gift of inspiration for what I consider to be one of my finest song lyrics.

What are you talking about? You wrote a song about farting?

Yes.

And you are proud of it?

As a matter of fact, yes. I happen to consider it a bit of a literary masterpiece, which is grossly underappreciated by posterity. I reckon it has many of the qualities that distinguish other great works in the same genre.

That genre being farting songs?

No. Comedy songs. Songs that combine eloquent and elegant wordplay with felicitous rhymes, alliteration and deft turns of phrase, conveying whimsical wit and humour. As exhibited by such masters as Gilbert and Sullivan, Noël Coward, Cole Porter and whoever wrote 'Eskimo Nell'.

Even if none of them wrote a song about farting.

Well, they should have done. But it wouldn't have been as good as mine. Actually, I'm not sure it is just a song. I used to perform it, accompanied by an acoustic guitar, in the manner of a talking blues, but I never really felt that it did justice to the subtlety of the rhythms, or allowed time to revel in the words, or relish the pauses, or to visualise the images. I really think it needs declaiming and acting out.

Like performance poetry?

Exactly. It is a poem.

And it was inspired by your granny?

To an extent, yes. I suppose it's sort of a tribute.

OK then, let's hear it.

You can't hear it, but you can read it. Preferably out

132

loud. With suitable actions and sound effects. It is called
...

BLOWING OFF by Bill Oddie

My birth brought tears to my mother's eyes
'Cos I was a wee bit oversize,
You know what goes in ain't nothin' to what
    comes out!
And though Momma pushed and shoved and
    squeezed,
I simply could not be released.
The whole thing looked like an all-in wrestling
    bout.
The midwife tugged and the nurses cheered
When on the eighteenth day my head appeared.
She said, 'Hold it right there, I'll just go get a
    rope!'
Well I must have heard that, 'cos my baby rump
Flexed and blew a mighty trump
And 'parrrrp!' I shot out, like a piece of soap.

Yep, jet-propelled I left the womb
And I farted around like a burst balloon,
Till the doctor caught me, and shoved a cork up
    my derriere.
When he dangled me down, I let one fly
And I shot that doc right between the eyes
And instead of crying I sang out then and there.

Chorus (you can sing this bit)
Blowing off, it's a gas. Blowing off, it's a trip
It's a sin to hold it in, so . . . let it rip!
Some folks like to hiccup, some folks like to
    cough,

133

But me—I blow off!

Well I blew off on my mother's knee
And I pooped my way to puberty,
And all through school, I still kept lettin 'em go.
I could blow off low, I could blow off high,
I could blow off wet, I could blow off dry.
I could blow off silent, so you'd never know.

My mother said: 'Son, it would make sense
To capitalise on your flatulence.
Maybe you could join a band and make us rich?'
So I tightened my cheeks, and I bent my knees
And I found I could fart in several keys!
And whadya know? I had perfect pitch.

I soon developed a nice round tone,
A bit like a tuba or a bass trombone,
I got amplified, and I widened my repertoire.
With a ton or sprouts, and a barrel of beans,
I cracked off down to New Orleans.
And lordy lordy! I became a star!

Chorus
Blowin' off, it's a gas. Blowin' off, it's a trip.
It's a sin to hold it in so . . . let it rip!
Some folks like to hiccup, some folks like to
    cough,
But me . . . I blow off!!!

(Optional repeat of chorus, in which the
audience gets to sing—and fart—along.)

And you wrote that about the same time as Bob Dylan and Joni Mitchell were at their peak?
Yup. If what they do is poetry, then surely …

Bill, I have to be honest, I can't tell if you are just being silly. Do you seriously think that is a great lyric?
Yes, I do.

You take your songwriting pretty seriously, don't you?
Yes, I do. Though I started off just singing. You know, other people's work.

So your first experience of performing in public was as a singer?
Yes, it was.

When was that, and how did it come about?
I must have been about five or six years old. I was definitely less than seven, because I was still living in Rochdale. I think it was some kind of parents' evening at primary school, and I had to do a duet with a little girl called Jean Mawson. You always remember the name of whoever you were with the first time you were really embarrassed!

You farted!?
No. Worse than that. We had to stand on a table and hold hands and sing 'Christopher Robin'. You know: 'Little boy kneels at the foot of the bed' and so on, and 'Hush! Hush! Whisper who dares. Christopher Robin is saying his prayers.' Which is appallingly soppy anyway. But then there's this really cringeworthy bit where we had to look at each other and sing: 'God bless Mummy. I know that's right. Wasn't it fun in the bath tonight!? The cold so cold and the hot so hot … Oh God bless Nanny—I quite forgot.' Something like that. God bless Nanny! She was probably supposed to be babysitting, keeping an eye on us, certainly not letting a couple of

curious six-year-olds who weren't even brother and sister take a bath together! 'Wasn't it fun in the bath tonight?' I dare say it was, but I'd rather not have to share it with a roomful of grown-ups!

But it didn't put you off singing?

Apparently not, although it was often associated with embarrassing circumstances. I remember my dad telling my first wife how when I was a little boy I used to spend hours singing whilst sitting on the toilet. Thanks, Dad.

And when did you first appear on stage?

That would have been in a school production when I'd moved to Birmingham. It was *Beauty and the Beast*, but it must have been a strange version because I played Mikey the baby dragon.

That even sounds embarrassing.

Oh yes. It was. Particularly when the teacher who was directing was trying to get me to dance around when I was singing. What she wanted me to do was what we'd refer to now as 'shakin' that ass', but she couldn't bring herself to say a rude word such as 'bottom' or even 'behind'. I genuinely couldn't understand what she was on about. Or was I being purposely obtuse ? I honestly don't think so, but either way she finally gave up and almost shouted: 'Just waggle your bum!' Which of course brought the house down. 'Miss said bum!' 'Bill Oddie doesn't know where his bum is!' 'Bill Oddie's bum!' Embarrassed? Of course I was. And yet . . . is it entirely coincidence that one of my finest compositions during *The Goodies* years was 'Black Pudding Bertha' which we performed on *Top of the Pops* and contained the irresistible chorus 'By gum, shake your bum!' You see, nothing is wasted by the sensitive songwriter. What's more—as with so many of my creations— apparent frivolity masks deeper and sadder feelings.

Only joking. Nearly.

When did you start actually writing original songs then?

When I went to King Edward's School, Birmingham. It all began on the school rugby coach. We used to play a lot of away games, and on the way back there would be the traditional singsong featuring the traditional repertoire of traditional rugby songs, all of which were incredibly gross and disgusting, although often incongruously literate.

Like 'Blowing Off' in fact?

Quite so. I told you it belonged to a genre.

You mean it belongs on a rugby coach.

If you say so. Look, do you want to hear about this or not?

Yes, I do. Sorry. Do carry on.

Thank you. So, every week we'd be singing the same songs. I can't remember any of them properly. There was something called 'I Ziggy Zumba', which I think had a chorus of 'Lay me down, you Zulu warrior, lay me down, you Zulu chief chief chief', but I'm sure it wasn't about African tribal warfare, any more than 'Eskimo Nell' was about Inuit culture. There was also one about a 'ruddy great wheel', which was an incredibly complex saga involving what I suspect was a giant metallic dildo! I swear the chorus went something like: 'Round and round went the ruddy great wheel, in and out went the prick of steel!'

Anyway, the thing is, rousing and ingenious though these depraved anthems may have been, they also got a bit tedious when it was all we ever sang, week after week after week. I suspect I may be a bit snobbish about the choral 'traditions' of Rugby Union. Am I the only one who is not so much elated as depressed by the Twickenham faithfuls wailing away on 'Swing Low,

Sweet Chariot'?

I hate that song. And what are those dreadful dirges Welsh blokes bellow out? 'Bread of Heaven', is it?

Yeah. And that one that sounds like 'Saucepan Bark, Merry on the Town', which is presumably Welsh for something supposedly inspiring. Like, 'Let's have a look at your leek, Taffy.' Actually, perhaps it's not so much tradition as repetition that narks me. I have the same trouble on New Year's Eve. Why do we always have to sing 'Auld Lang Syne'? I quite literally can't bring myself to join in. I just mouth the words and pretend. I think I am a bit obsessed with originality, which—in a musical context—is probably why I prefer singer-songwriters to people who just do 'standards'.

You mean you're more Bob Harris than Michael Parkinson?

Exactly. Anyway, the thing is, I got so bored with the same old rugby songs that I was inspired to come up with new lyrics for them all. It wasn't a big success because of course nobody knew the words so they couldn't join in. Also, they may have been new but they weren't half as filthy as the originals, which was probably the main attraction for pubescent schoolboys, very few of whom would have had any first-hand experience of the sort of activities they were singing about. In fact, I rather doubt that a single member of our first fifteen had actually done it! Except possibly the inside centre. But I'd rather not think about that, since I suspect the young lady he was doing it with was the netball captain from the adjacent girls' school, who I thought of as my girlfriend at the time.

Oh, that's sad.

Yes, but there you are - another example of sublimating sorrow with song. I no doubt incorporated some of my feelings in my reworking of 'Four and Twenty Virgins'.

Clearly, though, you were hankering after—and no doubt you felt you deserved—a more sophisticated audience than a coachload of rugger buggers.

I did. Fortunately I found a more appropriate outlet on stage in the school revue. Firstly, I have to acknowledge my good fortune that our school had a revue. Very few schools do. Concerts, plays, possibly even productions of musicals, yes, but not a lot of schools put on a whole evening of comedy sketches and funny songs! Back in the 1950s, King Edward's School, Birmingham did. In fact, it was a tradition. It happened twice, as far as I know. It was initiated by an extremely talented bloke called Nat Joseph, who went on to be a theatrical impresario, and also founded Transatlantic Records, which was a truly seminal folk label in the 1960s and 70s (compilations available in all good record shops). Nat wrote and directed the first school revue in 1957, which was his last year, and I wrote the second one in 1959, which was mine.

As well as the sketches, I came up with several songs. I am not making any great claims to wondrous originality, but I did break away from even the two-year tradition Nat had established. He too had written comedy songs, but he had conformed to a device that had already served its time in shows for many, many years and is no doubt still alive and kicking. It is called 'putting new words to old tunes'. It is a reliable staple in amateur shows, was exploited joyously by the Two Ronnies, and has been running gleefully for ages in 'Forbidden Broadway' type revues, in which the words to songs from famous musicals are changed to make satirical fun of the shows the tunes have been stolen from, which seems a bit ungracious to me. It also seems a bit of a 'cheat'. Here comes my self-righteous snobbery again! I remember reacting this way to the musical numbers in the first school revue, which consisted almost entirely of reworkings of Gilbert and Sullivan. I dare say you know the sort of thing. 'Three Little Maids' hardly needed a lyric change to be redirected at the young ladies from the next-door girls' school, plus it required three boys to dress up in gymslips and high heels.

Always a winner.

Similarly, there were such inevitable adaptations as 'I Am the Very Model of a Public School Librarian . . . or something else with four syllables'!

Er . . .

Not to mention 'A Wandering Whatsit I' . . .

Prefect, teacher, matron . . .

Whatever. The truth is—curse my pomposity—I used to hate Gilbert and Sullivan with a deep and bitter loathing, until I myself played Koko in the English National Opera's production of *The Mikado* in 1980-something. It was only then that I finally realised that G & S were pretty damned clever, and what I had really objected to was their ultra-pedantic aficionados—the ones who sit in the front row and follow the score!— and the plagiarisers who had highjacked their work and replaced their wondrously convoluted lyrics with all sorts of codswallop. No disrespect to the memory of Nat Joseph, mind you. Everyone did it.

But not you!

Oh no. I rapidly gave up using the same device to 'improve' the rugby songs, and set about composing an original score for the 1959 Kings Edward's School Revue. It was called *Let's Face It*. Even the title had a hint of rebellion about it, implying an intention to expose hitherto unconfronted truths and 'tell it like it is'.

Or at least like it was in the somewhat restricted world of well-educated schoolboys and their teachers in Birmingham in the late 1950s. So, what was in the show?

I still have the programme of *Let's Face It*. Some of the song titles remind me of some of the satirical targets. 'A Brit on Broadway' referred to our headmaster's 'research' trip to America. 'The Daily Espress' was about a coffee bar called El Sombrero, which the aforesaid headmaster deemed such a den of iniquity that it had been declared 'out of bounds'. In truth, nothing more sinister went on in there than the sipping of frothy coffee, which in those days was considered as decadent as cocaine. Other titles include 'Capital Punishment', 'Who Goes Where' and of course the opening number, 'Let's Face It'.

What were they about?

I've no idea but I'm sure they were terribly witty. I provided the lyrics and the tunes, whilst the piano accompaniment was provided by a young virtuoso called John Jordan, who went on to be the organist at King's College, Cambridge, which organ fans assure me is about as exalted as an organist can get. The cast of the show also included David Munrow, who became one of the world's leading proponents of medieval music. Clearly, the King Edward's sixth form of 1959 included some pretty highbrow musicians.

And you were one of them? What did you play?

The washboard. Although I did also possess a cheap acoustic guitar, and a mouth organ. I couldn't play anything properly. However, I did know the lyrics of just about anything in the hit parade, had accumulated a considerable record collection and become pretty much addicted to singing into a microphone. And I had finally discovered how to shake my ass.

But you were not highbrow. Definitely more rock and roll?

Exactly. I was also into comedy. These were not things that were normally or perhaps naturally connected, which is probably exactly what attracted me to the idea of putting them together. In 1960 I started at Cambridge University, where I soon got an opportunity to see if it would work.

Bill, forgive me if I misconstrue, but are you by any chance attempting to stake a claim to a niche in the evolution of humorous songwriting?

Would I do such a thing? Maybe. Meanwhile, allow me to put my efforts into context. The most prolific outlet for comedy or music—or indeed any kind of entertainment—after the war was, of course, the radio, commonly referred to as the wireless.

Which is odd 'cos it wouldn't work if it didn't have a plug, which was on the end of a wire.

Yeah yeah, old joke. Anyway, in our house in the terrace in Rochdale, the wireless was on more or less permanently, whether anyone was listening or not. I dare say the main reason for this was that it was the instant source of warnings of imminent air-raids. It was also constantly updating news of the war. Basically, were we winning or losing? I don't remember any specific bulletins, but it obviously made an indelible impression on me. To this day, I am unsettled by the sound of a lone male voice—especially a news reader—on radio. I immediately associate it with doom and disaster. Laura is in the habit of leaving the radio on in the kitchen. I keep turning it off. I know that she and indeed many other people regard the sound of a radio voice as comforting. But it physically upsets me, because it reminds me of wartime. Especially as news bulletins these days so often refer to death and destruction. The sad fact is of course, that in many parts of the world it still is wartime.

And this is relevant to comedy songs how?

Well, the wireless as a source of music and laughter I was totally addicted to, even as a little lad. I remember the names of lots of shows and entertainers: *Educating Archie,* Jewel and Warris, *Down Your Way, Family Favourites*, Wilfred Pickles, Charlie Chester, *The Billy Cotton Band Show*, the Crazy Gang and many, many more. Like me, anyone of my generation will recall them fondly. However, a couple of years ago I was asked to choose a selection of examples for a series about the history of radio comedy. I was sent extracts from maybe a dozen of the shows I had been entranced and convulsed by when I was a kid. As I listened to them I began to realise that they nearly all had the same thing in common. They were bloody awful! What was blatantly obvious on many of them was that the star comedian was still delivering his lines as if he were on the music hall stage. Most of them shouted, over-acted grossly, and seemed to virtually ignore those with whom they were supposed to be sharing the microphone. It wasn't until people started writing specifically for radio that comedies started to get subtle or inventive in a way we still appreciate today. The Goons, Hancock, Kenneth Horne and the like all relied on inspired writers: Galton and Simpson, Took and Feldman, Spike Milligan.

So that's the comedy. What about the music?

These shows had another thing in common. Two things actually. They all had music in them; but not all of it was funny. It wasn't meant to be. Invariably it would be just a musical interlude, featuring a lady singer, or a group of singers, usually blokes. They weren't a group, as in a

143

boy band, more likely a close harmony male voice quartet, who were long past being boys! They had racy names like the Smith Brothers, or the Frazer Hayes Four. Some of them were largely instrumental like the Morton Frazer Harmonica Gang, or the Ray Ellington Quartet, who were at least lively and jazzy. Not adjectives you could apply to the BBC Symphony Orchestra, who provided the half-time music on one of the lame comedy shows I listened to, and played a medley of patriotic marching music! I can only assume it was part of a musicians' union agreement with the BBC. They maintained several orchestras, which had to be guaranteed a certain amount of air time, even if what they were playing was completely incongruous and inappropriate. Comedian does mother-in-law jokes. Orchestra does extracts from the 1812!

Surely it wasn't that comedy songs didn't exist at all at the beginning of the 1960s?

No, but they were very rarely incorporated into comedy shows, either on radio or on the stage. There was indeed a considerable and largely British tradition of funny numbers stretching back to the bawdy ballads of the Edwardian music hall—'A Little of What You Fancy Does You Good' and the like—followed by the cunning innuendos of George Formby—'With My Little Stick of Blackpool Rock', or 'With My Little Ukelele in My Hand'.

What was he on about?

I can't imagine. And there were also witty 'concert party' numbers, usually sung by a bloke or possibly two blokes in dinner jackets, leaning nonchalantly on a piano. Noël Coward was justly famous; the Western Brothers less so.

Less famous or less justly?

Both. The 1950s was also the decade of the dreaded

144

novelty song single like 'Where Will the Baby's Dimple Be?' and 'Mule Train'.

They don't write 'em like that any more!

Thank goodness. However, the 1950s had seen some writers attempting to drag the comedy song into modern times. My personal favourite was an American professor called Tom Lehrer, whose compositions were not only verbally dazzling, but also in the worst possible taste. Lehrer was the brilliant musical representative of a new wave of 'sick humour' that was currently outraging the prissier side of society, and therefore appealed to me no end. I particularly enjoyed such gems as 'The Old Dope Pedlar', 'We'll All Go Together When We Go', and—one for us ornithologists—'Poisoning Pigeons in the Park'.

I've got a *Best of Tom Lehrer* CD—highly recommended. But how were you going to fit into all this?

When I arrived at Cambridge, I made a point of seeing some student revues, expecting them to reflect current comedy styles. The verbal and visual items generally did just that. There was some clever wordplay, some topical satire, occasional pre-Python surrealism, and some very inventive variations on mime and magic. I remember Graham Chapman's physically exhausting 'wrestling with himself' routine, and Graeme Garden's wonderfully dexterous 'Pets' Corner', when his sleight of hand transformed a piece of paper into a Vampire Bat which went straight for his throat. There were clearly lots of very funny performers and writers, and I could easily have been totally intimidated, except for one thing: the music, which wasn't intimidating at all. There were musical numbers in the shows, but they certainly weren't funny. And they definitely weren't meant to be. In fact, they were often quite the

145

opposite. I think the expression is 'bitter- sweet'. Bloody miserable, more like. They were invariably sung by a woman, or rather a girl, since most of the students were barely out of their teens. I think they really belonged in 'cabaret', which is I suppose a bit like a revue, but without the laughs. And with classier costumes. The girls often looked pretty stunning, in an old-before-their-time, Marlene Dietrich sort of way. Their dresses were invariably black, they wore high heels, and brandished a cigarette in one hand, and possibly a whisky glass in the other, if they weren't using a microphone. They were revealed by a spotlight suddenly slashing through the darkness, and they would often be leaning against a bar, or sometimes a white marble pillar. I suppose it symbolised sophistication, loneliness and melancholy. Which is exactly what they sang about, perhaps with a tiny wry touch of world-weary humour, usually directed at men. The genre was the 'torch song', the sort of slow jazz style found in musicals. Not for one second could I figure out why the fellas were allowed to do all the funny stuff, whilst the girls were lumbered with the miserable music, but boy was I glad it was so! I had spotted my niche, and my strategy was confirmed. I was going to be something completely different: a man, singing songs that were meant to be funny and were undeniably rock and roll.

It was indeed a cunning plan, and it worked. For over a year I monopolised the Cambridge comedy music scene, performing songs in various styles from Elvis to Chuck Berry, Eurovision, even Gospel. Frankly, I wouldn't claim that the lyrics to any of them were side-splittingly hilarious, but—and this was the secret of their success—they allowed snooty Cambridge students to tap and clap along and get their rocks off

146

to music that hadn't yet fully received the intellectual stamp of approval. It wasn't really rock and roll, it was a parody.

It was ok to boogie because it was satirical?
Exactly. It was also about to become a job.

Had you any idea what you would do after university?
I had no idea what I was doing at university, let alone afterwards. I was reading English Literature, but not because I particularly enjoyed it and certainly not because I thought it would lead on to any kind of gainful employment. I did English because it was what I was best at. Or at least it was the subject I got best marks for in exams. To this day I have no idea why. I felt then that I had conned the examiners, and I still do. I was good at waffling, which I think they mistook for original thought. I had no academic ambitions. I wasn't concerned whether or not I went to Cambridge, or got a decent degree. Dad was. My attitude was that I had three years in which I might discover what it was I wanted or was able to do to earn money. Meanwhile I played a lot of rugby and a lot of records and my newly acquired tenor saxophone and the fool! I also wrote my first 'hit' song.

What was that?
It was about Adam Faith. He was one of the most successful of the crop of young British pop stars of the 1950s that included Tommy Steele, Billy Fury, Cliff Richard and many more. History relates how these cleancut, besuited, homely lads with nice haircuts were nevertheless regarded as the spawn of Satan by politicians, parsons and parents, to name but three easily outraged self-appointed protectors of public morals. Adam Faith had decided to be, or had been appointed as, a spokesman for the young ones, and had

been granted an audience with the Archbishop of Canterbury for some reason, presumably involving publicity and selling records. It certainly worked. It was all over the newspapers and on the telly, and whilst I don't remember the Archbishop entering the charts, Adam certainly did. I wrote a topical satirical song about it which I performed at my Cambridge college end-of-term show. I sang in the style of Adam Faith— which wasn't hard as he didn't have much of a voice but it was characterised by a little Buddy Holly style hiccup that was very easy to impersonate. The song also had a sassy little beat which the undergrads could tap their toes to, and—though I say it myself—some quite canny wordplay in the lyrics culminating in the so-obvious-it's-good line: 'There's faith and hope and charity—and the greatest of these is . . .

fai-ai-aith!'

You got it! I knew it was a winner when it was included in the Footlights end-of-year revue at the Arts Theatre. I didn't get to sing it myself, as at that stage I wasn't even a club member, let alone in the cast of the official revue.

I soon discovered, however, that being in or writing for the Footlights was a potential portal to fame. Talent scouts from the BBC were in the habit of coming up to Cambridge on the lookout for comedy actors and material.

So, 'Have Faith' became the first piece of creative work you earned money from?

Correct. The first song I sold. It wasn't a hit in the *Pick of the Pops* sense, but it was performed on the hugely successful Saturday satire show, *That Was the Week That Was*, and appeared on a TW3 album.

You know, I've always said that the university years are a time when you might discover what you want

to do in life and it may be nothing to do with what you're actually there to study.

Exactly. What followed proved the point conclusively. The rise and rise of what became known as the 'Oxbridge mafia' during the 1960s, ... which has been documented to death in books, radio shows and TV programmes ...

Which is entirely justified. It was a remarkable decade, and history has confirmed that it was indeed every bit as extraordinary as it felt at the time. The names of individuals, the teams and their achievements are the stuff of legend. *Beyond the Fringe ... with Peter Cook, Dudley Moore, Alan Bennett and Jonathan Miller. That Was the Week That Was ...* with David Frost, Willie Rushton and many others. The Establishment Club, in Soho, again featuring Cook and Moore, and the slightly younger talents of John Bird, John Fortune and Eleanor Bron.

And there was my lot from the 1963 Cambridge Revue, Tim Brooke-Taylor, Graham Chapman, John Cleese, in a show that transferred to the West End, whilst a second team at the Edinburgh Festival included Eric Idle and Graeme Garden. At the same time, an Oxford revue introduced Mike Palin and Terry Jones into the mix. By the end of the decade, various permutations of these names, plus others from the same sources, had produced several TV and radio series including...

Don't tell me ... *Not So Much a Programme, More a Way of Life, Do Not Adjust Your Set, At Last the 1948 Show, I'm Sorry I'll Read That Again ...*
and more, until at the end of the decade they finally sorted themselves out into the two teams that sort of contested the British wacky comedy Premiership for

149

much of the 1970s: Monty Python and the Goodies.
Were you deadly rivals?
You know we weren't. If we were rivals at all it was never anything but a totally friendly rivalry.
Totally?
Nearly totally. Anyway, if you will indulge me, I would just like to conclude my personal musical Oddie-sey. Although I contributed lots of 'skits and sketches', it was the comedy song department that I felt was my speciality. It could be argued—even by me—that the keyword was quantity rather than quality, but that's what the work demanded. For a couple of years I wrote songs for *That Was the Week That Was*, including the unnatural practice of putting words to improvised jazz solos which Millicent Martin sang very fast and I always suspected the audience found a bit pointless.
So did I.
I also wrote an unbelievably huge number of daft ditties for *I'm Sorry I'll Read That Again*. We did over 100 shows, and for much of the time I produced two songs a week! At one stage I got so desperate for new ideas that I asked the audience to come up with silly titles and I would write a song to fit. It was when I heard myself singing some total nonsense called 'If Mao Tse Tung Was a Scotsman' that I cut down to one song per show. But no sooner had the *I'm Sorry* song production line decelerated, than along came *The Goodies*, for which I produced another vast library of material, much of which was buried beneath sound effects and audience laughter (which by the way was genuine and not a 'track'). *The Goodies'* soundtrack was my attempt to get away from the style of incidental music which had adorned TV comedy shows since time immemorial. Lots of fruity tubas and twiddly flutes and wahwahwahs at the end of each scene. I didn't really

150

care too much if anyone even noticed the lyrics of my 'incidental' songs. I just had a fabulous fun time recording them with some of Britain's best rock and jazz musicians. However, *The Goodies'* records—singles and album tracks—were more exposed. Apparently quite a few people actually listened to them. I know that, because I am still plagued by people who remember the words and sing them at me.

Heaven knows, I don't want to seem curmudgeonly or ungracious but ... I have penned lyrical narrative masterpieces like 'Blowing Off'. I have crafted the exquisite wordplay of my tribute to Joy Adamson:

> I'm not lyin',
> I'm relyin' on a lion,
> And a lion is lyin' on me!

Whoever thought bestiality could be so elegant?
Then there was the grandeur of 'The Policeman's Opera' on *The Goodies'* 'underground' album on Island Records, *Nothing to Do with Us*, now long since and lamentably unavailable.

And wasn't your rendering of 'On Ilkley Moor Bah Tat' in the style of Joe Cocker's version of 'With a Little Help From my Friends' in John Peel's favourite records box?
It was indeed. I'm not bitter but ... All that effort, all that inspiration, all that meticulous honing of lyrics, all that reverence for the beauty of the English language, melded felicitously to the magic of melody. And which of my hundreds and hundreds of songs am I best remembered for? 'Ooooh oooh ooooh, the Funky Gibbon'. Why did I bother?

2

From Fringe to Flying Circus . . . again

OK, I think that's quite enough about your songwriting ambitions. Let's face it, it's all just a teenie bit embarrassing. What I'd like to do is go back to the 1960s.

Wouldn't we all!

I doubt it. But anyway, I know you think everybody's read all these 'history of British comedy' books, but they haven't. And I know you think everybody knows about the Cambridge Footlights, but they don't. So please, answer a simple question in a simple way: what are, or were, the Footlights?

The Footlights were—and still are—a sort of drama society or club at Cambridge University, only they don't do plays and serious stuff, they do comedy.

And give us a few names of people who were in the Footlights during the 1960s. No comments, just famous names.

OK. Peter Cook, David Frost, John Bird, John Fortune, John Cleese, Graham Chapman, Tim Brooke-Taylor, Graeme Garden, Eric Idle, Jonathan Lynn, Clive James, soon to be followed by Hugh Laurie and Stephen Fry.

No women?

Women weren't officially allowed to be members, until I think it was the mid 1960s. But they *were* allowed to be in the shows . . .

. . . As long as they stuck to wearing black dresses and sang torch songs.

152

It wasn't a rule, but that's the way it often was, which may explain why not so many of them became as famous as the blokes! Nevertheless, a few slipped through the net of condescending male sexism. Eleanor Bron, Miriam Margolyes, Germaine Greer, Emma Thompson, but I doubt that many—or any—of them remember the Footlights as fondly as the fellas.

So it was a gentlemen's club?

Frankly, yes. Complete with a club room and a bar.

And yet it obviously wasn't just somewhere to go and snooze behind your newspaper. Especially during the late 1950s and early '60s, it was clearly a hotbed of creativity. Why do you think that was?

Maybe because there were no women to distract us or show off to, or to embarrass ourselves in front of? I don't know. One thing that I do feel was pretty crucial is that there was an actual club room. We didn't have to hire a hall, or meet upstairs at a pub once a month. A lot of us virtually lived in the Footlights club room. It wasn't enormous and it was a bit scruffy, but it had everything necessary for the survival of ostentatious young whippersnappers with pretensions of being funny. There was food, drink, ashtrays, toilets, tables, chairs, benches, and a small stage, with velvet curtains and a piano. Plus lots and lots of ambitious chaps . . .

. . . And the occasional woman. Who had to be signed in by a male member.

No, no, we just used a pen!

You never lose it, do you?

Unfortunately, no. Actually that's the kind of silly joke you'd feel embarrassed about in female company. I hate to be almost supporting the 'no women' policy—and I definitely didn't at the time—but I suppose it did mean that we were less inhibited or self-conscious, which is no bad thing if you are trying to be funny. Comedy is potentially excruciatingly humiliating. There really is nothing worse than metaphorically 'dying the death'. Come to think of it, I am sure that is another reason the 1960s Footlights produced so much genuinely original humour. People weren't afraid to try something different, because the audience were basically on their side. In fact, many of the audience were next up on stage, so it was a case of 'I'll laugh at you if you'll laugh at me'.

Couldn't that lead to delusions of funniness?

Probably, but it also encourages people to take risks. What's more, the audience hadn't paid to be entertained, and they were not going to turn nasty if they weren't. There would be no barracking, booing, heckling or cries of 'Give 'im the hook.'

Unlike some club situations.

Exactly. Any stand-up comic who has performed on 'the circuit', whether of the northern clubs or the more aggressive of the 'alternative' comedy clubs that sprang up in the 1980s, has chilling tales of hostile audiences, whose principal pleasure verged on sadism. In such venues, comedy could be classed as a blood sport. Akin to throwing the Christians to the lions. I have heard comedians refer to 'beating' the audience rather than entertaining them. A repertoire of 'put-downs' to subdue hecklers is as important as original comedy material, and rather than try new stuff, there is a big temptation to fall back on 'safe' jokes, even ones that are sexist, racist or smutty. The content at least of the early vanguard of 'alternatives' was invariably 'PC', but it's no coincidence that the delivery was rarely 'laid back', in the way that, for example, Eddie Izzard or Jack Dee can be these days.

I seem to recall Ben Elton being asked why he talked so fast, and so loudly, and with so much

154

swearing. His answer was to the effect that he didn't want to let the audience get a word in edgeways.

He wouldn't have had to worry about that at a Footlights show in the 1960s. The Cambridge audience even kept quiet during a mime act! Or maybe they were asleep.

Anyway, that is my convoluted theory as to why so many original 'humourists' flourished at Cambridge during the early 1960s. What it doesn't explain is why the same time and place also produced several eventually famous film and theatre directors such as Stephen Frears, Trevor Nunn and Richard Eyre. Not to mention quite a number of journalists and politicians. So I won't.

Blimey, and you said you didn't want to talk about the Footlights. I don't suppose you want to talk about *Cambridge Circus* either?

The 1963 end-of-year university revue, you mean?

Yes.

It wasn't called 'Cambridge Circus'. Not when we played the Cambridge Arts Theatre. It was originally called 'A Clump of Plinths'.

That's a snappy title. Why on earth did you change it?

Don't be sarcastic. Naming a show is much harder than writing or performing one. It's the same with band names and record albums. I wonder how many daft names the Beatles came up with before they became the Quarrymen, and how many more before they became the Beatles? Which, be honest, is a pretty crap name! Beat-les as in 'beat' music? Or is it because they had shiny black hair, like they were wearing beetles on their heads? I tell you something, I bet Lennon and McCartney wrote a whole album's worth of brilliant songs in less time than it took to come up with the title *Rubber Soul*. What's with the naff puns, boys? And, as it happens, I, Tim and Graeme spent weeks coming up with such gems as 'Superchaps Three' before I finally suggested *The Goodies*—which, by the way, I have regretted ever since, but that's another story.

I remember us labouring for days over the title of the 1963 show. Cleese was really irritating because he kept coming up with stupid things like 'Owl Stretching Time', 'You Can't Call a Show Cornflakes' and 'Monty Python's Flying Circus'—as if that would ever catch on. 'A Clump of Plinths' actually described the set, which was made up of a number of rather ingeniously interlocked wooden boxes. At least, I assume it was that way round. Surely we didn't tell the designer: 'It's called "A Clump of Plinths". It might give you an idea for a set.'

So when and why did it become *Cambridge Circus*?
When we transferred to London and we were in a theatre on Shaftesbury Avenue. The Lyric.

Which isn't particularly near Cambridge Circus, is it?
No. It's much nearer to Piccadilly Circus.

So why didn't you call it 'Piccadilly Circus'?
Because we didn't go to Piccadilly University. We went to Cambridge. Haven't you been listening to a word I've said?

Yes, of course. It's just that quite a lot of this is in those 'history of comedy' books.
I told you that.

Yes, but as I told you, *I've* read them, but not everyone has. So, please, very quickly, tell us what happened to *Cambridge Circus*. The show. Not the London landmark.
We started at the Arts Theatre in Great Newport Street. Then we transferred to the Lyric, Shaftesbury

156

Avenue, where we ran for nine months. Then we had a little break and got together again to do a six-week tour of New Zealand. Then in the autumn of 1964 we went to New York and opened at the Plymouth Theater on Broadway!

So what had started out as the end-of-year Cambridge University Footlights Student Revue ended up on Broadway!?

You got it.

Wow!

You knew that. You said, you've read the books. And anyway, you were in it.

Yes, I know. But I can still hardly believe it. Anyway, I'm sure what everyone wants to know is: how did it go?

Fan-bloody-tastic! After the opening night, we did this thing everyone did—and maybe still do—of going to an all-night theatrical bar called Sardi's. The walls there were covered with those caricatures, with big heads, of all the legendary Broadway stars from the past, like Ethel Merman, and Judy Garland, and Gene Kelly, and Fred Astaire, and Al Jolson—I recognised all of them, as I was a big fan of American musicals. There must have been legendary straight actors too, but I didn't know them so well. So now here's this bunch of English college students, giggling at the idea that we might become caricatures with big heads, sipping New York cocktails like 'whisky sours' and 'Manhattans', and waiting for a guy to burst in with a load of morning papers with the reviews of our show. Also with us were our British producer and director, Michael White, an impresario who went on to produce *Hair* and lots of other shows, and Humphrey Barclay, our Cambridge director who became a very successful producer in radio and TV. There were also a couple of Americans representing the stateside end of the management. They kept warning us about how vitriolic the notorious New York critics could be, and how vital it was to get good 'notices'. They told us there were one or two individual critics who could close a show overnight. This might have seemed exaggerated pessimism, were it not for the fact that, no sooner had the curtains closed after our last encore, than the theatre manager had posted a 'Notice of Closure' on the stage door pinboard. Imagine how confusing and deflating that is! We have still got the audience applause ringing in our ears, and are feeling as if we have a foot on the stairway to paradise, only to be brought crashing to earth by being told, 'The show closes tomorrow.' The Americans must have sensed our feeling of slight anticlimax, because they rapidly explained that this was standard practice on Broadway. No sooner have you been hired, than you are fired; and in this way the management will only be liable for three weeks' wages if the show is a flop.

And if it isn't a flop . . . ?

You are still only guaranteed three weeks' wages. Then they'll hire and fire you again. And so it goes on. Not what you'd call a secure future. But hey, did we care? We all had Cambridge degrees in various vocational areas. Graham Chapman was a medic. Tim, Johnny and John were destined to become lawyers, a training Cleese had already put to good use by writing the hilarious comedy court scene, with which we ended the show. David Hatch was surely a natural born history teacher. The only ones who might have even for one moment been drawn towards 'treading the boards' professionally were Jo Kendal—because she was a drama student—and me, because my English degree qualified me for bugger all. I suspect the truth of it is that, by the time we hit New York, all of us had a tiny inkling that we might be destined to jettison whatever proper jobs we had spent three years training for at university, and follow the lure of the spotlights.

Shouldn't that be the Footlights?

'Spose so. We may even have been discussing our future, when the man arrived with the morning papers and announced: 'It's a hit!'

So you got rave reviews?

Fantastic! I was likened to a young Mickey Rooney. To be honest, I had no idea who Mickey Rooney was at the time, but I presumed it was a compliment.

I didn't mean just you. The show?

The New York Post called us 'hilarious'. *Time* magazine 'indescribably funny', the *Tribune* 'glorious', NBC said 'critics were doubled over with laughter'. *Cue* magazine said …

Ok, ok. I get the picture.

We were instantly invited to appear on one of the most legendary TV shows of all time: the *Ed Sullivan Show*. I can't imagine how or why Ed Sullivan himself was so famous, since his general demeanour would have made George W. Bush look like Liberace. Ed wore a slightly ill-fitting grey suit, had slicked-back, thinning hair, a rather toothy smile and a slightly hunched back. He didn't tell jokes or banter wittily. He tended to introduce his guests—especially the non-American ones—as if he had no idea who they were, or what they did. In our case fair enough, but I recall he didn't seem any more excited or knowledgeable when the Beatles were on. Which they had been, along with other groups in the 'British Invasion', as it came to be called. We shared the bill with the Animals, presumably singing 'The House of the Rising Sun'. At the time, I was clean-shaven, and being quite small I could be mistaken for Eric Burdon, the Animals' lead singer. At least I assume that's who hordes of screaming teenage girls thought I was when I appeared at a fourth-floor window, waved, blew kisses and generally basked in a fantasy—one that sort of came true ten years later when *The Goodies'* popularity was at its peak. That too is another story.

We'll get to it. Meanwhile, you were the toast of New York!

Except for one rather puzzling fact. No one was coming to see us! Well, not literally no one, but the houses were such that—put it this way—nobody was rushing to take down the 'closing in three weeks' notice. We hadn't been axed after one night, which did happen to some shows, but it was obvious our days were numbered, and it wasn't a very big number either. But why? We'd had the raves, we'd done Ed Sullivan and Jack Parr. We had even heard word that you couldn't get tickets. This, it turned out, was true— not because the show was sold out, but because it wasn't even listed in some of the ticket agencies. We conducted a little research of our own, rather pathetically trying to buy tickets for our own show, only to be told there weren't any, or—even more bizarrely—that *Cambridge Circus* didn't exist. Inevitably, audiences got smaller and smaller and, just as our first-night notice had foretold, the show closed, we received three weeks' wages, and we were sent packing. Nobody could explain it, but I had and still have my theories.

Which are?

This is one of them. The American impresario who put us on was called Sol Hurok. Unlike Michael White, he was not known for taking risks with 'left-field'

160

'The Family Album.' Except there never was one. I don't remember these pictures being taken or how they came into my possession. In fact, I am having to assume the people in them really are who I think they are!

Apparently this is me, presumably late in 1941.

No, I don't remember the cuddly toy. And I can't believe I ever looked like this!

Lance Corporal Harry Oddie.
He was stationed at Bury St
Edmunds in Cambridgeshire.
Not exactly the front line!

Pre-war, Lilian Clegg.
Later to become Harry's
wife, and my mother.

Mother about to launch me
in the annual baby throwing
contest. Presumably my
landing took the smile off
my face.

I think I do remember this session. The photographer was amusing me with his woolly monkey. Really.

Me and Dad on holiday in Salcombe, Devon. I look about ten, and presumably was.

Lapal Primary School football team 1950-51 season. Me on the floor, on the right. I played right half (midfield nowadays), apart from one disastrous game as Britain's smallest goalkeeper. I let in two goals, one through my legs, and the other—where else?—over my head.

LET'S FACE IT!

AN ORIGINAL REVUE

presented by
THE KING EDWARD'S SCHOOL
DRAMATIC SOCIETY

JULY 20th and 21st, 1959

Signed by the cast. It wasn't that John Peel. But Robin Duval did become the British Film Censor—the bloke who signs the certificate before the movies—and therefore got his name on every screen in the land.

The school revue, written entirely by me!

A page from my bird diary from September 1956. A rather good day on the north Norfolk coast. Dad was my chauffeur.

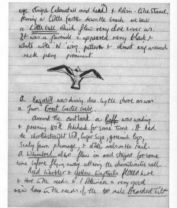

KING EDWARDS SCHOOL
RUGGER XV 1959-60

The K.E.S. 'rugger' team. They really did call it that! That's me with the ball. Yes, I was captain, which meant I had to be made a prefect, much to the disgust of the Chief Master, I suspect.

Our skiffle group. Every school had one in the 1950s. I eventually played washboard, but at this stage we had a proper drummer. I presume he exploded and I took over. (Only fans of *Spinal Tap* will get that one!)

Late 1950s. King Edward's unbeaten second Eleven. A bunch of jolly sloggers who had far more fun than the first team.

1960. My room at Pembroke College, Cambridge. Every room I have had since has had a wall like this featuring birds, music and comedy, with a few bits of my own 'artwork'.

1959. At Fair Isle Bird Observatory. Note the local knitwear and antique brass telescope, and is that a hint of a beard? How rugged.

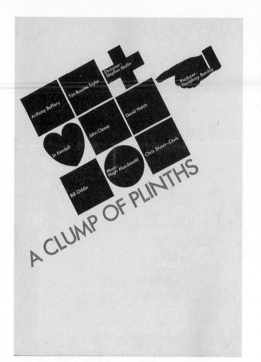

1963 Cambridge Footlights Revue. Weird design. Weirder title. A wee bit pretentious, perhaps!

Autumn 1963. Same show, but weird no longer. Jester icon designed by Humphrey Barclay.

Budding comedians 'pretending' to be boozy undergraduates. Tim Brooke-Taylor, Chris Stuart-Clark, John Cleese and David Hatch.

The cast of Cambridge Circus larking about in London. Hatch, Jo Kendall, Graham Chapman, Brooke-Taylor, me, Stuart-Clark, and Cleese as a fake policeman. Plus real policeman about to say, 'hello hello hello, what's all this then?'

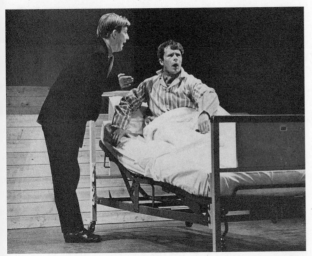

Tim's robot hospital visitor. A masterpiece of physical comedy and totally knackering. He couldn't do that any more. I, on the other hand, could easily reproduce my role.

More iconic artwork from Humphrey Barclay. A 'smash' that lasted three weeks!

The Plymouth Theatre

PLAYBILL

the magazine for theatregoers

CAMBRIDGE CIRCUS

'Hilarious. Fresh, disarming and inescapably engaging.'*

SAYS WATTS OF THE POST

* and just about all the critics agree!

CAMBRIDGE CIRCUS

SMASH MUSICAL REVUE

PLYMOUTH, WEST 45TH ST. Clr 6-9156

TICKETS AVAILABLE. See Stage Play Directory below for details.

October 1964. Brits on Broadway! Johnny Lynn, me Hatch, Kendall, Cleese, Brooke-Taylor and Chapman.

Jean Hart and Bill Oddie. Or is it Barbra Streisand and Mickey Rooney? Were we turning American?

TW3 on the road. 'Cushion caricatures' by the greatly talented and much missed Willie Rushton.

1965. Flying the flag. English, yes. Original, hardly. One of the few pieces of publicity that didn't feature David Frost. But then, he was the famous one.

4331

Emu

TRIPLEKNIT
•
32 to 44 inch
chest sizes

THE EMU

PURE NEW *wool*

SWEATER
AS WORN BY
BILL
ODDIE
IN
"THANK
YOUR
LUCKY
STARS"

NINEPENCE

Mid '60s. Promoting my latest single: a parody of the 'Clapping Song', called the 'Knitting Song', which involved me funkily 'rapping' knitting patterns, whilst perched on a giant ball of wool. As you do.

In full, late '60s faux hippie gear. But I didn't smoke dope. Honestly. More's the pity.

The first of several of my records to be banned. Maybe I should be grateful?

PARLOPHONE RECORDS R5153

BILL ODDIE

nothing better to do

E.M.I. RECORDS LTD., E.M.I. HOUSE, 20 MANCHESTER SQUARE, LONDON, W.1

The original – and perhaps a teensie bit legendary – cast of ISIRTA. Fans will know what those letters stand for. Non-fans won't care. Oddie, Graeme Garden, Brooke-Taylor, Hatch, Kendall and Cleese.

Oh dear, still harbouring dreams of becoming a pop star. But hey, dreams sometimes come true. Just be patient. Wait till the mid 1970s.

My original 'designs' for the Goodies' 'basic' costumes, which were largely accepted, except for Tim's bowler hat.

A historic ticket for the very first show in 1970, probably now utterly worthless on eBay. Poster for another hit single and, as it happens, my favourite. 'By gum, shake your bum!' They don't write 'em like that anymore.

The international language of music. What's 'oo oo oo' in German? It wasn't a hit anywhere except Britain. And a tiny bit in America.

The Goodies in 'Punkerella'. Tim has, of course, had his head turned into a pumpkin. Don't ask. It made sense at the time. Possibly.

The rock life. Late nights in the studio. Crappy take-aways. Playbacks, reel to reels, rebakes, overdubs and remixes. You see, dreams do come true.

And we still had time to have children! Tim and Ben and Edward. Graeme with John and Sally. Me with Kate and Bonnie.

1979, birding abroad. Not sure where. I never really noticed anything except the birds.

ITV Super Sports. Celebrities pull muscles for charity. Who do you recognise? We were the 'Comedy Team.' We won! Beating drama, current affairs and others!
Me, Roy North, Alfred Marks, Mickey Dolenz, Robin Asquith, Jeremy Bullock, Robert Lindsay, Lisa Goddard and Linda Haydon. I think.

More bruises for charity, but ah, the joy of scoring a hat trick for the Top 10 Eleven! A touch of the George Best's, don't you think?

The first of what were to become traditional Oddie-themed Christmas cards. Subsequent years featured *A Christmas Carol*, with Rosie as Tiny Tim being battered by Scrooge (me), Harry Potter and friends (I was Harry), *The Blair Witch Project*, Band- Aid revisited, and the three of us suspended in a glass box like David Blaine. Alas, the passage of time has taken its toll on our enthusiasm for such Yuletide whimsy. In other words, in recent years, we can't be arsed!

Me and my gals. Bonnie, Kate, Laura and Rosie. About twenty years ago. They are all even lovelier now. Except me.

July 22nd, 1983. Our lavish confetti-free white wedding. Laura's mother, Sally Barnes, was a singer/comedienne who had her own TV show back in the 1950s. One of her biggest fans was . . . my dad!

1986, Auntie Margery holding a recently arrived Rosie. A rare encounter, sadly not repeated for about fifteen years.

Simon King, me and Kate Humble. The Spring and *Autumnwatch* team, and yes, we all love it, and get on great. Thanks for watching.

1997. Birding with Bill Oddie in Shetland. If I look happy, it's 'cos I am. I can't speak for the Puffin.

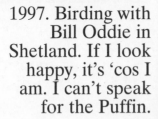

1994. With Peter Holden presenting *Bird in the Nest*. Undoubtedly a precursor to *Springwatch*.

With Jelly from CBBees. A serious rival to Kate Humble.

16th October, 2003. Buckingham Palace. A unique photo recording several very rare events. Bonnie in a hat. Rosie in a dress. Laura inconspicuous, and me in a suit. I considered wearing a tie, but I thought it would look silly with that shirt. Spot the O.B.E.

More than grand children. *Great* children. Thanks to Kate, Bonnie and Laura for having them, and to the relevant fathers. Including me! Me, Rosie, Ella, Kyle and Gracie.

productions. Quite the opposite. Sol specialised in 'safe bet' spectaculars, often imported from outside America, such as the Milan Opera, or the Russian Ballet, or the Moscow State Circus. Theory number one is that there was a case of mistaken identity. I don't suppose for one minute Sol ever bothered to personally check out the shows that were going to make his fortune. Why bother? Seen one opera or ballet, and you seen 'em all. Sol assumed that if Moscow had a Circus, why not Cambridge? We only ever met Sol once, when we were rehearsing at the theatre. It was a brief encounter, and I recall he seemed a little bemused. Presumably, he was puzzled by the lack of performing elephants and tight-rope walkers. He smiled and waved us good luck, but we never saw him again.

Frankly, I think it was a little inflexible of him not to respond to the fact that we had got such great reviews. He could have extended his stable of productions. 'Sol Hurok presents ... the best in Opera, Ballet, Circuses—and student revues'. Nevertheless, I just love the idea that he was expecting a real circus. No wonder he made sure we got taken off before anyone found out his little mistake. Imagine the headlines in *Variety*: 'Sol goofs again! Sol Hurok, the man who put money into the Marx Brothers because he'd heard they did a night at the opera, realised he had made a similar mistake when he discovered six kids from Cambridge University did not include a single acrobat or lion tamer. Mr Hurok told *Variety*: "So I screwed up, but hey, that title was misleading. *Cambridge Circus*. Why couldn't they have called it 'A Clump of Plinths'?'"

Great theory, but surely not true. Any others?

Yes, I have a second theory. You know Mel Brooks'

wonderful film and stage show, *The Producers*? Come on, sure you do. You know, it's about these guys who need a tax loss, and they put on this sure-fire disaster musical called *Springtime for Hitler*—and it's a hit! OK, maybe this is a conspiracy theory that Al Fayed would be proud of, but imagine a big-time New York producer, such as Mr Sol Hurok, has been told by his accountants: 'Sol, you need to put on a flop.' And somebody tells him about 'this bunch of posh English kids who do parodies of Oscar Wilde, and sing songs about London buses'. 'Hell,' says Sol, 'if that doesn't bomb on Broadway I'll eat my cigar.' So Sol puts on *Cambridge Circus*, and what happens? The English kids get raves! So if Sol is not going to be ruined by their unexpected success, he has to sabotage the show. So, he slips a few dollars to the ticket agents *not* to sell tickets. *Cambridge Circus* gets taken off, and Sol has his tax loss.

I have yet another theory. Maybe you weren't as good as you thought you were!

Maybe. Perhaps the critics were just jumping on the 'British Invasion' bandwagon. I will never be able to explain what happened, but as it turned out it was for the best.

After a few days' break in which we drowned our sorrows by taking a trip to the gorgeousness of New England in the fall, *Cambridge Circus* moved forty blocks south and reopened in a smaller theatre, called Square East, on 4th Street, just off Washington Square, downtown Manhattan, slap bang in the heart of Greenwich Village. My future wife, Jean, and I moved into a tiny apartment, owned by Mark Murphy, a jazz singer who is still scatting with the best. In fact, some jazz fans would say he *is* the best. Mark's place came with a massive record collection and a thriving community of hundreds of hot and cold running cockroaches. It was also within sauntering distance of some of the world's most legendary jazz and folk clubs. In the mid 1960s. How hip could this get? We heard live music by John Coltrane, Bill Evans and Charles Mingus, at clubs like the Village Gate, the Blue Note and the Village Vanguard. There were ground-breaking American stand-ups like Dick Gregory, and it's more than likely we heard singer-songwriters whom I have since come to worship, but at the time wouldn't have heard of. We lived no more than 100 yards from a club called the Bitter End, the New York showcase for such as Bob Dylan, Joni Mitchell, Neil Young and so on and on and on; and just across the road was Electric Ladyland, the studio where Jimi Hendrix recorded.

Wow!

Wow indeed. Square East itself was not without its associated stars. There was a considerable tradition in the States of improvised comedy. It took rather longer to cross the Atlantic, but it eventually emerged in such TV shows as *Whose Line Is It Anyway?*, and is still alive and fairly kicking in 'theatre sports' events, where the audience is asked to call out objects, adverbs, adjectives, acting and musical styles and so on, and teams come up with a hilariously inventive and entirely improvised piece. Or not. When it works, it's very impressive. When it doesn't, it's a bit of a cringe. Either way, I'd find it totally terrifying. In America in the 1960s it was all the rage. Square East was the New York home of an improv group called 'The Second City', because they were actually from Chicago. I presume that's where they went back to when we moved in. They may even have been sort of booted out, in which case I'm sorry, but thanks for the loan of your space. Square East was a much more appropriate home for us than on Broadway. The audience capacity was about 400, mostly seated at tables, as in a night club, and they were encouraged to buy drinks, which made them generally more responsive, but never raucous. New York audiences in the 1960s were a pretty civilised bunch. I reckon they still are. Loud Americans they are not. Just appreciative.

You are a big fan of America, aren't you?

There is a lot to loathe, but there is also a lot to love, and it was during my time there in the mid '60s that I first experienced so many of the best things. In New York, it was largely the American culture: the music, the comedy, the theatres, the clubs, the energy and the creativity. When the *Cambridge Circus* group finally left Square East in January 1965, I set out on a journey that gave me a taste of the vastness of America and made me realise that, yes, it really is a mighty big country! During the next three months I saw quite a lot of it.

Hold it! Before you set off on your trans-American tour, can I ask one question?

Sure, go ahead.

Did American audiences understand the British sense of humour? Or have trouble with your accents?

Good question. What do they say? 'Britain and America: two countries divided by a common language.' And what's that song? 'Let's Call the Whole Thing Off'—'I say tomato, and you say tomarto. I say potato, and you say potarto!' Which is ridiculous. Nobody says 'potarto'. Not even Julie Andrews. Of course that was written by an American. Cole Porter, was it? Maybe Americans can't hear the differences between British regional accents, but I honestly don't believe they can't understand normal English as spoken—for example—by a bunch of students from

Cambridge University.

Even if one of them did have a swanky double-barrelled name like Brooke-Taylor. But Tim doesn't speak posh. Actually, come to think about it, one of Tim's great strengths in that show was that he didn't have to speak much at all. A lot of his bits were visual. In one sketch he played a mechanical robot hospital visitor, who kept going out of control, breaking down, and speeding up. It's exhausting being a robot! Tim will tell you. In the big court scene he played an incredibly old court usher, who doddered on very, very shakily—and very funnily—with Exhibit A, which was some kind of portable washbasin with collapsible legs like a deckchair, which Tim took ages to set up. John Cleese asks the witness: 'Do you recognise this object?' The witness says 'No'. Cleese says: 'No further questions', and Tim dodders back on, takes another minute to dismantle the thing, and dodders off again. He managed to spin that bit out for five minutes some nights!

Mind you, talking of spinning it out—it's all coming back to me now—also in the court scene, I played the accused, 'Sidney Bottle, a dwarf'. Cleese calls him to 'take the stand'. 'Call Sidney Bottle.' Then there's quite a long pause in which nothing happens, except the audience begin to titter. Then Cleese carries on: 'You are Sidney Bottle, a dwarf.' And he's talking to the witness box but nobody is visible, because it's a dwarf, and he's too small to see over the side! So the audience are laughing at absolutely nothing happening; and the longer nothing happens, the more they laugh! Now that's my kinda job. Being totally invisible and getting huge laughs for doing nothing! Then comes the spinning it out bit. Cleese asks: 'Can we have something for Mr Bottle to stand on?'

Tim's usher comes doddering back on with what you assume is a box, which he puts in the witness box, so I can get up higher, but I'm still not high enough. All you can see are the tips of the fingers of one hand, gripping the edge of the witness box, and then the next hand appears, and I manage to pull myself up, so you can just see the top of my head. Cleese starts to speak to me, but I lose my grip, and fall down out of sight. Another big laugh. The I struggle up again, and fall again. And so it goes on. By the end of our time at Square East, I reckon I could drag that routine out for getting on for ten minutes. In fact—here's a bit of trivia for you— there is a live original cast album of *Cambridge Circus*, recorded in London by George Martin (yes, *that* George Martin, the fifth Beatle), and, legend hath it, the sound of an audience laughing uncontrollably on *Sergeant Pepper* is from our court scene.

I say 'our'. If you read the credits it says 'written by John Cleese'. Which basically it was, but how much talent does it take to write: 'Tim drags out old man bit for ages' or 'Bill stays hidden, and then falls down for five minutes'? OK, Cleese was absolutely brilliant as the lawyer—'My learned friend appears for the defence, and I appear for the money'—and David Hatch was a splendid deaf judge, and . . . hey, let's just call it one of the best examples of team comedy in the history of theatre. You had to be there.

From what you're saying, it seems to me that the reason *Cambridge Circus* 'travelled' so well is that it was a very visual show.

Yes. And there were quite a few musical numbers, and they do say music is a universal language.

They do, but that really refers to the instrumental part. I presume there were lyrics in your songs.

Of course, but nothing as sophisticated as 'Blowing

Off'. There was also quite a lot of movement, sort of choreographed movement.

Dancing?

I wouldn't have called it proper dancing, though we did do a parody of *West Side Story*, which ended up with Cleese as a tap-dancing policeman.

An English bobby?

Yes.

The Americans liked that, I imagine.

Yes, and they liked us doing the 'Hallelujah Chorus' as a Beatles medley, dressed as choirboys. 'I Wanna Hold Your Handel.' Oh yes, and they liked the 'slapstick humour lecture', which was written by Mike Palin and Terry Jones, which had lots of custard pies and plank routines, and was very complicated, and quite painful, especially for me, as I had to be clouted over the head several times every night with a wooden plank. Which, by the way, taught me a valuable lesson about audiences. Audiences like to watch people in pain. But it has to be real pain. I was beginning to get a really bad bruise on the back of my head, and I was seriously becoming a bit worried I might get some kind of permanent damage. So, one night, I wore a cloth cap with a bit of padding in the back. When the plank whacked me, it was much less painful, but it didn't get a laugh. So the next show I did it without the cap, and they laughed. What they found funny was the authentic 'bonk' of wood clouting real human flesh and bone. And my genuine wince, and the fact that I obviously wasn't faking it! That wasn't just American audiences. Pain is a universal language. As is music. And so of course is visual comedy. So, yes, looking back on the *Cambridge Circus* experience I guess that is why it was such a successful show. Just as you said.

Exactly. Thank you. It also makes sense of where

that visual stuff took some of you.

How do you mean?

Well, John Cleese . . . silly walks in *Python*, Basil Fawlty goose-stepping or giving his car a good thrashing. And you and Tim in *The Goodies*, running around, falling over . . . Need I say more?

I'd rather you didn't. This is beginning to sound like one of those books about the 'history of comedy'.

Perish the thought. Anyway, I am willing to bet there's nothing much in those books about what you did during your last three months in America.

You mean the tour?

Exactly. Surely that was a hell of a risk. I mean OK, the show was pretty visual, but there were some words in it, sketches and stuff.

And my witty song lyrics.

I mean no problem in New Zealand, where they're used to British accents, or indeed in New York, where the audiences are pretty hip. But what about 'old' America, like the Midwest or the Deep South. Surely back in the 1960s most Americans wouldn't have even known where Britain was.

They still don't.

Maybe, but I imagine nowadays there's a fair chance that most of them are aware of some British TV programmes, and British TV comedy stars. Sasha Baron Cohen—as Ali G or Borat. Or Ricky Gervais maybe, or at least *The Office*, or the American Office. And Hugh Laurie's a big star in the States.

Playing a depressive doctor, not camping about in *Blackadder*.

Talking of which, they know Rowan Atkinson.

As Mr Bean.

And Benny Hill was huge in America. And of

course most of them would know John Cleese from *Fawlty Towers*, and *Monty Python*. At least you had Cleese in your show.

But he wasn't a star then. And anyway he didn't go on tour.

So what British comedy people would Americans have known in 1965? Who was the Benny Hill of the time?

David Frost.

You're not serious.

Deadly. He was the host of the American version of *That Was the Week That Was, TW3*.

And he was the host of the British version as well.

Yep, both of them.

At the same time?

Yep. Not literally simultaneous. But he used to do the British show and then leap on a fast plane, do the American show and then fly back again.

Just in time to do *Through the Keyhole*.

I'm sure he would have done had it been on then. That's true, though, Frosty used to commute between London and New York every week.

So he was a big star in the States?

Exactly, and everyone knew *That Was the Week That Was*.

So if you went out on tour with a stage version of *TW3* with David Frost's name on it, that would pull in the audiences?

Yes. So that's what we did.

What *you* did? But you lot were from *Cambridge Circus*.

Oh, yes, and so was 90 per cent of the material in the show. We did have a couple of people join us who had been in the British *TW3*: Al Mancini, who was actually an American, and Willie Rushton.

And of course David Frost.

Oh, no. He wasn't actually in it. If you saw any of the posters or adverts you might have assumed he was in it, because they said 'David Frost's *That Was the Week That Was*'. Except it was more 'DAVID FROST'S *That Was the Week That Was*'.

So didn't the audiences expect him to be in it?

Oh, yes.

And didn't they get cross when they realised that he wasn't ?

Yep. In Louisiana I thought they were going to lynch us. The thing is, if only they'd realised, the show was so much better without him! But seriously though—as if I wasn't—David did do, I think, two of the dates. One near New York, because he could do that one and still do two versions of *TW3* on the telly in the same weekend; and there was some other place where he had an early morning breakfast meeting at a local hotel, so he might as well do a show the night before whilst he was in town. You gotta give it to him, he was a worker that boy. What's more, let's face it, he enabled me to see more of the United States in three months than I've seen in the rest of my life! And it was a wonderfully bizarre experience.

Who was in the cast then?

Tim Brooke-Taylor, Willie Rushton, Al Mancini, Sandra Caron (who was the sister of Alma Cogan, who'd had the hit with 'The Baby's Dimple'—see, it all links up), Jean Hart (singer, actress, my eventual wife) and me.

And where did you play?

Just about everywhere. Sometimes we flew, and other times we were in a coach, just like a rock group in a band bus. Which it literally was, because our road manager was a bloke called Ira who had done the same job for the Beatles when they first toured

America. Which was something Ira reminded us of about ten times a day, usually by telling us what present the Beatles had given him wherever we happened to be. 'Hey guys, we need to fill up at the next gas station. There's a nice little diner next door. I remember it 'cos that's where the Beatles gave me a gold watch.' We bought him a packet of crisps.

I'm not sure if it was Ira who had organised our itinerary, but it was someone with little grasp of geography. Instead of following a logical, circular route, we zigzagged all over the country. I drew a line on a map connecting the venues and thus tracing our journey. By the time we'd finished, it looked like America had a very serious heart condition. The worst planned bit involved us playing Chicago one night— where the temperature was sub zero and the snow a foot deep—flying down to Florida—where it was baking hot—doing the show in Jacksonville, and then flying all the way back up north for the next one. Which was disorientating in itself, but became almost surreal when our plane was diverted by ever-worsening snow storms and frozen runways, and we ended up having to hire taxis to plough for several hours through blizzards and fog, till we finally reached that night's venue somewhere in the deepest Midwest. It turned out to be not so much a theatre, as an assembly hall at a small mining college. The audience consisted of a couple of hundred engineering students. They were somewhat rough hewn—they might even have qualified as rednecks—but though we were nearly two hours late arriving they seemed far from resentful. In fact they were jolly to the point of raucousness. We thought this was particularly forgiving since by the time we got there it was the interval. The interval in what? You may well ask. We discovered that

Al Mancini—who had taken a different plane back from Florida in order to drop in on some relations—had managed to arrive more or less on time. Finding himself confronted by 200 beer-guzzling lads—I don't recall any women—he'd decided not to risk their wrath, and had duly kept them entertained for over an hour. Al didn't say how, and we didn't ask. We were just very, very grateful to him.

Thus, at last, the full cast took the stage and we launched into the opening number. It didn't go very well. The second sketch was no better, and the third was met with almost no response at all, except we sensed some unrest, with shuffling and muttering. It was only when some of us were cowering in the makeshift wings whilst Jean did a solo song that we discovered why the audience were so unenthusiastic. They had heard it all before—about an hour ago! Having presumably exhausted his limited repertoire of jokes, Al had resorted to performing the material from the whole of the first half and part of the second ... by himself! He must have done it awfully well, since none of the audience looked as if they were muttering, 'Ah, this is more like it!' Instead, there was a surprisingly polite yet disappointed air of bemusement. They certainly hadn't turned nasty. I guess mining students don't get many travelling comedy shows dropping by, so they were grateful for what they'd got, yet clearly they had hoped for something a bit less repetitive. Happily though, once we'd realised what had happened, we went out and chatted with the audience, had a good chuckle about it, and mutually resolved that the most satisfactory solution was to indulge in a session of community joke telling! In other words, we got the audience to join in the sketches, especially the punchlines. Altogether now! In the best sense, it was a riot. The buzz was better than Johnny Cash at San Quentin!

Of such things are showbiz memories made. Especially when the hall with 200 students was followed the next night in Texas by an astrodome holding 5,000.

From Cash at San Quentin to the Beatles at Shea Stadium! And nobody asked where David Frost was!

That tour must have left you with lots of unforgettable images.

Indeed. Many of them classic Americana, which is still available, as long as you don't mind sharing it with a few hundred tourists, but it will never be as it was back then. I stood on the rim of the Grand Canyon. Just me and Jean. We had it to ourselves. We saw the lights of Las Vegas. There were other people there, but nothing like as many as there are now! We went west and we went south, saw the Golden Gate Bridge, and the iron filigree balconies of New Orleans—now all rusted?—and we drove through Louisiana in spring with the magnolia trees in blossom. The countryside was only spoilt—according to our cab driver—'by the niggers picknicking.' We decided not to risk the Klu Klux Klan jokes in that night's show. There was also an extraordinary surreal visit to a sort of safari park for breeding endangered species near Calgary in Canada. The sky was dazzlingly blue, but the chill of the air literally took our breath away. Minus 10 Centigrade. That's cold. The landscape was almost featureless. Solid relentless white. The only warm colours were the orange flames in the eyes of a pair of Siberian tigers prowling along the boundaries of their enclosure. I'll never forget those eyes, glaring at me with what I suspect was hunger. Nor will I ever be able to erase the horrifying moment when a keeper went into a cage to feed a grizzly bear and it literally tore his arm

off. Blood on snow. You don't forget images like that!
Any more than you forget blood on white crockery.

**You've encountered Grizzlies on your wildlife
shows haven't you?**

Yes, I had an opportunity to redress the image of
Grizzlies in 2006, when I hit upon the cunning device
of retracing the 1965 tour, but this time seeking out
the wildlife I didn't have the chance to see as we
rollicked along in our Beatles bus. I called the series *Bill
Oddie Back in the USA*, and it was one of the most
enjoyable and satisfying projects I have ever done.
Whatever your feelings about American humans, there
is no disputing that American wildlife is fabulous.
Wherever our tour took us, my binoculars never left
my side, and the result is that I still have a bigger
American bird list than British. Indeed, my American
sojourn ended in May 1965 with two birdy spectacles
right in the heart of New York City. One was when I
went up to the top of the Empire State Building at
night and saw what I at first assumed were hundreds of
moths flitting around in the floodlights. When I looked
through my bins I realised that they were migrating
birds. On the final morning of the trip I went into
Central Park at dawn—despite the warnings—and
found myself in the company of, not muggers or mime
artists, but gaggles of birdwatchers, who like me were
gazing up and around, as birds literally cascaded from
the sky like shower bursts of fireworks, and just as
colourful.

**So, only Tim, Jean and you went on the *TW3*
adventure?**

Correct. Other members of *Cambridge Circus* had
returned to England. With Jo Kendal it was to get back
to proper acting (and eventually some improper acting
in *I'm Sorry I'll Read That Again*), while Graham

174

Chapman had resumed his medical studies in London. John Cleese, however, had chosen to stay on in New York. We weren't entirely sure why. He had mentioned something about trying to be a journalist. I'm not sure how seriously we had taken him, since the fact was that over the years we had become accustomed to John taking up something, and not necessarily sticking at it for very long. It was a bit of a running tease: 'What are you doing this week then, John? Learning Russian?' Which he did. 'A crash course in brain surgery?' Which he didn't. We did confirm later that he had indeed done a stint as a journalist, or at least he'd written for some publications, one of which had introduced him to Terry Gilliam. The rest, as they say, is history.

What is not so well recorded by history is what John chose to take up as his final employment in America. It was, to say the least, a little out of character. I'm sure John wouldn't be offended if I said that he was not naturally musical. Indeed, he was naturally unmusical, to the extent that his attempts at singing were very funny. It was something we—and he—exploited on *I'm Sorry I'll Read That Again*. I refer you to Cleese's unforgettable and almost unbearable rendition of 'I've Got a Ferret Sticking Up my Nose' (no doubt still available on a BBC CD). Neither was he what you would call a rhythmic mover—despite his tap-dancing policeman. He *was* a hilariously physical performer, and maybe still is, though silly walks and goose steps are not appropriate or prudent after a certain age. So what on earth—one might wonder—possessed John, in 1965, to join the Broadway cast of *Half a Sixpence*?

Half a Sixpence? **The musical?!**

Yup, the very same, seminal celebration of cockney jolliness. The starring role of a cheeky, chirpy, toothy, singy, dancy photographer, often attired in a blazer and

175

boater, was played in London and on Broadway by Tommy Steele, who by 1965 had already forsaken rock and roll for 'showbiz'. As well as lovable Tommy, the show inevitably featured a chorus full of other chirpy cockneys. They didn't have to do as much as Tommy, but they were called upon to sing and dance, which is of course what people normally do in musicals.

Did John do an audition?

I can't imagine how! Even his famous dancing policeman wasn't meant to be good. Maybe Gilliam had known someone at the theatre, and tipped them a few dollars to offer John a part. Presumably for a laugh. I can easily imagine Terry right now, guffawing like Goofy: 'I didn't expect him to actually do it!' Mind you, I can also hear John explaining very earnestly: 'I thought it would be an interesting experience.' Tim, Jean and I made sure that it was.

Imagine this from John's perspective. He is waiting in the wings, adjusting his jolly cockney braces, tying his red and white spotted neckerchief, and making sure his cheeky cockney cap is tilted at the correct jaunty angle. Around him another dozen chorus boys are doing the same. On stage, Tommy is belting out a merry knees-up of a number. He gets to the second verse, the key rises a semitone, and the trumpets blast a fanfare, and on prance the jolly cockney chorus. Cleese is in the front of the bunch, and is clearly concentrating on his feet (which are unfamiliar with the concept of control) and he is appearing to sing along (probably just mouthing the words, I reckon). Then the routine calls for the chorus boys to whip off their neckerchiefs and brandish them gaily, much in the manner of Morris dancers. At which point, John executes a genteel twirl and looks up towards the dress circle in approved theatrical manner. Never forget to play to the punters in the gods. Even as he waves his hanky as if in greeting, his eyes alight upon a box that is almost overhanging the stage. Leaning over the quilted edge are three familiar faces: Tim, Bill and Jean. We wave back. John turns red, and away.

I don't know if he was traumatised by the experience, but as far as I know he never again appeared in the chorus line of a Broadway musical. I would like to think that Tim and I can take some credit for making him accept his limitations, and stick to comedy. If we hadn't embarrassed him that night, he might now be working for Andrew Lloyd Webber. You owe us one, John.

Sounds like a punch line to me! End of American episode.

I just want to get things straight now. By the middle of 1965, the *Cambridge Circus* people are all back in England, where the slightly younger generation, such as Eric Idle and Graeme Garden, are deciding whether to carry on with whatever they were studying at university or go into comedy; at the same time, there's Mike Palin and Terry Jones, who'd now left Oxford, and were also working in comedy; and there's Humphrey Barclay, who is now a producer at the BBC, and I believe David Frost reappears as a producer as well, and . . . Bill, are you listening?

Oh, sorry, I'd fallen asleep. I know what you're doing. You are trying to lure me into going into all that 'comedy family tree' type stuff, but I am not going to. I've been interviewed about it so often my mouth actually refuses to release any more words on the subject. So, unless you want this book to grind to a halt, ask me about something people don't know about. Come on, eke out some little known facts. Interesting ones.

177

OK, OK . . . you asked for it. Is it true that, when you got back to London, you tried to have a career as a serious rock star?

You bastard. You know that's really embarrassing.

Tough shit. Tell us about it.

OK. Well actually, now I think about it, it wasn't so much me as my agent who thought I could be a pop singer.

Bollocks. Don't blame your agent. It was you.

Well, people kept telling me I had a really good voice, but that it was wasted on comedy songs, and I ought to try something serious.

I can't believe you went along with it. What did you sing?

I wrote my own songs.

You wrote serious pop songs? Rockers or ballads? Oh my gawd, you didn't write love songs, did you?

One or two.

I suppose you used to imagine yourself crooning to the lay-dees.

No. One of them I based on the words of a Shakespeare sonnet.

Oh! You wrote love songs to fellas. Bill, are you sure you're not just saying this to sell this book? It'll certainly get in the red tops. You happy with that? Actually, you're a bit old to come out, aren't you? Or was it just a phase? We've all . . . experimented.

I haven't.

Yes you have. I happen to know that when you were fourteen, on holiday, you shared a caravan with that bloke from school, what was his name?

I don't remember.

You may not remember his name. But I bet you remember . . . his kiss.

He didn't kiss me. I kissed him.

So, you admit it!

Look. I fancied his sister, all right? He looked very like his sister.

Except that he was a boy.

He had very smooth skin.

Where?

On his face. Oh, for gawd's sake. I closed my eyes and pretended it was his sister, OK?

And who was he pretending you were?

I have no idea!

Maybe he wasn't pretending at all. Did you go on holiday with him again?

Yes. We went camping in the Lake District.

Say no more!

It was with his whole family. Including his sister. I was hoping I might get to . . .

Do to her what you did to her brother? Do you think she knew?

Knew what?

That you'd asked her brother if you could kiss him. Only, if she did know, I imagine she might have had mixed feelings if you then tried to kiss her. Did you ever kiss her?

No. As a matter of fact, I later discovered she was actually 'doing it' with one of my best mates.

Ah, was she the netball captain then?

No.

So that's two of your girlfriends that went off with your mates?

Yes, yes. Thank you so much for reminding me. Can we get back to whatever you were asking me about? I've forgotten what it was now.

I haven't. You were telling me how you wanted to be a pop star, so you could impress girls, and you

wrote a love song based on a Shakespeare sonnet. Which one?

That one that starts:'My love is nothing like the sun.'

Was that the title of your song?

No. It was called 'Because She Is My Love'.

Ah so you changed the sex. Shakespeare would have written 'because he is my love'. Except he was cleverer than that, because in the sonnets you can't tell if he's writing them to a bloke or a girl, can you?

Can't you?

You did English Literature at Cambridge! You must have known Shakespeare was gay.

It was 1965, for God's sake. I'm not sure anyone knew Shakespeare was gay. Even if they did, they probably kept quiet about it. It was a long time ago. People had hardly got over Oscar Wilde!

And you have never got over not becoming a pop star, have you?

Well, that is where you're wrong. Because I did become a pop star. The Goodies were pop stars.

Well, sort of. Anyway, we'll come to that later.

Maybe.

Meanwhile, what happened to 'Because He— sorry, She—Is My Love'?

It came out as a single, I think. And another singer did a cover version, which I think was a bit of a hit in Germany.

You are always going on about how you were into rock and roll.

I still am.

But this was a slow soppy ballad, wasn't it?

Yes, it was.

And, let's face it, you haven't naturally got what you'd call a soppy ballad type voice.

180

No, I admit that, but what I used to do in those days was sort of impersonate somebody else's voice which suited the song. So I sang 'Because She Is My Love' a bit like the Righteous Brothers. Well, one of them. Lots of wavery vibrato. I did another song—which may have been the B side—which was rockier, so I sang that like Georgie Fame.

Nothing like confusing the listener, eh? Is it true that you had the same producer as the Beatles?

George Martin, yes. And we had some really famous musicians on the demos—except they were young session men then, who became famous later. Rik Wakeman on keyboards (eventually of Yes), John Paul Jones on bass (Led Zeppelin), Mitch Mitchell on drums (Jimi Hendrix). I remember Mitch was wearing a very neat sort of herringbone tweedy suit and a tie and his hair was quite short. A couple of years later he's in full hippy beads and a giant afro, and playing bigger venues than we did on the *TW3* tour! Bigger than the big ones, I mean, not the mining colleges and converted gymnasiums.

Any more names you'd like to drop before we move on out of Lala Land?

I did a radio broadcast with David Bowie. He was in a suit and tie too. Actually so was I. Bowie was probably about fifteen. We just mimed to our records, though I'm not sure why we bothered to do that on radio! It was in a cellar, with an audience of a couple of dozen teenage girls.

Did they scream at you?

They screamed at anyone. The director told them to.

So you never had a hit?

Not as a solo artiste, no. Of course, as the Goodies . . .

Sh. Later.

We'll see.

181

Anything else you want to tell us about your abortive, misguided pop star phase?

Well, I did have two singles banned by the BBC!

Not just that they refused to play them because they weren't very good? Actually officially banned?

Yes. Actually. The first one was called 'Nothing Better To Do'. I sang it in my Gene Pitney voice. It was about the battles between Mods and Rockers that went on every weekend down at Brighton. They were really pretty nasty. The song was what you might call a social comment. Totally serious. It was a 'big' production. Big brass section. Dramatic key changes. Complete with sound effects of motorbikes and lambrettas, and with a double-tracked chorus about these kids who had 'Nothing Better To Do'. The BBC refused to play it, because they considered it a potential 'incitement to violence', and they felt there was a danger that the gangs would use it as an 'anthem', and all be singing it as they beat each other up! I was quite cross it got banned, but in a way I suppose it was a compliment, because presumably somebody at the BBC must have considered the chorus to be catchy enough to become a sing along! Personally, I don't think it would ever have happened. They would never have reached the high notes in the last line. Mind you, they did wear really tight trousers.

If it hadn't been banned, do you think it would have been a hit?

In all honesty, no. Unlike the second single that got banned, which I am absolutely certain was going to be a hit. I wrote it the day after England won the World Cup in 1966. When they beat Germany 4–2, after extra time, and Kenneth Wolstenholme created one of the great moments of sports commentary when he said, 'There's people on the pitch. They think it's all over'—and then, when Geoff Hurst slammed in the fourth goal, 'It is now!' Brilliant. I missed it at the time. Ask me why?

Why?

'Cos I was there! With Eric Idle. Oh happy day. Anyway, one of the most memorable TV images was of Nobby Stiles—a tough little defender—dancing about with his shirt off and flashing a huge smile, but without his false teeth in. Come to think of it, he looked a bit like my granny! Except Nobby had just a couple of teeth, so it was more like Sean thingy from the Pogues, or the sort of mouth witches always have in Disney movies.

Nobby was a truly iconic, heroic figure. He deserved to be feted in song. So I wrote 'The Nobby Stiles March'. It had a rousing chorus, and an Alf Ramsey impression in the middle, when he confessed he loved Roger Hunt more than Jimmy Greaves—and, though I say it myself, some of my finest lyrics. Pressings were rushed out and distributed round the record shops in anticipation of a sure-fire hit, the quickest seller ever. I was booked to perform the song on all the big TV and radio shows, including an exclusive launch on the *Eamonn Andrews Show*, which was the biggest plug you could get in those days. Like a British Ed Sullivan show. Nowadays, it would be Jonathan Ross maybe.

So there I was, on the brink of nationwide fame. All we were waiting for was Nobby himself to approve the release. It wasn't a send-up, it was a tribute. I don't know if Nobby ever even heard it, but of course his agent did. He refused to allow its release! Can you believe that? I and the record company were threatened with court action, and they took out an injunction which in effect killed it stone dead. As far as I remember, the reason the agent gave was along the lines of the song is 'holding my client up to ridicule!' or 'undermining his dignity' or something. I have no doubt a percentage of the considerable anticipated profits were offered, and I would have been happy to donate the lot to the old footballers' home. But all to no avail. 'The Nobby Stiles March' was assigned to the bin marked 'so near and yet so far'.

Obviously I still think it was a pretty crass decision. That song was a celebration of England's victory. The whole country would have joined in. I can't imagine that Nobby himself was too concerned about his dignity, judging from the way he discarded his shirt and his teeth, and pranced around like a gibbon on hot coals. But I think my deepest regret is that the nation was deprived of arguably the most felicitous compliment I ever created:

> We love Nobby Stiles.
> We love the way that Nobby smiles.
> Tough and ruthless,
> Rough and toothless.
> Nobby Stiles.

Now that's what I call a love song! Shakespeare ... pah!
That's quite a sad tale, that is. What a shame. I almost sympathise. So have you had anything else banned by the Beeb?
Well, obviously 'Blowing Off' didn't stand much chance.
Obviously.
Island Records did release it as a single, presumably only because they thought it would be good publicity if it got officially censored. It didn't get censored. They just didn't play it. Well, D'oh! So much for that cunning piece of marketing. Mind you, there was one time I wished that song had got banned!

I was doing one of those big Amnesty International shows. *The Policeman's Fifth Ball* or something. I got a little band together, plus a couple of backing singers, and we'd rehearsed a rousing rendition of 'Blowing Off', complete with a joyously juvenile new intro, and peaking with a final chorus involving audience participation. So there we were, waiting in the wings, just about to rollick on to the stage with our paeon to bad taste and frivolity, when the director told us to hang on because first 'they are just going to play a short film to illustrate the work of Amnesty International'. Obviously, from a serious issue-raising point of view this was laudable. From a programming point of view, it was the kiss of death. We and the audience were stunned into as sombre a silence as you have ever experienced as we witnessed ten minutes of horrifying images of torture, mutilation, starvation, and human rights abuse. The film finished with a heartfelt plea for us all to do whatever we could to recognise and alleviate the appalling injustices of the world. 'Meanwhile ... Here's Bill Oddie with a song about farting!' So much for my social conscience.

Fall through the floor time?

Indeed.

Bill.

Yes?

Can I ask you to do something for me? Or rather to not do something?

Yes. Of course.

Can I request that we—or rather you—resolve never again to mention that bloody song?

Yes. Sorry. What would you like me to talk about?

The Goodies.

No.

3

'Superchaps Three'

Hang on. You can't say no. A couple of pages back you were looking forward to boring us—I mean telling us—about how the Goodies were pop stars.
Well yes, but that's not what you *want* me to talk about, is it? You want me to tell you how Tim, Graeme and I got together in the first place and how we did other shows and then became the Goodies. And were we surprised it was a success? And did a bloke really die laughing at it? And what's our favourite show? And will I tell you about the giant kitten and Ecky Thump and black puddings? And why haven't there been any repeats? And do I think people would like it now? To which the answer is why don't they buy the bloody DVDs and find out?!

Why don't they?
Some of them do. And they look us up on the internet. And they buy those flippin' books about the history of comedy.

Bill, why are you so bitter about the Goodies?
I am not bitter! You really don't understand, do you? I'm just not good at repeating things. What I've enjoyed about writing this book is writing about stuff I have not written about before. Thinking about things I haven't thought about before. Even discovering a few things I didn't know or didn't realise before. What I don't enjoy is being asked the same questions and giving the same answers. I don't mean to be uppity. I mean I realise that if someone is interested enough to ask, then I should be gracious enough to answer. And normally I will do. If

it's an interviewer or a journalist asking the questions, then I try to be as interesting or entertaining as I can, though I admit if I don't feel they've bothered to think of anything but the same old questions, or they're not really listening to the answers, then I can get pretty tetchy. I do often wish I wasn't quite so stroppy, because if I'm honest I don't really like the idea of anyone thinking I am an awkward little bugger, even though I know I can be. But that's exactly why I decided to ask myself the questions. If I don't like them I can say fuck you. Fuck me.

My sentiments exactly. OK, so you are not bitter about the Goodies.

Of course I'm not.

Are you proud of the Goodies?

Of course I am.

Do you think people in general are aware just how successful the Goodies were?

Probably not.

Do you want to tell us?

OK. Why not? Can I include the records? And the books?

Include whatever you like. I tell you what, let me put the question this way: how famous were the Goodies? Blind us with a few dazzling facts and figures.

Right. Prepare to be dazzled. *The Goodies* ran for over ten years. The first show was on 8 November 1970 on BBC2. They put it on late at night because they assumed it was esoteric, far-out, intellectual, ex-university type humour!

In other words, childish!

Frank Muir (legendary comedy script writer) called it child-like humour, which he correctly pointed out is quite a different thing from childish. As he put it, 'The

187

kind of world where you know a bloke is a burglar because he's wearing a striped jersey and carrying a bag marked "Swag".'

Like in comics or cartoons.

Exactly. Both of which, as we all know, can have 'adult' versions.

Such as *The Simpsons*, *South Park*, *Viz* and so on.

Quite so. Do you want dazzling statistics, or a discussion on the nature of comedy genres?

More facts and figures, please.

Right, as I was saying, the first series was put on late at night. Then the BBC realised that it was indeed 'child-like' and so they went the other way and put us on really early in the evenings, I think about 6.30 p.m., which was really a kids' slot. We weren't happy about that and told them so. They asked us: 'So when would you like to be on?' And we said about nine o'clock on BBC2, on a Thursday. And to this very day that is considered sort of the traditional BBC2 comedy night. I think they've even got a slogan about it, haven't they? 'Thursday night is comedy night' or something. As well as the BBC2 'origination', we were also repeated each week on BBC1. The final series we did was actually for ITV.

And for a lot more money?

Indeed. The last show went out on 13 February 1982. Which means that we were peak viewing on British telly for over ten years. In fact nearly twelve years.

What were the audience figures?

At its peak, which was 1975, the audience was regularly over 10 million on BBC2, and one evening in April hit 11.9 million, which is still probably one of the highest audience figures ever on BBC2. In the same year on BBC1, we hit 15 million!

Bloody hell!

Indeed. Nothing gets audiences like that any more, except soap operas and Rugby World Cup Finals, but even then it was most definitely 'bloody hell!' As well as the telly, there were three *Goodies* books—which we wrote and illustrated ourselves—all of which topped the bestsellers charts in both hardback and paperback. In the *Sunday Times* bestsellers chart for 1975 we had two books in the top ten. *The Goodies Book of Records* in hardback, and *The Goodies File* in paperback. There was one week when we were number one in both the hardback and paperback charts. That year our books were considered essential reading, topped only by Bronowski's *Ascent of Man* and Alistair Cooke's *America*. Neither of which were as funny, or had coloured cartoons and silly photographs. Not to mention the records.

But you're going to, aren't you?

You asked! We had five top 20 singles, and a top 20 album. We appeared on *Top of the Pops* many, many times. In 1975 the Goodies was the seventh bestselling group in Britain— just above Gladys Knight and the Pips—and I was the eighth most successful songwriter. I was sandwiched between David Essex and Barry White, which is a position many a housewife of the time would have killed for!

And how would the housewives have felt about you, seeing as you were also pop stars? Did you have groupies?

I can't speak for Tim and Graeme. Myself? Well, I wouldn't have used the word 'groupies' and, as far as I know, I didn't have any dalliances with any housewives. Or indeed any other kind of wife, since my own marriage was in trouble by then. Not, I hasten to add, because of my 'carrying on'.

So you did 'carry on' then?

There were young ladies who chose to express their gratitude for my part in the Goodies entertaining them with song or laughter in a manner that was, let's say, not merely verbal. Which is all I am going to say, except that my gratitude was I'm sure much greater than theirs. It still is. To any and all of them: thank you, thank you, thank you.

There were three of them, then?

There were more than three.

At the same time?

Oh, for heaven's sake. We may have had a few hits, but we were hardly the Rolling Stones.

Are you implying the Stones went in for 'orgies'?

Stop it, right now. You are just trying to trap me into saying something scurrilous so you can whip up a bit of business for this book. 'Bill Oddie—not so Goody after all!' 'Funky Gibbon? Fu*ky Gibbon more like?' 'Ecky Thump, show us your pudding, Bill'. Well, forget it. It won't work. There is nothing to 'reveal', and even if there was I wouldn't.

Sorry, sorry, sorry. In fact I am being neither cunning nor contentious. I just thought you might like an excuse to reminisce about some fun times, or remind us that you may be a podgy old codger now, but in your time you were a bit of a lad.

I was never ever 'a bit of a lad'. For gawd's sake, I was in my mid thirties, my first marriage—which had been great for ten years—was obviously over, and I was simply doing what I hadn't done when I was the age most blokes do it.

Except that most blokes don't have the advantage of being pop stars.

Are you saying that that was the only reason girls might have fancied me?

I am not saying that, but you must have wondered.

190

I didn't wonder at the time. I'd like to think it wasn't the only reason, but if it was, then lucky old me, I say. Oh, bugger. Why the hell did you have to put that thought into my head? Why can't you just leave me with my memories? Even if they are perhaps a bit . . . what's the word?

Delusional?
They are NOT delusional! Stuff happened. It was lovely. The girls were lovely. All of them. I hope they enjoyed whatever happened as much as I did. If I didn't thank them at the time, I'd like to thank them now. Very much. Thank you. I hope whatever has happened in the rest of your life has been good, and that you are safe and happy.

Hang on a minute. How the hell did we get into this? You asked me to give you a few facts and figures about how famous the Goodies were in their time, and somehow we've ended up discussing my sex life in the mid-1970s. Actually, I say discussing—undermining more like. Is there anything else you'd like to undermine?

Well, since you ask. Can we just go back to the Goodies records?
If you must.

You know you said that in 1975 you were just ahead of Gladys Knight . . .
. . . and the Pips. Don't forget her Pips.

You always have to be facetious and silly don't you? I am trying to make a serious point here.
That's what I'm afraid of.

No need to be afraid, but can I just ask: you were above Gladys—and her Pips—but who was above you?
You mean in the top ten bestselling pop groups in 1975?

Yes. Who were those famous names we presumably all remember so well?

I've got a feeling I know where this is going.

Just answer the question. The names of the famous bestselling groups, please.

OK. We were at number seven. And above us were Hot Chocolate, Showaddywaddy, Kenny, the Bay City Rollers, the Stylistics, and number one was Mud.

Yes. Well. There you are then.

What do you mean by that?

Hardly household names, are they?

They were then.

Yes, and so, I'm sure, were you.

Your point being?

Well, all those bands were what you might call one hit wonders.

Or four or five hit wonders. Some of them maybe even nine or ten hit wonders.

Yeah, OK, but they have hardly gone down in history as seminal icons of rock.

They are pop groups, for gawd's sake. They were of their time. They come, they go.

Exactly. As did the Goodies.

As a pop group, yes, but we weren't a pop group, we were a comedy group, but considering we were a comedy group, we were a pretty successful pop group. Maybe the most successful comedy pop group.

Nothing like as successful as the Monkees. Whose name, come to think of it, is not dissimilar. Is that a coincidence?

Of course it wasn't a bloody coincidence! The Goodies were meant to sound like a pop group, like the Monkees were meant to sound like the Beatles. The Monkees didn't do comedy songs, they did straight pop numbers written by famous pop songwriters, like

Neil Diamond. We did songs that sounded like straight pop songs but were actually comedy songs.

That's debatable.

You are just being nasty now. Look, if you've got some kind of theory as to why the Goodies haven't gone down in history, as you put it, in the way that, say, Monty Python has, then out with it.

OK. Here goes. I accept that the records, and the books, were what you might call offshoots, merchandising, which still goes on of course, plus these days there are videos and DVDs—bet you wish they'd been invented in the seventies, eh?

There are Goodies DVDs now.

Yes. But they don't sell like Python, do they?

Probably not.

Definitely not. And why not?

You tell me.

I'm going to. It's only my theory of course but, how shall I put it? Let's go with the musical analogy. It's as if you made pop singles . . .

Which we did.

. . . but Python made classic albums.

Which they didn't.

Maybe not, but if you translate the TV comedy into music terms, it's like the Goodies were a pop group, and Python were proper rock artists. One is of its time, the other lasts.

You mean like we were the Bay City Rollers of comedy, and they were the Steely Dan? Our Mud, to their Stones? Our Gary Glitter, to their Led Zeppelin? Our George Formby, to their Jimi Hendrix?

Exactly. What do you think?

Fuck off. We were famous.

You *were* famous. No one could argue with that. In fact, I have a question about fame. Bill, you used

to have a bit of trouble with it, didn't you?

That's not really a question, is it? You know I had problems. How can I put it? 'I used to have this weird feeling that I was being followed. Then I realised that I was.' Woody Allen said that, but I wish I had, because it was true. I know we weren't real pop stars, but during the mid-seventies we certainly got treated as if we were. Which could be quite nice, even exciting, but it could also be scary. I'm not sure the screaming fans thing happens quite so much these days. Kids are probably 'cooler'. Do they mob pop stars? Certainly it's not on the news or in the papers, which it was all the time back in the sixties and seventies. We've all seen those black and white clips of the Beatles or the Stones concerts, with thousands of hysterical teenage girls clawing at the stage, bursting into tears, being armlocked by policemen or carted off by the St John's Ambulance people. That used to happen to just about any group in the seventies. Especially the young boy bands like The Rollers, The Rubettes, Kenny—which was a group, not just one bloke!—and, believe it or not, it used to happen to us.

You were *not* a boy band.

No. We were a thirty-something band. OK, a middle-aged band. I very much doubt if there was any hormonal element involved, it was just sort of Goody mania, and to be honest it could be pretty exciting, if not just a wee bit intoxicating. I defy anyone to be paraded along in an open-top vehicle with thousands of people waving and cheering and singing your signature tune, and not to develop delusions of omnipotence. I can easily imagine, when the Queen is feeling a bit less than revered, when people are calling her a 'redundant anachronism', or accusing her of being mean to Diana's memory, or re-editing her documentary, that she thinks to herself: 'My God I could do with Trooping the Colour right now; I might even have to go to the Cup Final or something.' You can't bit a beat of adulation set to music. Our fans didn't actually sing 'God Bless our Gracious Goodies' but, believe me, several hundred people chanting 'Give us an oo' sends shivers down your spine.

So you did enjoy some of the attention.

As long as our public appearances were properly organised it was fine. No, let's face it, it was bloody amazing. We did the open-top bit when we switched on the Morecambe Christmas lights, and 'be honest'— as Eric would say—we revelled in it!

What we found harder to revel in were the book and record signings which inevitably involved physical contact with the fans. You can't sign autographs without being within arm's reach, and this is when you can start to feel a bit vulnerable. It's not that Goodies fans weren't polite and well behaved, and anything tactile that occurred was usually affectionately intentioned, and gratefully received.

However, when several hundred people are crammed into a small space trying to get at three middle-aged fellas, who are in there somewhere, but no one seems to know exactly where, or has thought about a safe and sensible queueing system, things can get out of hand, and a bit scary. This happened once at the Arndale Shopping Centre in Manchester. Some people began to panic. Unfortunately, those people were the police. They were supposed to be escorting us—in a caring but platonic sort of way—but alas, as has so often happened in history when custodians of law and order are confronted by youthful high spirits, they seem to lose all sense of humour and proportion. In the Arndale case, instead of marshalling the crowd,

195

they grabbed a loud hailer and cancelled the whole event, which naturally made things a lot less cheery. They didn't resort to batons and water cannons, but suddenly the whole atmosphere didn't seem terribly appropriate at an event featuring the Goodies. We were supposed to emanate ... goodness, not chaos!

Actually, I don't suppose anyone feels comfortable being crushed in a crowd, whether you've been caught in it or caused it. In fact, it wasn't the 'special events' or public appearances that I really had trouble with. What freaked me out, as we used to say in the seventies, was the fan in the street.

Oh dear, sounds like your attitude is contrary to showbiz tradition, which dictates that the correct response to being asked 'Do you mind being recognised, followed, shouted at, chased or generally molested?' is to reply: 'The day I am *not* molested is when I will worry!'

I know, I know. I also know there's some logic in that, but I'm afraid that for much of the time I hated the off-screen attention. It wasn't, I hasten to add, because the fans were unpleasant. It was my problem, and I did have an excuse. You may not consider it a very good excuse, but it was genuine. It was—that word again—panic. Not the fans, not the police. Me. To go back to that Woody Allen line: 'I felt people were following me ... because they were.' I don't mean stalkers. I don't even mean it was one particular person, and it wasn't always being literally followed—though that did happen. It was a cumulative effect. Some days I felt as if I was being hunted. By a pack. They were surrounding me, and there was no escape. It would maybe start when I went into a local shop. The shopkeeper would simply greet me as a familiar customer, but then the next person in the queue would say, 'Hey, aren't you

196

that bloke in the Goodies?' At best I'd mutter 'Yes'. At worst, I would deny it. I would actually say 'No'. Not a good idea, since the response was almost certainly 'Yes you are.' Whereupon, I could admit it or deny it again. Either way, I would appear perverse, paranoid or hostile. As the day progressed, things would get worse and worse. I'd go from ungracious to aggressive.

I would defend myself by going on the attack. If a bunch of kids kept calling my name even though I was ignoring them, I would turn on them. 'What do you think I am, a fuckin' dog?' Yes, I swore too. 'How would you like it if people kept yelling at you?'

Bill, this is not good.

I know. My most absurd and shameful riposte was when I turned on a lad who had been pointing at me and repeating 'You're Bill Oddie, you're Bill Oddie'! I could have said 'Yes', or even 'No'. Instead, I pointed back at him and yelled, 'You're a schoolboy. Look, everyone, he's a schoolboy!'

And how did he react to that?

He said, 'You're mad, you are.' I wasn't mad, but...

Which one of you was the schoolboy?

Quite. I am not proud of how I used to react, but I do maintain that my excuse was very real. I felt hunted, I felt claustrophobic, and I was resentful that I couldn't just carry on shopping, or going for walks, or to the cinema, or even on holiday, especially with my daughters Kate and Bonnie. They hated it too. In 1975 they would have been seven and four, and as a dad I wanted to spend time with my children, and vice versa, simply doing normal things that parents do with their kids. It was rarely possible. Kate and Bonnie too felt hunted, embarrassed, and perhaps even a bit frightened. Why were all these people pointing at their dad? I will never forget a morning in Penzance. We had just come off the Isles of Scilly, one of my favourite places in the world. We'd had a great hassle-free week there, and now we had a couple of hours to kill before catching our train back to London. It was two hours of such stress and agony that it almost obliterated the joy of our holiday. It was as if, wherever we went, a spotlight was being shone in our eyes, and—to change the metaphor—we were the 'frozen' animals and we could hear the hounds approaching! In truth, all I was being asked to do was sign autographs or pose for photos, but there was simply no respite, no escape. To the girls, it must have been almost as if their dad was being snatched away from them. They were reduced to tears. So was I.

How did Tim and Graeme cope?

I don't really know, since I was rarely with them except when we were actually doing the shows. Contrary to common belief, we did not all live together in real life, any more than Morecambe and Wise shared a bed. When we were outside filming, we were 'protected' from the public, in the interests both of safety and of getting some work done! It wasn't an easy job for those who had to do it. Wherever we were on location, word would get around, and crowds would gather. Since most of them would be youngsters, they were prone to shouting out in the middle of a take, or running across the shot and ruining it. This did not please us. Areas were roped off, and several of our crew were put on crowd control duty, which would include gathering up autograph books to be signed when we had a break. Book signings and photo sessions were even incorporated into the day's schedule. The whole thing was organised like military manoeuvres, but location filming was not what you could call a relaxing experience.

Surely, nobody could deny that the public had a right to hang around and watch, or indeed to complain that their lives or neighbourhoods were being disrupted.

Of course, but you rather hoped they would voice their discontent quietly to one side, rather than yell out: 'Bloody BBC. You think you can do what you like! Bugger off!'—right in the middle of a take—but they have the right to do that too. And they quite often did. Nevertheless, anyone who goes location filming accepts that they will have to deal with the public. What you don't have to do is actually invite them along.

That sounds like a very bad idea.

It was. It happened in Winchester—or was it Dorchester? Anyway, we were due to film a scene which—especially for the Goodies—was extremely subtle. The story was that we had fallen on hard times, and had been reduced to the level of down-and-outs living on the street, or in this case in the local park. The scene involved us sitting shivering round a small fire, bemoaning our lot. There was a smattering of typical Goodies sight gags involving collapsing benches, newspaper pillows, and a tulip reading lamp, but the scene was as near as we ever got to sensitive acting. There were to be tears and pathos, and our dialogue would be strictly *sotto voce*. The shooting of the scene required atmosphere and above all perfect silence, except for the crackling of the fire, and our almost whispered words. Intimate. That's the word. So you can imagine our surprise when we arrived at the park to find that two large banks of temporary seating had been installed. Where that morning there had been an empty sward, there was now a grandstand. On asking if there was to be an outdoor rock concert, we were told that the mini stadium was to accommodate our audience! What's more, a full house was guaranteed, since the local schoolchildren had been given a day off to come and watch the Goodies filming. Thus we played our intimate, atmospheric little scene in front of a crowd of a couple of hundred kids and their parents. It is a tribute to them, and us, that it was—though I say it myself—rather moving.

Mind you, talking of moving, it was also in Win or Dorchester that we had what we all agree was our scariest 'mobbing' experience. It may even have been later that same night. We must have been on a break, possibly supper, because we had retired to our Winnebago, which is film-speak for caravan, which is a euphemism for a mobile dressing-room. We had been smuggled inside, so that the crowds didn't know where we were, but they had found out. We knew this because they kept battering on the doors and windows and yelling out our names, 'inviting' us to come outside. Call us lily-livered cowards if you like, but we were reluctant to accept the invitation. The crowd's response to this was to start rocking the caravan backwards and forwards, and from side to side, so that it felt as if we were being tossed on the high seas in a small boat, or buffeted by an earthquake. Fortunately, our 'production manager' must have been watching, presumably with growing concern, and we heard his voice yelling for us to let him in. This we did, probably snapping off a few fan fingers in the door as we slammed it shut again. So now there were four of us trapped in there. As our prefabricated prison cell continued to rock and roll, our manager walky-talkied for reinforcements, and eventually we were escorted, or possibly bodily carried, out of the Winnebago and into the nearby pub.

Big mistake. Awaiting us in the pub were another batch of Goodies aficionados—older and stronger, since they were of drinking age—who made a mass beer-fuelled lunge in our direction. Whereupon we were escorted or probably thrown across the bar, and into a very small back room, little bigger than a broom cupboard. In fact, it probably was a broom cupboard. Another door was slammed shut, leaving us wondering how we would ever get out alive. However, we soon realised that the most imminent dilemma was not us getting out, but the fans getting in. There were two doors in that cupboard, one that was slammed shut, the other one that led outside, presumably into the back yard. That door was wooden and worse for wear and, though it was padlocked, it did not look strong. What happened next was like a classic scene from a horror movie.

As we cowered in a corner, the door handle began to rattle and turn. The padlock quivered, and the whole door began to shake on its hinges. There was banging, battering and scratching. Something was trying to get in. It could have been a werewolf, or a pack of werewolves, or maybe vampires or zombies. Whatever they were, they surely had claws rather than hands. At any moment we expected the door to crack, splinter and finally crash to the floor. There would be dust, mouths, eyes, talons, fangs ... fast cutting, cacophonous chords ... screams, blood, then the screen would go blank. Mix to next morning in the park. The sun shines. All is calm. There is no sign of any temporary seating. Birds sing. Children laugh and play. Everything is back to normal. The Goodies have gone. It's as if it was all a dream.

Surely that sort of thing is way in the past. It doesn't happen now does it? Now you are no

longer a Goody.

We don't get mobbed. Well, I don't. I can't speak for Tim and Graeme. I have heard the *I'm Sorry I Haven't a Clue* audience can be a bit boisterous. And when the three of us got together a couple of years ago for a short tour in Australia we certainly got mobbed there, but in a very nice, gentle, friendly Australian way. But I do think it's a case of 'once a Goody always a Goody.' Hardly a week goes by but a cheery scaffolder or cab driver bellows out 'Goody Goody Gumdrops', which is of course inaccurate because it's not 'gumdrops', it's 'yum yum'. I have learnt not to correct them, however, in case it leads to violence.

Violence from fans. How do you mean?

Ah, well, what you have to understand is that not everyone who shouts to a TV personality in the street is a fan. Some of them just want to hit you.

How do you know?

Because they have done. So you mustn't give them a reason.

So you should just ignore them?

No, no. That's a reason. That's one of the worst things you can do, especially if they shout out your name—or my name—which is usually pronounced 'Biw'. As in 'Oi, Biw!' If I don't turn and acknowledge them—and sometimes even if I do—the next thing they'll do is call me a 'wanker'.

Why?

Because they want to hit me. So now it's really difficult. If I ignore being called a wanker, they'll probably say, 'Oi, you wanker. Just 'cos you're on the telly . . .' and start moving towards me in a threatening manner, which may lead to them hitting me. Or I can answer back, for example I might say: 'Don't call me a wanker, you wanker.' In which case they'll definitely hit me.

202

And does that sort of thing still happen?

Occasionally. These days, if I get called a wanker, I do the sensible thing and look terribly old and frail (which is getting easier), because I figure there's not much fun thumping an old geezer. Thumping a thirty-something is apparently much more satisfying. The people that shout out 'Wanker!' are not fans. They don't call out the names of celebrities or footballers because they like and admire them. They do it because they hate them, and what they are looking for is an excuse to thump them. Listen, this is all getting a bit negative. I'm coming over as a bit of a grumpy old man.

I won't argue with that.

I admit I was a grumpy middle-aged man, but I'm a lot mellower these days. If there is anyone reading this who I was horrible to back in the seventies, or the eighties, and possibly quite a lot of the nineties ... I am really, really sorry. Especially if they were youngsters. I am not sure I appreciated it then, but it is perfectly understandable that people on the telly get shouted at in the street. TV personalities are not real. Especially if they do daft comedy shows which have catchphrases, like *The Goodies, Python, The Young Ones, The Fast Show, Little Britain* or *The Mighty Boosh*. We are all cartoon characters escaped from the screen. We are no more human than those Disney critturs with big heads. You don't get parents at Disneyworld telling their kids: 'Don't stare at Mickey and Minnie, there's a human being in there!'

OK, you reckon you are more affable these days— though other people will be the judge of that. Let's face it, you needed to improve! You have admitted that you were at times grumpy and aggressive, and that you had something of a reputation for being awkward to work with.

Apparently, yes. I honestly didn't realise that until somebody told me that some people on the Goodies production team found me a bit scary.

In other words, they didn't like you.

I guess not.

Does that worry you? Is it important to you to be liked?

You bet it is. It always has been, which may surprise you, since I obviously didn't do a very good job of being likeable if people found me scary! The thing is, I could—and I'm afraid I still can—be very abrasive, especially in a work context. Somebody once said about me, 'He doesn't suffer fools gladly.' That really upset me. I hate that word 'fools'. It's a horrible, cruel word. People aren't fools. I honestly have never thought of anyone I've known or worked with as a fool, but I fear there have been times when I have made someone feel like one. I don't mean to. I will concede that I do tend to have strong opinions on how things should be done, and if I think something is wrong or not good enough, or even simply could be a bit better, I tend to say so. Often out loud, with several people listening, including the person responsible for whatever it is I'm stropping about. It may seem an extraordinary thing to plead, but I don't mean it personally. I honestly don't mean to embarrass or humiliate any individual, but I am afraid I often don't realise that I have made them feel foolish or upset them. I think—I hope—that I am getting better, more aware, more sensitive, but alas it still happens.

Give me an example.

Must I?

Yes, please. You may find it cathartic.

I may find it embarrassing!

And cathartic. Come on, 'fess up.

OK. Mid August 2007. At the annual Bird Brain of Britain quiz (a sort of ornithological *Mastermind*) it was my job as chairman to read out the questions. Last year many of them were so esoteric—full of literally unpronounceable Latin names and scientific jargon—that I began to wax sarcastic to the point of skipping ones I couldn't understand or pronounce, and adding increasingly profane comments such as 'as if anyone gives a stuff', or 'whatever the fuck that means'. My motivation was that I felt that the mainly non-expert family audience (a couple of hundred of them, including kids) was being almost entirely excluded. Quizzes are surely more fun if the audience can at least have a stab at the answers themselves? On that point, I think I am right. However, where I was utterly wrong was to be so publicly scathing, especially because sitting next to me was the learned fellow who each year spends many a long and arduous evening trawling through vast tomes to come up with over a hundred questions and answers. Anyone who has organised a pub quiz will agree, it ain't done in half an hour. I was told later that the gentleman in question had been quite upset by my facetious criticisms. Added to which, several parents had justifiably complained about my bad language. I know it's too late now, but I am really, really sorry. I was a complete prat.

Did that teach you a lesson?

Alas, no. A few months later, I made a similar distasteful, inappropriate and I fear possibly hurtful *faux pas* on the final evening of *Autumnwatch*. Fortunately, it wasn't live on the telly. It was at the 'wrap party'. This is a traditionally joyful event celebrating the end of any entertainment project, be it a theatre run, a movie shoot or, in this case, two weeks of challenging, exhausting but fulfilling natural history television. There will be food, drinks and dancing. There will also be speeches. Often funny and frivolous, but nevertheless genuinely appreciative and congratulatory about what has been achieved. At the *Autumnwatch* wrap the executive producer went first, followed by the series producer. Both were eloquent, witty, silly but, above all, sincere. Then it was my turn. I got it really, really wrong.

Professional public speakers call it misjudging the audience. Like telling blue jokes at a Women's Institute supper. Or booking Bernard Manning to do a closing speech at the Notting Hill Carnival. Back in the 1980s, I myself came close to committing a misjudgement that could have gone down in showbiz history. As it is, I may well be the only TV personality who was banned from a major charity concert.

You were banned from a charity concert!

Yup. The event was one of the first Aids Benefit evenings, to raise funds for the Terence Higgins Trust. I had been invited to perform a humorous song of my own choosing—already a risky request, if you recall my penchant for revelling in contentious ditties. I rummaged in my repertoire to come up with something that was not only comedic, but also satirical and relevant to the theme of the evening. At this point, you may well be thinking: 'A comedy song about Aids? That could be paddling in dangerous waters.' Paddling? I was preparing to plunge in from off the top board. I had the very thing: a little number about irresponsible promiscuity. Surely that was appropriate to the cause? The song was, in fact, a parody of a 1980s soul hit called 'Me and Mrs Jones ... we've got a thing going on'. The singer basically boasts about having it off with other blokes' wives, with no more excuse than an uncontrollable libido. Lenny Henry concocted a perfect prototype with the character of Theosophilus P.

Wildebeest, crooning about his unsatiable 'lurve' for the 'laydees'. I didn't physically quite match up to Lenny, but nevertheless I was more than willing to play a diminutive, white version of a 'sex machine'. My song was called 'She Wouldn't Understand'. There was one of those statutory talking bits in the middle, when the singer reveals that over the years he has come to the conclusion that he has 'an irresistible tendency to shag everything in sight'. He would like to assure his wife: 'Honey, that doesn't mean I love you less. Just less often.' However, he hasn't actually confessed his carryings on to his spouse because, as he sings in the chorus: 'She wouldn't understand. That a man must be a man.'

Now I am not going to disown the song. I think it is pretty good, and sends up a genre that deserves it. Plus, I loved singing it in my best Barry White type voice (only a bit higher). What's more, I had assembled a small band, complete with backing singers. In the afternoon, we did a pretty funky 'soundcheck' in the big London Theatre, in front of a sparse audience of a few of the representatives of the Terence Higgins Trust, and the director of the charity show, no less than the inestimable Stephen Fry. We didn't expect a standing ovation. Indeed, we weren't even sure if anyone had been listening. But they obviously had. We became aware of the familiar sound of muttering that indicates that a 'confab' has been called. This is rarely good news. Heaven knows, I sympathise with Stephen (now, if not then!), who called me over and made the nonchalant enquiry: 'Bill. Have you got anything else?' Which was instantly translatable as: 'You are not singing that one tonight.' He went on to explain that some, well, all the people from the Trust did not feel it was appropriate to sing lustily about irresponsible sex, when the front row of the audience would be at the very least HIV positive, and some had terminal Aids. My plea that the song was obviously a satire, not a celebration, may well have received an inner nod of understanding from Stephen, but he was not about to argue my case with the Terence Higgins people. My response was inevitably and sadly typical of my stroppy years. 'We do that song, or we do nothing!' The fact that, even as I spoke those words, we were already packing up and leaving relieved Stephen of the embarrassment of having to make a decision. Clearly we would be doing nothing. I left with a final flourish—or was it a flounce?—flinging the music in a nearby rubbish bin, and muttering something like 'Well, you're better off without us—charity shows always overrun anyway.' I also growled something along the lines of 'I bet you won't be asking Ben Elton to run through his act in case he gets a bit distasteful. Or the bunch from *The Mary Whitehouse Experience*.' I was probably trying to convince myself that I had been fired because these young upstarts all preferred *Python* to *The Goodies*, and only they—the so-called 'alternative' comics—were allowed to do rude or contentious stuff. I could almost hear them saying 'Why doesn't he stick to the Funky Gibbon?' Now that's what I call offensive!

Looking back on that debacle now, I have to admit it was about as fine an example as you could get of 'misjudging the audience'. Thanks, Stephen, for preserving my image. Indeed for improving it!

Bill, that was twenty-odd years ago!

Yes. How did I get on to that?

You were going to tell me about the *Autumnwatch* wrap party 2007. Was that worse than the Aids Benefit gaffe?

Oh blimey, I went off on a bit of a detour there, didn't

I?

A lot of a detour, but at least it proves you've always been a liability. So what exactly did you cock up at the *Autumnwatch* party that you are now so ashamed of?

Oh, I just got it all wrong. I pretended I had hated the whole thing, and I was glad it was over, and I said I wished I'd 'buggered off in a chauffeur-driven car, like Kate always does as soon as we finish', and that I was 'sick to death of bloody whooper swans, honking away like a troupe of drunken buglers', and that 'if I ever have to pretend to be excited by another V-shaped skein of pink-footed goose, I'll shoot the lot of them'. And the really really worst bit was . . .

Go on. Confess.

I was horrible about the public, the fans, as it were. I said they 'freaked me out'.

I thought you got over that back in the 1970s.

I did really. I wasn't serious. It was meant to be funny. I said something really appalling like: 'I hate going out there when the public are in, because I am suddenly surrounded by people in wheelchairs, or misshapen, or with speech impediments. It feels like I'm at bloody Lourdes! Like I'm supposed to sign an autograph, and they'll leap up and sing: "Praise the Lord, I'm cured!"'

That really is an awful thing to say.

They knew I was joking.

Did they?

Maybe not. Not all of them. And anyway, it's a pretty sick kind of humour. I must have seemed so bitter and twisted. I can't remember how I finished off. I hope I said something nice! I felt awful. I just went and sat on my own in another room, till a lovely girl who is one of our researchers came and asked me if I was all right.

And were you all right?

No. Definitely not. I felt terrible.

You sometimes just don't think, do you?

No.

It's anything for a laugh, isn't it?

I'm afraid so. Which makes it pretty ironic when nobody finds it funny.

It never crossed your mind that you might be hurting someone's feelings, did it?

No.

And now do you feel really guilty?

Yes.

And you will apologise?

Yes. Yes. Definitely, yes. That is one thing I am good at. I always, always apologise. I just wish I didn't have to so often. And I wish I didn't swear so much in public. Who do I think I am, Billy Connolly?

You wish. But you see people expect a sprinkling of F-words from him, because that's what he does in his act. It's hardly headlines, is it? 'Read all about it. Billy Connolly swears in front of audience!' But if David Attenborough started effing and blinding . . . Or you—ex-Goody, family favourite, cheery wildlife presenter, and with kids in the audience. Why do you do it? Are you showing off? It's not clever, and it's not . . .

. . . All right, all right! Please stop attacking me.

I am not attacking you, I am simply telling the truth.

You know, I am beginning to really dislike myself.

Ah. Now that sounds like depression talking.

Funny you should say that. Well, actually, it's not funny at all.

4

Brain stopped play

Message to the reader:
I am not making this up. I'm afraid this is really happening.
And, yes, I am afraid.

Time: 10 March 2008
Location: My office

Well, here's an irony. I began writing this book early in the New Year, and for two months I wrote just about every weekday, usually from about ten in the morning until early evening. It is not for me to say if it is a good read, but I was certainly finding it—to coin a phrase—a good write. I was enjoying it. Words were coming easily and I was well on schedule to 'deliver', as publishers say, by the end of March. However, now it is 10 March, and I can barely produce a coherent sentence. These few lines have taken me ten minutes or so. I keep slowing down, sometimes stopping. My fingers feel heavy, my head is fuzzy, my eyes keep closing and I am yawning a lot. I feel very, very tired, but worse than that. Frankly, I feel frightened. Not because I don't know what is happening, but because I do. Or rather, I know what might happen. Anyone who has had, but recovered from, a serious illness or injury will, I am sure, confirm that the fear that never leaves is of recurrence or relapse. A sportsman feels a twinge and it reminds him he has a weak knee. He remembers the time it collapsed completely and he was out for months. This time it might just be a passing tweak, but the fear will always be there, because that is what happened before: first a twinge, then a total collapse. Next time it might end his career.

Having had three serious clinical depressions, I am all too aware of the early symptoms. I cannot ignore the fact that I am experiencing some of them right now. If I tell you what they are, I wouldn't blame you for thinking, 'Oh, come on, I feel like that every morning!' or 'most of the time'. Indeed, I feel embarrassed to be complaining, since none of them sounds exactly life-threatening. So what are they?

For the last few days, I have been waking up early with feelings of anxiety. Not terrified, but nervous. Slightly fearful. My mouth is very dry. Most of my body—especially my back—is very wet. Heavy perspiration, hot sweats. I am finding it hard to roll out of bed, though if I do, the sweating usually abates. Instead, I begin feeling the cold, which normally I don't. Anyone who has been outdoors with me in chilly weather would confirm that I often seem oblivious to the temperature, wearing only a light jacket, whilst others are wrapped in several fleeces. But now I am shivering, even inside a well-heated house. I am also being frequently overwhelmed by a general weariness, lethargy and apathy. I try to force my mind to wander into the future, to anticipate things I will enjoy, but I am not convinced. It is not yet a feeling of dread or utter pointlessness, but there is a worrying blankness. I have been feeling this since the last day of February. The 29th. If it hadn't been a leap year, that day would never have existed! Bad luck that. At least I still seem to have a sense of flippancy, which is hopefully a sign that the Black Dog is not about to take over. At the moment, this is more like the black puppy, but it's snarling rather than wagging its tail. The truth is, though . . .

I am scared. What is happening? And why? Can I do anything to stop it getting worse? On the advice of my therapist I am trying to acknowledge that there are logical reasons why I am feeling under pressure. Somebody once said: 'The aim of therapy is not to make you feel permanently happy but rather to enable you to deal with being sad.' You could say the same about antidepressant medication, which is why dubbing them 'happy pills' is not only dismissive but inaccurate. So what might be beginning to stress me or depress me now? I don't often find it hard to handle my 'workload'. However, what I do get very edgy about is the anticipation that I am being pressured into a future schedule or a   job that I have doubts about. It is choices and decisions that give me problems. In my old age, I am getting better at saying 'no', but I still feel guilty if I do. I won't trouble you with the details—if only because you would be justified in saying, 'He should have such problems!'—but what I can't ignore is the fact that I am feeling distinctly wobbly, and I am very scared that I am about to relapse into the depths. My therapist offers advice and reassurance: 'Think of these symptoms as a warning signal,' he says. 'I'd be concerned if you didn't feel anxious.''You are allowed to be sad.' 'You've been here before, and you've been fine.' These may sound almost like platitudes, but they are things that I need to believe are true. I have already written about other truths in this book. How much I love and am fascinated by my family, how much I enjoy my work, how much pleasure I get from music. Those are the truths. The doubts and 'don't cares' are the insidious 'false truths' of depression. If I start to believe them, I could be in serious trouble, and there have been times during the last week when I have lain in bed or on the backroom sofa, half sleeping, and half thinking, believing and accepting the worst.

Three days later: 13 March 2008

I have been down all day, but right now I feel better, which is why I am able to type! May this continue. If it doesn't, I fear I probably won't finish this book. I certainly won't meet the delivery date I have agreed with the publishers. That was, by the way, probably one of my big mistakes. How and why on earth did I have the (over)confidence to say that I reckoned I could write my autobiography in less than three months? In January I believed it. Now I don't!

One month later: 14 April 2007

It is still going on. I haven't been able to concentrate enough to write any more of this book for six weeks. What I have found myself doing is scribbling down odd thoughts and phrases to try and describe what this depression feels like, because it is not the same as the previous three. I haven't felt utterly despairing or suicidal, and I don't keep bursting into tears, or become totally uncommunicative. And I definitely don't feel I would be better off in hospital, which I certainly did before.

The overwhelming feeling is still of weariness, lethargy and apathy. There have been several days—this is one of them—when I have stayed in or gone back to bed till the late afternoon or early evening. I presumably sleep some of the time, but there are also long periods when I don't. My mind won't let me. Not that my thoughts are particularly dark, disturbing or even stressful. There are just too many of them. Constantly buzzing, quite randomly, often recalling scenes or situations from the past that are not so much distressing as uncomfortable. I think of places where I have been previously happy, but my brain is saying, 'No, you weren't. It was actually rather uncomfortable.' I remember walking in the Scilly Isles when I was warm and content, but now it's cold, wet and windy. It is as if I am trying to cheer myself up by thinking about things I enjoy, but my brain is refusing to see the bright side. The result is an overall mood that feels not so much catastrophic as blank. No enthusiasm, no motivation, no energy. It is very much a physical feeling, which is why I went and had a series of blood tests to check out the illnesses that can cause extreme fatigue. Can you understand why I felt almost disappointed when I got 100 per cent clear results!? No anaemia, no diabetes, no thyroid problems, no prostate cancer; my cholesterol was actually quite a bit better than a few months ago, and my rather high blood pressure was no worse. I know it is perverse, and indeed insulting to those who do suffer from any of these physical conditions, but I have to admit I had been thinking: if the tests reveal I do indeed have a specific, identifiable physical problem, there is most likely an appropriate specific cure or treatment. It would make things 'simpler'!

The doctor's conclusion disabused me of that one. 'The tests I did are not totally exhaustive,' he said, 'but I'd have to say that things overwhelmingly point to all your symptoms being connected to your depression recurring, albeit in a rather different form.'

That much I wouldn't deny. It does feel different. Frankly, it is not as bad as the previous three. I'm aware that I am as much angry and resentful as depressed. And there are logical reasons. I had been rollicking along writing, and now I have had to stop. I resent that. I am also due to do a couple of days filming in Norfolk to set up this year's *Springwatch*, and I am not sure I can face it. I resent that too. I was also being put under pressure to sign up for an ITV series travelling round remote British Islands. My agent had been negotiating the contract for weeks, but I had to call him and ask him to tell the ITV folks that I was having doubts about what was frankly an extremely arduous schedule, that would possibly exhaust me before *Springwatch* and certainly would after it. Their response was to work out a new schedule and offer a bigger fee! But postponing a quandary doesn't solve it, and money is no consolation for wrecked health: physical or mental. I feel terrible about backing out, but I knew I had to. So I did. I told my agent to be totally honest with ITV, to tell them I was feeling pretty dreadful, and that I was withdrawing for their sakes as well as mine. My anxiety and stress was now augmented by a large dollop of guilt, but I hoped that having made a decision would clear my brain and revive my energy.

It didn't. A lot of this stuff peaked during the Easter week when my therapist was taking a break. As soon as he was back in the office, I was back on the couch. I told him I was still feeling exhausted and pretty low, and I recounted the recent events. His response—his analysis, if you like—was predictable. 'You feel rotten. You are tired, anxious, and sad.' I almost joined in the chorus, 'I'd be worried if you weren't.' I, on the other hand, was worried that I was. More than worried. I was scared.

I don't think it is appropriate for me to write in any great detail about the content of my therapy sessions, but nevertheless, I assure you that I am well aware that I have already blown my initial resolve about this book. I have already said that I don't want to be thought of as a 'celebrity depressive', and here I am being exactly that. My excuse is, I didn't mean to! It is what has happened, and believe me—as I am sure you do— I wish it hadn't. Should I continue to write about it? Well, let's face it, I also said that young autobiographers have the advantage that they don't have to remember stuff from long ago. Well, at least, on this topic, neither do I. It is happening right now. And—that's right—I wish it wasn't.

More than one person has made the classic comment, 'What you need is a holiday.' Fortunately, I am about to get one.

17 April 2007

Just before midnight, I and a large percentage of my family boarded the Cornish Riviera Express sleeper from Paddington Station. By 8 a.m. we were in Penzance, where we ate a hearty breakfast before catching the little bus down to the heliport. By mid morning, we had landed on Tresco in the Isles of Scilly. One of my favourite places in the world. Even more so in the company of my wife Laura, daughters Kate and Bonnie, and grandchildren Lyle, Gracie and Ella. Only Rosie is missing. She has several gigs to do with her band. Nevertheless, surely if anything could be a 'pick me up' or a 'rest cure', this would be it?

Alas, it was neither. Fresh air and walks can—and indeed should—make you tired, but in a good, healthy way. But my compulsion to retire to the bedroom didn't feel healthy at all. Just as I had done for the previous six weeks at home, I sometimes slept, sometimes read a little, but most of the time just lay there staring out of the window. At least the view was one of the best in Britain. I tended to perk up in the evening, but most of the day I simply slouched around, feeling like the worst grandad in the world. Frankly, I don't think I'm that good at the best of times, but I couldn't even summon the energy to go rock-pooling or beachcombing with Lyle or the girls. It was my loss, and that added more sadness to the mix. But it was when I went on one of my long walks that I felt worst.

I have often thought that there is a thin line between solitude and loneliness. Heaven knows, I got used to being alone when I was a kid. I used to spend day after day searching for nests in the local woods, or wandering round the bleak reservoir I called my local patch. I occasionally had the company of a birdwatching chum, but mostly I was by myself. I didn't mind at all. I used to talk to myself. Not out loud. I kept a sort of running commentary going in my head, anticipating what I might see round the next corner. I used to try to will rarities to appear by the power of autosuggestion! 'There was a westerly gale last night. As I scanned with my binoculars across the bay, I saw . . . can it really be? Yes . . . it is ! A Leach's Petrel! Storm driven on to my local patch. A first for Bartley Reservoir!' At least once it worked, when I predicted a Great Northern Diver and, bang on cue, one came drifting out of the fog.

For most of my life I have remained pretty at ease with my own company, especially in the great outdoors. I don't just watch the wildlife. I often 'work', or at least have 'creative thoughts', which get jotted down in my notebook along with whatever birds I've seen that day, and whatever CDs I must buy next time I go to HMV. Many's the daft lyric or wacky comedy routine I have come up with whilst doing the birding rounds on Hampstead Heath. In recent years, however, the solitude has been less productive. It is not that my brain has emptied. Quite the opposite. There are days when it feels crammed full to bursting point, but not with anything constructive. Thoughts, images, phrases. Nagging, relentless and repetitious. Round and round. Not meaningless. Not crazy. Often making sense, voicing logical concerns, telling the truth, over and over again, till I feel like shouting out: 'I know! I know! Now leave me alone!'

By the end of the week on Tresco my notebook was full of my attempts to express some of the feelings I had experienced during March and April, both back in London and on Scilly. Here are some of them, transcribed from my jottings:

On lying in bed

'This inertia thing: I just can't be arsed to shift position. If I do turn over, it's a reason to sigh and relax into it for another stretch.'

'I lie there and look round the room for cures and answers. Objects can be potentially helpful, or so I then believe. If I gaze at that door for ten minutes, I'll feel better! Meditate on the lampshade. Focus on that pot plant. Mainly I stare out of the window until I'm drawn out of bed as if by a magnet—an urge to go outside takes over. But when I am out, everyone seems to be doing something I can't or couldn't do. Even just walking! Running certainly. Going to work. Doing the crossword in the local café. Chattering and being cheery and silly—as I do when I'm OK. Whatever people are doing, it seems to intimidate me. I can't do that. I couldn't do that. I never have. Even if I know it's not true.'

How do I feel?

'In this condition, I am basically bored with myself. Why would anyone want to know about me? I find myself boring.'

What's in my head?

'Constant awareness. Do I feel better? Worse? The same? Awareness. Will I enjoy the future? Did I enjoy the past? Aware. Aware. Me, me, me. I, I, I.'

'Constantly conscious of doubts about worth and status. Why am I any good at anything? Instead of relishing time, I will it to pass. Clock watching.'

'When the phone rings, I jump! What am I afraid of?'

On holiday on Tresco

'I can't believe I am sitting in the sand dunes looking at one of my favourite views, and at this moment it means nothing to me. I feel I have lost touch with who I am. I have lost my ambition, and therefore my sense of future.'

'I am bored with myself. Possibly bored with my life—or aspects of it. But I am NOT bored with living. Various suggestions from my family include: Get a dog. Learn to use a computer. Get more regular social routines. But what? I am very bad at trying things. Negative about new stuff. It can't be healthy to be so self-obsessed. Am I addicted to negativity?'

221

What am I afraid of?

'Loneliness? Repetition? Feeling "I've done that"? Lack of feelings? Lack of control? Intimidated by my ignorance of modern IT? Death? Probably only got a year or two left? Can I only be happy when I'm working? Can I work? Will I be able to do *Springwatch*, or not?'

That is a pretty worrying possibility. Worrying not only to me, but presumably to quite a lot of BBC folk, such as my producers and the head of BBC2. Should I warn them right now? Should I trust myself to be OK? I had after all managed to do those few days' filming before the holiday, two days in Norfolk checking out our new location, plus speaking to the press and local radios, and also a couple of pre-recordings to show how things were in April. The 'real thing' is due to begin in mid May. I've got about a month to recover. I am concerned, but not totally pessimistic. Over the past years, I have had to cancel or postpone quite a number of jobs when the big depressions struck, and believe me, in the condition I was in, there was no way I could have stood up or spoken, let alone done a public performance. However, I reckon I have become a realistic judge of what I can and can't do, and indeed I have managed quite a few appearances when I have been in a bit of a state. I am rather proud of the fact that I landed a very lucrative voice-over contract with B & Q after doing an audition for which, not feeling confident enough to drive, I had walked the not inconsiderable distance from Hampstead to central London in the rain, thinking it would do me good! I suppose it must have, since despite sweating buckets and feeling thoroughly spaced out, I got the job!

Only once have I actually broken down on the job, as it were. Frankly, looking back at the circumstances now, it was hardly surprising.

It was late November, and depression number three was beginning to take over. I was due to do a photoshoot for Country Innovation, the outdoor clothing company I endorse. It would only involve standing still, striking a few outdoory poses, and changing jackets and fleeces a few times. That morning I woke up telling myself, 'Surely I can manage that.' I was also aware that there was an imminent deadline for publication, and no doubt Maria, from Country Innovation, and the photographer were already on the road to London, halfway through the considerable drive from Somerset where they were based. It really wouldn't be fair to phone them and tell them to turn round and drive back. However, by mid morning I was crouched halfway down the stairs, still in my dressing-gown, now and then bursting into uncontrollable tears. I was still in that state when the doorbell rang. Maria was totally compassionate and understanding, but I could sense that even so her inner voice was pleading, 'Oh please, Bill, all you have to do is stand still and wear clothes. It'll only take half an hour.' I assured her that I'd be OK, tottered back up to my bedroom, got dressed, and tottered back down again, by which time I had decided that, though wearing a fleece was not beyond me, what I really couldn't face was doing it in public. The shoot was

223

meant to be out on Hampstead Heath. It was only about two hundred yards away, but I doubted whether I could walk there, and I certainly didn't want to be seen weeping and trembling. Although, to be honest, I might well have been in good company, since the Heath is a well-used sanctuary for melancholics, alcoholics and druggies but I doubted that it would enhance my image if I were to join them. Fortunately, there is a 'communal garden' in our road, which has several big trees with sturdy trunks that I could lean against, in typical outdoor male model fashion. Maria got her photos and went back to Somerset. I went back to bed.

However, as I lay there, my mood and confidence improved enough for me to convince myself that I would be up to fulfilling the next day's appearance, albeit that it involved rather more than leaning against a tree. Laura thought I was crazy. Looking back now, I think I was crazy. You may well think I was crazy when I tell you what it entailed. The next morning, I had been booked to give a lecture and a slide show to a roomful of oil industry workers at a conference in Edinburgh. This meant setting off that afternoon. Almost instantly. Laura would drive me to Paddington, where I could catch the Heathrow Express, and board a late afternoon plane to Scotland. I would stay in an Edinburgh hotel overnight, be picked up next morning at 7 a.m., briefed about the event, driven to the location, and be ready to face my audience at 8 a.m. I was sure I could do it, and indeed that I should do it. My agent, David, didn't try to dissuade me. Understandably, since I was contracted and he had negotiated a considerable fee—oil companies can afford it!—which he might well be liable for if I cancelled at so late a stage. I packed an overnight bag and my carousel of slides, took a Diazepam, and assured Laura I'd be fine.

During the journey I was fine, albeit in a slightly disconnected haze, rather akin to being jetlagged. There was a driver waiting to meet me at Edinburgh airport, holding up a card with my name on it. I had already phoned the event organiser and politely declined supper with assorted oil executives, pleading tiredness as an excuse. I was dropped off at the hotel around 9 p.m. It was, of course, dark. It was also very, very cold. There had been recent snow, pavements were icy, and the ponds in the hotel garden were frozen. I went straight to my room. It wasn't unpleasant, but it didn't exactly emanate cosiness. Everything in it was chrome, glass or black. No colour at all. All black. I remember thinking it was kind of appropriate, considering my condition, and I took some solace from the fact that I was capable of chuckling inwardly at the irony. I called room service. I ate in the black room, at a glass and chrome table. I took a sleeping pill, crawled under the black duvet, and was asleep by 10.30.

My alarm woke me at 6.45 a.m. I was sweating profusely, but I got up, had a shower, and brushed my teeth in the black bathroom. I got dressed, slung my bag (also black, by the way) over my shoulder and went down to the foyer, where I was met by a cheery man who drove me through the frozen Edinburgh streets—black and shiny with ice and frost—until we arrived at the Botanical Gardens.

This was a surprise to me, and apparently a surprise to whoever was in charge of the gardens. There was no sign of life, let alone greeting. Basically, the gardens seemed closed, or—considering the earliness of the hour—not yet open. After wandering up and down the street for maybe ten or fifteen minutes, becoming increasingly chilled by the arctic wind and in constant danger of skidding on the icy pavement, we finally found a doorman, and were allowed inside. As we crunched, slipped and slithered along snowy pathways, past bare and barren flower beds and empty greenhouses, I began to feel rather less than confident that I had made the right decision. After tea, toast and 'briefing' in a small canteen, I became convinced that I hadn't. It was explained to me that the oilmen's conference was going on for two or three days, during which there would be all manner of workshops, seminars and talks, and no doubt social events in the evenings. The early mornings, however, would commence with lectures from prestigious keynote speakers. I was to be the first. I explained that I intended to talk about *Springwatch*, which had been a huge success earlier in the year. I would answer questions from the audience, who I assumed would be thirsty for inside knowledge of such a popular show. 'That sounds fine,' said my host. He did, however, feel that he should mention one little detail that I might care to take into consideration. My audience would consist almost entirely of men who spent much of their year marooned on oil rigs far out in the ocean. They may not therefore be typical television viewers—more into satellite and videos—and a fair percentage were not British. I may well have visibly blanched at hearing this information. Certainly he felt compelled to assure me that 'they'll be thrilled just to see you here'. I wasn't so convinced, but at least I was armed with my carousel of slides, which as it happened included plenty of seabirds. Including species that might fly past an oil rig. My host assured me that they'd be fascinated by whatever I chose to show them. We finished our tea and toast. He looked at his watch and cheerily enquired: 'Shall we go then?' One hundred per cent of me wanted to say, 'No! I absolutely and definitely do not want to go!'—or possibly 'Yes, I do want to go, but not in there. I want to go home. Now. Please.' But there was no escape, no excuses, no choice. He led me to the lecture theatre.

Theatre? If only. It was more like a huge conservatory than a theatre. It may even have once been a greenhouse. At least it wasn't cold in there. In fact, quite the opposite. Despite the freeze-up, a watery winter sun was filtering through the huge glass windows, which were concentrating the rays like a giant magnifying glass. No doubt my ever-tensing body was exaggerating the effect, but again I began to sweat profusely as soon as I entered the room. The layout made me feel even more panicky. There was no stage, and no rows of seats for the audience. Instead, there were small groups of people—all men—sitting at little round tables. It looked like the clientele of a 'gentlemen's club' awaiting the first stripper. Except it was 8.30 in the morning and, instead of the lighting being soft and seductive, it was blindingly bright. And instead of a lap dancer they were going to get me!

Mind you, lap dancing would have been an easier option. Years of doing slide presentations have made me ultra-aware of the factors that can make showing slides much more difficult than it should be. This set-up was almost a showcase of flaws, obstacles and deficiencies. The screen was tiny. The projector was balanced precariously on a small table. The audience were strewn round the room and facing in different directions. Worst of all, the windows lacked opaque curtains or blinds, which meant that a black-out would be impossible, which in turn meant the slides would be almost invisible.

Even as I was being led to the front (I would more willingly have been led to the electric chair) I made an instant decision. Forget the slide show. I would stick to *Springwatch*. *Springwatch*, essential viewing for all the family. *Springwatch*, which for three weeks had attracted an audience of over four million. *Springwatch*, the show that surely even dour-faced, bewhiskered men of various nationalities, who spent most of their year in a totally male environment, isolated on storm-battered oil rigs, would surely have a soft spot for. I didn't expect a roar of approval, a round of applause or even a few whoops of recognition, but I did expect a slightly more comforting reaction than I got when I began by asking the audience: 'So, who saw *Springwatch*?' One person put his hand up. Eventually. He was right at the back, and I suspected that he was the organiser's best friend. Maybe he was auditioning to be my best friend! Bless him. Otherwise the room was immobile and silent. Totally unresponsive. Barely a blink of interest or familiarity. It crossed my mind that not

228

only had 99 per cent of this audience (there were about 100 of them) not seen or probably even heard of *Springwatch*, it was perfectly possible that they had no idea who I was. Perhaps they had a few Goodies DVDs out on the rig - a bit of seventies nostalgia for when they'd exhausted *The Office*, *The Best of the Two Ronnies*, classic movies and porn. Or if they were Scandinavian (many oilmen are) perhaps they were more into Ingmar Bergman. Oh yes, I could look back in frivolity, months after the event when I had recovered my sense of humour, but at that moment I was utterly overwhelmed by a humiliating, all-consuming sense of panic.

I tried to talk. I don't remember what I said. I think I attempted to explain what *Springwatch* was. Three weeks of live wildlife TV, based on a farm in Devon. Not a location oil rig workers instantly identified with! I barely stumbled through a couple of sentences before breaking down completely. I muttered profuse apologies and almost collapsed into the arms of the organiser, who led me from the room whispering words of comfort. 'It's OK. It's OK. Don't worry. They'll understand.' I can't for one minute believe they did understand. I am not accusing them of being unsympathetic, but if you have just spent three months in the middle of the North Sea, I can't imagine that sitting in a glorified greenhouse at eight in the morning, watching a bloke you have never heard of having a nervous breakdown, is your idea of big fun!

As it happens, the organiser himself did understand. He led me to an anteroom, gave me a cup of tea, and rightly diagnosed my problem. 'You suffer from depression, don't you? So do I. That happened to me once. At a conference. Just like that. Don't worry, we'll get you back to London.'

It is never less than comforting to be reminded that you are not the only one who gets zapped by these things, but it isn't a consolation for public embarrassment. Even as I said, 'I need to get my slides, they are on the projector', I felt myself making another daft decision. The oilmen were by now having a quick coffee and fag break, allowing us to slip back into the room to recover my carousel. Even as I touched it, I felt a surge of misplaced confidence.

'There are some really nice seabird slides in here. I could do this talk in my sleep. I'll go for it.'

'Are you sure?' asked the organiser.

'Yes, definitely. Can we darken the room?'

Why did I need to ask? I already knew the answer was 'we'll do our best', but in a word 'no'. But did I accept defeat and leave? Oh no. I waited whilst the audience shuffled back into their seats. I was given a second introduction. I announced that I would recount the story of my first unforgettable experience on seabird islands. 'The Farnes, just off Northumberland. In the North Sea.' At least they'd be familiar with that! I clicked up the first slide. The screen might as well have remained blank. The sunlight was by now streaming through windows shaded only by improvised curtains of tablecloths and coats. It was completely hopeless. The slide show wasn't going to happen either. For the second time that morning I apologised, but this time I retrieved my carousel, whilst the organiser assured the unfortunate oilmen that it wouldn't be long before they could rest assured that 'Mr Oddie has left the building'. I imagine they were relieved.

So was I. I even took some consolation from the fact that the room they'd provided was totally unsuitable for a slide show, except at night. Even in darkness, it was hardly the venue I would have expected for a world-famous oil company's conference. I took the train back to London, on a line that runs parallel with some of the most stunning coastal scenery in Britain, including appropriately the Farne Islands. I wasn't miserable, and indeed I was cheered by the care and understanding I had received. I was even more grateful a few days later when my agent called to say that they had phoned him to ask if I was OK, whilst waiving any compensation. I was also relieved that if there had been any press in the room (there might well have been), they didn't sell the story to the papers. Then again, I had nothing to be ashamed of. I had tried. I had failed. And I had learnt a lesson.

The truth is that in the deepest state of depression one is virtually catatonic. In a less extreme condition it may be possible to work or 'put on a show', but even then it is wise to stick to your comfort zone. Unfamiliar places and faces can faze a performer at the best of times. I recall one comedian telling how one night on stage he was going down so badly with the audience that he pretended to faint and allowed himself to be carried off into the wings! At the Edinburgh Botanical Gardens, I wasn't pretending. I simply couldn't do the job. I didn't want that to happen on *Springwatch* 2008. No disrespect, but collapsing in front of 100 oilmen is one thing. Doing it in front of four million viewers is quite another. That would get into the papers!

*   *   *

Meanwhile . . . Back to late April 2008. At the end of our week on Scilly I was supposed to stay on for a weekend's filming for CBBees—the excellent pre-school branch of the BBC. It is a job I love doing. Who wouldn't enjoy cavorting with a spiky-haired green character called 'Jelly', operated by a delightfully sparky young lady, who is capable of improvised banter and can chat as naturally as if she herself were a three-year-old child, which is how she thinks of Jelly. It is true of all the best puppeteers, they literally become their puppets. (Jelly is a puppet, but please don't tell anyone. I don't think she knows.) Frankly, I was cautiously optimistic that I would have been OK for the filming, but in effect Laura wouldn't let me. It was entirely for my own good. 'I don't like the idea of you being stranded on Scilly without family,' she said. 'There is obviously something wrong, and I think you should get home as soon as possible, and travel with us.' So I did.

I enjoyed the weekend in London more than the week in Scilly. How perverse is that? I was glad to get back to Rosie, and my garden. There was some decent rugby on the telly and, best of all, I was able to go to the fortieth birthday bash of Kate, my eldest, which was exactly the sort of thing I had not been able to do in my gloomiest state. I thoroughly enjoyed it. This fact added further weight to my feeling that the extreme fatigue and low energy level I had now been experiencing for two months could be as much physical as psychological.

On Monday, I arranged to have a second round of blood tests and a full check-up at what was, let's be honest, a very expensive Harley Street clinic. Alas, waiting for the NHS really wasn't an option. The fact that I had pulled out of the CBBees filming meant that the BBC, including the *Springwatch* office, would be well aware that I was not fully functional. Indeed I had not been withholding progress (or lack of progress) reports throughout March and April, so I presumed they must have been considering contingency plans in case I didn't recover. What they really needed was some good news. So did I.

At this point, I may as well accept that many of you will know that I did make it. I am writing this in my caravan at Pensthorpe, in Norfolk, on Monday 9 June. It is the first day of the final week of what has been one of the best, most enjoyable and successful *Springwatch*es so far. So yes, sigh of relief etc, not only have I been able to do the show, I have felt no anxiety, no hot sweats, no excessive fatigue, and I have even regained my enthusiasm for writing, including finishing this book! So how did this happen? You tell me! All I can do is relate what I did once I returned from Scilly, and make a few suggestions as to what may have led to recovery.

a) I went to my psychotherapist nearly every day for the first week of May.
b) I got the results of the second lot of blood tests, which included a low testosterone level. The doctor explained that this in itself wasn't particularly worrying, but that combined with a low level of the 'carrying agent'—the sexual

hormone binding globulin, no less!—it could explain symptoms of extreme fatigue and heavy sweating.

c) Consequently, I had a testosterone injection. This cost £50 from another private doctor. The Harley Street clinic would have charged £450! I have to concede that it was the Harley Street doctor—Doctor Two—who discovered the condition. Doctor One hadn't tested my SHBG, but when I called him he agreed with the theoretical diagnosis. He also added that his standard charge for a jab was £400 cheaper! I suppose I could have taken the attitude that Doctor Two deserved a £400 bonus, but then again, since I will require top-ups several times a year . . . the BBC don't pay me that well, and it's not covered by insurance, and you can't get testosterone on the NHS either. What I was getting was sort of the male equivalent of HRT for women. The male menopause at sixty-six! I was almost proud. On the other hand, Doctor Two put it less flatteringly: 'Your results, Mr Oddie, are much the same as a patient of mine who is nearly eighty!' OK, that might well explain the two and a half months of weariness. On the other hand, it might not.

d) The fourth factor is that my mood may well depend on the circumstances of my work. Week after week, alone at my word processor—as I was in January and February, writing this book—could indeed contribute to lethargy and apathy. A month outdoors, with a team of cheery workmates—as on *Springwatch*—could indeed make me feel happier and more energetic. Well, D'oh!!

e) There is a fifth factor that surely must have

helped. Believe me, there are few weirder experiences than trudging dolefully through busy streets feeling grim but being constantly told how well you look, or how much people enjoy what you do. Try as you might to be grateful, it doesn't have the cheering effect it should have. An inner voice—your own—whispers, 'If only they knew.' I considered wearing a badge saying: 'I know I look ok, *but* . . .' Nevertheless, a few days after returning to London, kind words and compliments finally began to sink in. So much so that I began to jot them down in my notebook, so I could read them when I felt the need for a confidence boost. Here is a selection of comments that I reread now, not through vanity but to record just how charming, friendly and supportive 'the public' can be. I can't help wishing I had been so appreciative of it back in the 1970s. Excuse me, please, whilst I bask in this lot!

From a little boy: 'Are you Bill Oddie? Wow!'

From a young woman: 'Bill Oddie! I love you!'

From two 'grungy' teenage girls: 'You do a wonderful job, mate. It's great to see nature in all its glory!'

From a cab driver, a *Big Issue* seller and a traffic warden (not all at once!): 'All right, Bill? Love the programmes!'

From a well-spoken gentleman, with an air of authority and wisdom: 'Your programmes enrich life.'

I'd like to think that bloke was God! And there were folks with longer memories.

Three blokes in a taxi who leant out of the window and sang 'Goody Goody Yum Yum' in perfect harmony!

From a lady of a certain age: 'I loved Black Pudding Bertha!' (So did I, it was one of my finest compositions.)

And a welcome bit of street cred from a young woman canvassing for Amnesty International in Oxford Street: 'I thought you were fantastic on *Buzzcocks*!' That one might or might not mean anything to you, but it meant a lot to me!
They all did. To all those people, and to anyone who has said nice things to me: thank you, thank you, thank you.

*   *   *

There was one more exchange that perhaps did more than anything to focus my determination. It was in early May, and again I was walking through the middle of London. I had just been to the doctor's. A pretty woman was walking towards me (I notice these things!) and as she passed she gave me a great big friendly smile. It was so lovely that I had to tell her, so I did: 'Thanks, I needed that.' She stopped, smiled again and spoke. 'I've got to tell you, *Springwatch*, my husband and I love that programme. So bursting with life. The birds, the buds . . . Love it!'

'So do I,' I agreed. 'I need to get myself OK to do it.'

She didn't enquire what I meant. Maybe she knew. Instead, she gave me what amounted to an order. She spoke with mock severity. 'You must do it. Nobody else is going to do it like you. So get on with it!' She smiled again. 'Please.'

Clearly I had no option.

*   *   *

So what did lead to my recovery? Was it physical, chemical, psychological, injections, medication, family, friends, company, encouragement, kindness, love? One of these, some of them, or all of them? Right now, I don't care what the explanation is, I am just mighty glad to be back to my version of normal. As I wrote earlier in this book: 'recovery happens'. Phew!

5

So where was I?

I said, so where was I?

Are you talking to me?

Yes. I'm OK again now.

That's a relief. I was getting worried.

Really?

Yes. The publisher keeps calling me and asking, 'Is he going to finish in time to get it out before Christmas?' She's driving me nuts. I keep telling her: 'I don't know. I don't think he knows. He's

237

not putting it on, you know.'

She *does* know that, doesn't she?

Yes, I'm sure, but you know what publishers are like. I even tried to make them feel guilty. I said, 'Look, it's quite possible that writing the book is one of the things that made him break down.' You know what she said to that? She said: 'Oh, I'm not surprised it's happened. It happens to most people who write their own autobiographies!'

But now that he's OK again, can he finish it as soon as possible?

Exactly.

No pressure there then! I suppose I could just not bother with the rest of my life and cut to the end—the end of the book, I mean—but I don't suppose they'd like that. How far did we get?

The end of the 1970s.

Bloody hell, is that all?! We'd better get a move on. Next question ...

To a lot of people the end of *The Goodies* was the end of your comedy career. The next time you appeared on TV you had become a wildlife presenter. Was there a bit of a gap between the two?

Yes. It was called the 1980s! In fact, I did a big variety of TV work during the eighties. All sorts of different things.

Was that diversification, or desperation?

I'd call it an intentional change of direction. A couple of things sort of forced it. One was that, for what turned out to be the final Goodies series, we'd transferred to ITV. We felt a wee bit unappreciated by the BBC. They were planning a series of *The Hitchhiker's Guide to the Galaxy*—which was great—but they told us that they didn't have enough special effects people to do *The*

Goodies as well.

So you were fired.

No. They told us they weren't firing us, but they did ask if we'd mind hanging around for a year to see if *Hitchhiker's* was a success or not. If it wasn't, they would want us to do another series. Maybe. If it was, they definitely wouldn't.

An offer you had to refuse!

Exactly. Somehow news of the situation reached London Weekend Television—I can't remember which of us phoned them—and the result was that we signed a three-year contract. In fact, we only lasted twelve months, but during that one year we earned more than we had in the previous ten! Alas, a 'new broom'— called John Burt—took over at LWT and immediately swept us out. We were in good company. Stanley Baxter got axed too.

I was a big fan of his.

Me too. Anyway, we had a decision to make. We could crawl back to the BBC, or try and move to another ITV company. In either case, we would sacrifice the money due for the remaining two years. Or we could take the loot, and declare the Goodies finally defunct.

That is what they would call these days a 'no brainer'.

Quite. So at last that headline we'd joked about whenever the three of us had any tiffs came true: 'GOODIES SPLIT!' This coincided with two other events. Graeme—my writing partner for about fifteen years—had divorced, remarried, and moved from Cricklewood to a more countrified abode beyond Oxford, near Chipping something. I had also divorced, taken up with Laura, and moved about 100 yards down the road in Lower Hampstead.

Tim had not divorced (he still hasn't) but he was

now languishing in a rather grand mini-mansion, complete with tennis court and swimming pool, deep in the Thames valley, barely a champagne cork's pop away from several other famous showbiz personalities. He began to play a lot of golf. Rather well, so I'm told.

By him?

Amongst others. Anyway, in 1983 Laura and I got married. In doing so, I acquired not only a lovely wife, but also a new writing partner. No disrespect to Graeme, but it was logistically so much more convenient working with someone who lived in the same house, and indeed slept in the same bed. And the sex was much better.

Did you and Laura get work immediately?

Pretty much so. She hadn't written that much at that stage, but she was full of ideas. The first half of the 1980s was a very happy and productive time for Laura and me. We co-wrote eighteen (three series of six) half-hour TV comedy dramas for a 'younger audience'. These were technically for children's television, but our and the producers' attitude was that above a certain age—seven or eight?—kids' sense of humour is much the same as adults', certainly when it comes to 'wacky zany' comedy, as opposed to 'grown-up' sitcom.

I'll support you on this one.

Good. It's still true, isn't it? In recent years playgrounds and school buses have echoed with catchphrases, funny voices, and re-enacted routines not from 'children's TV', but from *Little Britain*, *The Fast Show*, *The League of Gentlemen*, *The Catherine Tate Show*, *The Mighty Boosh*, etc etc.

Exactly, just as they echoed with kids quoting *The Goodies* back in your heyday.

True. Mind you, there were also some very sophisticated kids' shows then, like *Do Not Adjust Your*

240

Set, with Eric Idle, Mike Palin, Terry Jones, David Jason and the Bonzo Dog Doo-dah Band. What a cast! That couldn't happen now. Current children's TV budgets are so small that very few ambitious or original programmes are being made these days.

But there were in the 1980s?

Oh yes. In fact, one of the shows Laura and I wrote was arguably one of the most elaborate TV productions I've been involved in. It was called *From the Top*. It was based on Laura's childhood experiences at a stage school, and it featured myself as a 'mature student'. A bank manager who had always dreamt of 'treading the boards'. We had an extremely talented young cast (none of whom, incidentally, had theatrical training). A lot of the storylines were developed pretty authentically from Laura's memories, and it was quite satirical about star-struck kids, theatrical mums and indeed middle-aged men with undignified ambitions (like me). There was also a surreal element in that, at least twice in every show, there was a 'fantasy' musical number. This covered just about every style we fancied: from rock and roll to punk, funk, gospel, music hall, even 'Busby Berkeley' extravaganzas, featuring ranks and ranks of young dancers in elaborate costumes. Kids are cheap! The director of the first series was Mickey Dolenz—yes, that Mickey Dolenz, ex-Monkees. Here's one for Trivial Pursuit: when is the only time a Goody and a Monkee worked together?

From the Top?

So you *were* paying attention. Laura and I were very proud of that show, and eternally grateful to Lewis Rudd, the then head of children's TV at Central, for having the nerve—and the money—to put it on! Had we pitched such a concept at an adult level, I am willing to bet we would still be arguing what department it should come under. 'Is it comedy? Is it drama? Is it music? Is it light entertainment?' I'll tell you, whatever it was, it . . .

Bill, sorry to interrupt this torrent of somewhat self-congratulatory nostalgia, but doesn't it strike you that rattling on about shows that none of your readers remember—mostly because they didn't see them in the first place, or maybe they weren't yet born—might be just a teensy bit tedious?

Oh. Is it? Sorry.

It's OK—once! I just hope 'what I did in the 1980s' isn't going to be all about programmes we've never heard of.

Of course not. Well, maybe a few. Actually, quite a lot. OK. More or less entirely.

Mmm. I feared as much. Have you got any photos?

Of what?

You. In forgotten shows. Preferably wearing silly costumes.

Well I have, but I'd rather people didn't see them. Some of them are a bit embarrassing.

Excellent. That sounds exactly what's required.

Can't we just skip to the wildlife years?

All in good time. Meanwhile . . . bring on the funny photos!

Shall I tell you what they are of?

Please do. I'll just look at them and smirk a little!

From the Top

Of course every performer has their own personal list of roles that they would love to play. Mine included the John Travolta part in *Grease*, Howard Keel's role in *Calamity Jane*, and of course Dorothy in *The Wizard of*

Oz.

Does this indicate your love of diversity, or a serious identity problem?

You decide! And try not to interrupt. I'm doing the explaining, OK? Heaven knows, I have been called 'childish' and an 'eternal schoolboy' often enough . . .

That's true.

. . . so the part of William Worthington, the bank manager turned drama student, was pretty much typecasting. By the way, did you spot the theatrical allusion in the name Worthington? As in 'Don't Put Your Daughter on the Stage, Mrs Worthington'? Only in this case, I was a son. Geddit? Clever stuff, eh? Or maybe you are not familiar with the song. Never mind. Indulgence in such minutiae amused Laura and me. Actually, *From the Top* was one enormous indulgence, but it was also pretty popular with the young viewers, regularly attracting an audience of four or five million and—as Lewis Rudd gleefully informed us—it often outperformed *Blue Peter* and the regular cartoon slots.

So why does nobody remember it except you?

And Laura.

What about the five million?

They grew up. And lost their memories. I don't know.

I recognise that bloke top left, don't I?

You see, I wasn't making it up. That is the real ex-Monkee, Mickey Dolenz, asking us to translate the script into American so he can understand what the heck we are on about. As you can imagine, ex-Monkees and Goodies are used to having large budgets, lavish sets, and unlimited numbers of 'extras'. Ironical then that only 'kids' TV' could oblige us! I think I can safely say that everyone involved in the two series of *From the Top* had a pretty enjoyable time! It was a lot of fun.

Saturday Banana

Saturday Banana was theoretically Southern TV's answer to *Tiswas*.

It must have been a pretty silly question!

Shut up. Of course, when I was a kid, we were packed off to Saturday morning pictures. A typical bill would include comedy from the Three Stooges (who were more retarded than funny!); a cowboy adventure featuring Hoppalong Cassidy, or the Lone Ranger and his 'friend' Tonto (gay or what? and this is fifty years before *Brokeback Mountain*); and a number of cartoon 'shorts', with plenty of violence and gratuitous racial stereotyping. Any character who had been blown up by dynamite instantly acquired a black face, grabbed a banjo, and burst into a chorus of 'Swannee Ribber'.

As you would.

If we were really lucky, we might also get a *Look at Life* or a *Pathé News*, with a commentary from ☐that man whose voice instantly brings back the era of black and white newsreels. Fortunately, he is easy to impersonate, which means people are still doing him whenever a programme wishes to conjure up a 'post-war' atmosphere.

Yes. I've heard you do it. And Tim. And Harry Enfield. And . . .

Sh! Saturday morning pictures were of course eventually replaced by Saturday morning telly, which was no doubt originally based on the cinema 'magazine format', but by the early 1980s had evolved—or was it mutated ?—into the garrulous, cacophonous, untamed beast we still know today.

Oh, hello. Here we go! I sense a dose of Bitter Bill.

It's a strange phenomenon. Weekday children's TV is subject to all sorts of 'guidance' rules and regulations. Words that can't be used, subjects that can't be covered, health and safety warnings—'Don't try this at home', etc, etc. However, Saturday morning telly seems to be totally immune from such restrictions. Indeed, it seems to exist specifically to undermine any concept of politeness, good behaviour, taste, safety, or self-control. It is as if the TV company's brief is to educate and inform for five days, and then, on the sixth day, destroy all the good work that's been done during the week. Sunday morning telly doesn't need to exist, because the young audience is presumably experiencing the consequences of the TV-induced hyper-activity and subsequent Saturday night misbehaviour, and are either still out, in bed, or grounded. It could be argued that *Tiswas* should be credited—or blamed—for pioneering this genre, that still plagues our screens nearly thirty years later.

Hang on, hang on. Saturday morning programmes are not meant for grumpy old men like you.

Yes, of course, I know that, but the extraordinary thing was that *Tiswas* was! At least, that's how it seemed. For a start, it was presented by grown-ups. OK, Chris Tarrant, Lenny Henry, Sally James and Bob Carolgees were younger in the early 1980s, but they weren't kids. They weren't exactly adults either, of course. Or rather, they certainly didn't behave like adults. There were a lot of 'slapstick' ingredients—custard pies ('flan flinging'), 'gunge tanks'—and a fair smattering of *double entendres* or references you felt must surely have gone over the kids' heads. I'm sure there were people who hated *Tiswas* with a vengeance, but it was hugely popular, and had an almost intellectual credibility about it. It attracted complimentary words like 'anarchic' and 'irreverent'.

The Goodies used to get called that.

Indeed. Which may explain why I was called upon to present *Saturday Banana*, which was intended to be a rival for, and possibly take over from *Tiswas* in ITV's coveted Saturday morning slot. It was not a success. *Tiswas* was anarchic, *Banana* was chaotic. *Tiswas* was messy, *Banana* was just a mess. I have only vague memories. If any traumatic experience justified 'blanking', presenting *Saturday Banana* was it! The show was 'live'. I recall an awful lot of breakdowns. Cameras, microphones, outside broadcast links, and several producers. However, I learnt lessons that were to prove very useful in my newly sprouting career as a

presenter, mainly about what I myself could and couldn't do. I learnt that I could not feign enthusiasm, especially when attempting to interview monosyllabic pop groups. After one attempt, I refused to do any more. Neither could I be in a studio full of screaming youngsters without wanting to scream myself. I decided I would try and avoid that in future. But by far the biggest revelation for me was that I didn't get nervous doing live television, and it didn't 'throw' me when things went wrong. In fact, I rather hoped they would! I feel the same about *Springwatch*!

I noticed. Who or what is the shiny creature in the middle that looks like a reject from *Doctor Who*?
It, or he, is a robot called Metal Mickey, who got his own series, which was directed by Mickey Dolenz! Spooky connections, eh?

Was Mickey named after Mickey, or vice versa?
Don't be silly.

Sorry. And the next show you did, was?

Tickle on the Tum

After my bad *Banana* experience you might have assumed I would have vowed to avoid all children's TV, but the truth is I love doing things for youngsters—and indeed with youngsters, as long as it's 'under control', as it were. *Banana* wasn't. *Tickle on the Tum* definitely was. It was a sweet little show for a younger audience, which involved songs and storytelling. The songs were provided by legendary folk singer Ralph McTell ('Streets of London' etc). Ralph played not only the guitar, but also the shopkeeper of the general stores in the village of—did you guess it, children?—Tickle on the (river) Tum!

248

I'd got that.
Well done. Good boy. If Ralph was, let's say, 'imaginative' casting, how about me playing a physician?!
Seriously?
With a name like Doctor Dimple? It was a lovely show, with lovely people, and an even lovelier total absence of a studio audience. Mind you, the presence of other people might have made Ralph and me behave a wee bit more responsibly.
Explain please.
We are both terrible gigglers, as was demonstrated when we attempted to record our very first scene together. Up to the moment of the first take, Ralph hadn't seen me in full costume, and I hadn't noticed how much his voice sounds like Tommy Cooper's!

(Talking, I mean. I never heard Tommy Cooper sing folk songs!) Actors call it 'corpsing', when you start giggling and find it hard to stop. We found it very hard indeed. It wasn't as if the dialogue was exactly side-splitting. All I had to do was enter the shop. Ralph would look up from the counter and say, 'Oh, hello, Doctor Dimple', and I would reply, 'Hello, Ralph'. There is no way I can convey to you why it was funny. You might try saying 'Oh, hello, Doctor Dimple' in a Tommy Cooper voice. I just tried that, and started chuckling immediately! But it was Ralph who started it. He simply couldn't get past the first line. Maybe it was the word 'dimple'! Or maybe I just looked daft (which I did). I tried not making eye contact, which made him laugh even more. We got to about take six or seven, up to which point I had managed to keep a straight face. However, the next time I entered, I was confronted not with Ralph's front, but with his back. He was pretending to stack things on shelves so he wouldn't have to look at me! That's when I went! On to take eight. I was now expecting Ralph's back, so I was fine—until I noticed that his shoulders were beginning to shake. His laughter was silent, but mine wasn't! Take nine, and I came in to find that he had abandoned the shelves. Instead, he now had his head hidden completely, and was rummaging in a big cardboard box. At least his giggles were now muffled! Mine weren't. So on and on it went. Another take we both got through, but it was spoilt by the cameraman who'd started laughing because we'd got it right! At which point, the director's voice came over the tannoy telling us to 'get a grip'. He then collapsed into giggles himself. It took us twenty-six takes, which has to be some kind of record! I can honestly say I have never enjoyed myself so much in all my life!

250

Koko in *The Mikado*

If there are two things I can't stand they are opera and
Gilbert and Sullivan. So what kind of masochism was it
that led me to accept the role of Koko in the English
National Opera's production of *The Mikado*? Was I
trying to face my demons? Or challenge my prejudices?
  Or was it vanity?
Probably. I was, after all, following in the footsteps of
Dudley Moore, who had given his Koko in New York,
and Eric Idle, who'd done it in the original London
production, directed by Jonathon Miller, whom opera
aficionados will know as a director, but I can only think

of as one of the cast of *Beyond the Fringe*, which had inspired us all in Cambridge in 1960.

Peter Cook, Dudley Moore, Alan Bennett and Jonathon Miller. Right?

Right. Not a bad line-up, eh? I think I must have figured: if Koko is good enough for Dud and Eric, then surely it is the role for me.

Was it?

No. Frankly it wasn't. There was lots to dislike. For a start, the director. It wasn't Jonathon, but an ENO regular, whose name I have totally forgotten, but not his demeanour. Bitchy, abrasive, humourless and a little cruel, to the extent that he managed to reduce more than one of the female members of the cast to tears. And they weren't behaving like divas. *He* was. I think I can safely assume he didn't like me either.

Neither could I get used to the standard opera practice of 'putting in a dep'. I knew it happened in orchestras, where musicians will send a replacement if they can't make it one night. It generally works fine, as long as the 'dep' can read the 'dots'.

The music score?

Exactly. Apparently, opera singers have a similar attitude. They all know the tunes and the words, so they don't even need to rehearse. I found it a little disconcerting to find myself singing a romantic duet with a lady I'd never met before! I also took a deep dislike to the folks from what I believe is called something like the Gilbert and Sullivan Society. Every night, there was a contingent of them in the front row. They had a copy of the score and the 'libretto' in their laps, which they followed, presumably to make sure no one deviated by a single word from the sacrosanct original! As an inveterate ad-libber, I was often the target of audible tutting or sighing, and the occasional *sotto voce* 'boo'! Fortunately, Koko's big number, 'I've Got a Little List', allows—indeed, requires—the singer/actor to provide topical lyrics which he can change as often as he likes. I have no memory of the subtle satirical quips I came up with, but I got a fair number of laughs, and having that one solo kept me sane.

Any positive outcomes?

Oh yes. Most of the singers were friendly and helpful, and I did begin to appreciate how witty and dexterous Gilbert and Sullivan's lyrics were, and still are. I realised that the main reason I had disliked them was that it was a standard comedy revue device to put new words to Gilbert and Sullivan. Those readers with long memories will recall that I was whingeing about that in my last year at King Edward's School!

And Footlights auditions, I dare say.

Correct.

So would you do G & S again if you were asked?

No.

Much to the relief of the Gilbert and Sullivan Society, I imagine.

Actually I do have a last word for those pedants. Gilbert and Sullivan themselves were in the habit of constantly changing and updating their lyrics (and not just Koko's list), so it is totally against the spirit of the originals to stick rigidly to the score.

Oh dear, you are going to get hate mail.

Yeah, well, that'll teach me not to get involved with things I don't understand.

Or even like!

253

Titmus Regained

OK, I had dabbled in light opera, now how's about a spot of acting?

'Straight' acting?

I suppose it was, in so far as my part wasn't meant to be funny. *Titmus* was a TV drama series written by John Mortimer and starring David Threlfall. I played a militant bearded nature reserve warden.

So you didn't have to act at all really, and presumably they saved a bit on make-up, costume and optical equipment.

It wasn't a huge speaking part, but I got to shoot a couple of naked lovers for doing what naked lovers do in the middle of my 'patch'. That was fun.

'Sarah the Cook' in *Dick Whittington*

Panto! I suspect a lot of people would assume you did panto nearly every year.

God forbid! I hate panto. I always have. I won't rattle on about why, as I might come over as a bit of a scrooge, a killjoy, or even a curmudgeon.

We wouldn't want that.

I could even be accused of a touch of intellectual snobbery, if I were to dismiss panto as witless, predictable, exploitative claptrap.

It's a point of view. But some people would say it is traditional British entertainment.

So were witch-burning, cockfighting and gurning, but none of them deserves a place in modern society.

And none of them would cost as much as taking the kids to a panto.

And they wouldn't go on so long. I suspect you may agree with me about panto.

Let's put it this way: if Britain has one tradition it should be deeply ashamed of, panto is it.

Here here!

So was your decision to appear in *Dick Whittington* another exercise in theatrical self-flagellation? Was it aversion therapy? If *The Mikado* didn't put you off treading the boards once and for all, surely the panto would?

Well, it more or less did, but not because I didn't enjoy it. It was just so bloody knackering! I'd accepted the invitation to do the show at the Shaw Theatre in Euston, mainly because it was to be an original script with original music, which we would develop in 'workshop' over a full month. This was a far cry from

255

the 'traditional' panto, which is cobbled together in a couple of weeks from an ancient script, padded out with even more ancient gags and routines, current pop songs, and a few topical references to *Big Brother* and soap operas. What's more, the Shaw is barely ten minutes' drive from my home, so there'd be none of that 'theatrical digs' business.

If you are going to hate something, at least make it convenient, eh?

I didn't hate it, but never again. It was—as Laura pointed out—my own fault. I came up with a character that raced about like a dervish in drag, played air guitar like Freddie Mercury, and chased runaway 'freerange' sausages at a speed Linford Christie would have envied. That's all very well in rehearsal, but three times a day for six weeks! I was lucky to survive.

So that was it for panto.

No, actually. The following Christmas I was back at the Shaw, again doing the panto, but this time I had the more sedentary role of director, and co-author with Laura. We did our version of *Mother Goose*. It was more of a musical really, involving original songs, some splendid puppetry, courtesy of operators who had worked for Jim Henson's Creature Workshop, elaborate visuals, and excellent comedy performances.

And a fine inventive script, I dare say.

Anyone who saw it wouldn't be surprised that Laura and I were (and still are) huge fans of *Little Shop of Horrors* (the musical).

Great show.

Indeed. In fact, if there is one show I wish I had written, *Little Shop* would be it.

And your *Mother Goose* was that good?!

No, but it weren't half bad, and we felt it deserved a longer life than one short run. In subsequent years we tried to revive it, but never found a management interested in anything but a 'traditional' production. Puppets? A proper band? Rehearsal? No need for any of that expensive nonsense. Good old British panto, that's what people want.

Well, it's what they get!

Laura and I were disappointed at the relative failure of *Mother Goose*. People liked it, but it clearly wasn't going to go anywhere. We were feeling this about several of our projects. We had had a whole series commissioned by the BBC, six 'Scary Tales' for older children. We'd envisaged them as entirely on film, with the feel of *Ripping Yarns*. The BBC saw them as studio based, with the feel of *Rentaghost!* We withdrew the scripts, and gave them back the money.

Blimey.

We also had several 'grown-up' proposals going the rounds, and getting lost in 'development hell'. Looking back now, we were probably over-reaching and over-optimistic. Moreover, Laura was becoming increasingly miffed at producers assuming that I was the senior partner, as it were.

You were older.

I still am! But I am certainly not more creative and I wasn't then. If anything, Laura was the more prolific with ideas, and was every bit as competent as I was as a writer. She still is! Nevertheless, we would go to meetings where the questions were mostly addressed to me. I too would be miffed, especially as it was often Laura who had the answers. I could, of course, entirely appreciate her annoyance, and I also respected her wish—perhaps need—to do more of her own stuff. She had already shown me work in progress on both a children's and an adult novel. They were both extremely entertaining. She also wanted to revive her artistic talents. She is an excellent illustrator. She should have gone to art college. She now does, as a mature student.

Hang on, this isn't Laura's autobiography! It's yours. So, as the 1980s stumbled towards the next decade, it was clear that 'the times they were a-changing'?

Right song, wrong era, but yes, for me they were. Laura and I were working together less. She was working on her own a lot more. My comedy career was being replaced by more presenting jobs.

Fax

One programme I presented was *Fax*—which I think was a corruption of 'Facts' rather than a reference to a form of communication not then invented. Or maybe it referred to Filofax, which I think was around by then. Who knows?

Who cares? What kind of show was *Fax*?

It was a general interest information show, which basically answered viewers' queries in an entertaining manner. I suppose it was a forerunner of what we'd nowadays call typical daytime television. It involved guests, practical 'demonstrations', usually a bit of music, and lots of quirky, quick-fire facts and figures. Back then, it was a pretty refreshing mix. It also established a new peak viewing slot. Five till six o'clock in the afternoon.

That time used to belong to children's TV.

Well, for three series it belonged to *Fax*. Then Michael Grade recognised the potential and nabbed it for *EastEnders*. Fair enough.

Was there any wildlife in *Fax*?

There were occasional items, and I also wore a considerable selection of birds and animals on my custom-made, new-design-every-week sweatshirts, which are still doing a good job for charity as items for celebrity auctions.

Ask Oddie

Several elements from the 1980s combined on the next series I did for HTV. I presented *Ask Oddie*, in which I answered questions from young people about wildlife, the environment and nature.

Do I sense that the transition from comedy to

wildlife is gathering pace?

You surely do. If I may coin a tortuous and yet strangely appropriate metaphor, it was almost as if the caterpillar of comedy had crawled into the chrysalis of exploration, and was now emerging as the butterfly of wildlife presenting. What do you think?

I think that is not so much tortuous as bloody stupid. But I did like some of the embarrassing photos. Anyway, so that's the 1980s out of the way.

6

Work on the wild side

OK. Let's get on to the Bill Oddie that people know nowadays.

What, the ageing depressive?

No. We've heard more than enough about that one, thanks very much. You have been called 'Britain's best-known birdwatcher' . . .

Name one other *known* birdwatcher.

. . . and 'the country's leading twitcher'.

That's bollocks. I am not a twitcher. You know that. And you know why.

Yes I do, but maybe your readers don't.

So you tell them.

OK, I will. A 'twitcher' is obsessed with ticking off rarities. A sort of ornithological trainspotter. The media like the word because it sounds silly, but it isn't interchangeable with 'birdwatcher'. To make a sports analogy: every sprinter is an athlete, yes? But not every athlete is a sprinter. In the same way, every twitcher is a birdwatcher, but not every

birdwatcher is a twitcher. And you, Bill Oddie, are not a twitcher.

I couldn't have put it better myself. Oh, hang on, I have put it better, or at least I've put it exactly the same. About five thousand times. And has it made any bleedin' difference? No. Barely a day goes by when I'm not referred to as 'twitcher', in an interview or an article. Or there's a headline in the papers about twitchers' concerns about some bird conservation crisis, usually with a photograph of the wrong species and a bunch of inaccurate statistics.

I've hit a nerve, haven't I?

I should say so. I am all for the press covering wildlife stories, of course, but I'll tell you something: when you actually know about a subject, and then you read the press coverage . . . well, put it this way, I reckon about the only things you can guarantee are accurate in most newspapers are the football results. Look, it may seem strange but I am going to find my 'wildlife years' the least easy to write about.

Bill, do I sense a certain reluctance to—how can I put this?—go over old ground? Or in this case relatively new ground!

It's just that so much has been covered already. Otherwise, I am perfectly happy to talk.

So what do you want to talk about?

You should know. That's why you're asking the questions.

OK. Let's assume we have some basic knowledge. Do you mind if I précis it?

You better had, because I'm not going to.

Right, I'll keep it brief. You began collecting eggs when you were a little lad in Rochdale, and you continued to do that when you were a slightly bigger lad in Birmingham, until one day you tried

to blow a bad pheasant's egg, but it was so rancid you ended up sucking it. You swallowed some of the foul gunk that was inside, and threw up over your egg collection. Your dad made you throw away your eggs, but he bought you a pair of binoculars, and by the time you were eleven or twelve you considered yourself a proper birdwatcher. You've been at it ever since. You have written abstruse articles for ornithological publications and . . .

Sorry to interrupt, but if people want to know any more about that, it's all in my book *Gone Birding*, which is probably still obtainable from car boot sales, and I dare say traceable on the internet. And whilst I'm at it, there's also *Follow That Bird*, and *Gripping Yarns*, about birding trips further afield, and *Birdwatching with Bill Oddie*, and . . .

OK, OK, cut the commercials. I hear what you're saying. Would I be right in deducing that rather than talk about Bill Oddie the private birdwatcher, you'd prefer to delve into Bill Oddie the public wildlife presenter?

When you put it that way, it sounds a bit egocentric.

Well, aren't you?

I suppose so. But it would be an angle I've not written about before.

Good. For gawd's sake, can we get on with it now?

Yes.

OK. Phew. My first question is: when was the first time you realised you might be able to make birding a job rather than just a hobby?

Ah. Good question, actually.

Thanks. I try.

I can thank a publisher called Christopher Falkus of Eyre Methuen for that. He'd been involved with

Goodies' books in the 1970s. Maybe he sensed that I was going to need another career soon, because he asked me if I'd ever thought of writing a book about birds. Frankly, I hadn't, and my first reaction was that I had no great ambition to. I think probably I felt that I wasn't entirely washed up in the world of comedy yet. Perhaps I even thought that switching to birds might be seen as some kind of admission of defeat! Then, in October 1979, I had one of life's little revelatory moments. I was spending a couple of days on Portland Bill in Dorset, the site of a permanent bird observatory, and a rarities hot spot. One day a rare bird was indeed in the area. Something typically small, brown, and boring, and complete with a daft name: a red-throated pipit, no less. Even the 'red throated' bit is a gross exaggeration. 'Dull buffish throated' more like. Not that anyone was getting a decent view of it. It was a flighty little thing, given to zooming way overhead now and again, giving its almost inaudible but distinctive call, and then plunging down into an impenetrable cornfield and remaining totally invisible, until it chose to do another tantalising and frustrating flight. Boy, was there a lot of frustration on the Bill that day! There were twitchers (correct use of the word here) 'burning up and flogging' the area (galloping around searching), working themselves up into a right old lather and muttering about 'dipping out' (failing to see the bird), or 'gripping off' their mates (seeing the pipit when their friends hadn't), beaming if it was a 'lifer' (a new species for their list), and all in all clearly demonstrating that birders of this intensity are a unique subculture, complete with its own lore and language. I spent the rest of that weekend ignoring the birds and watching the watchers.

When I got home, I rang Christopher and

announced that I would indeed write a book, but it would not be about birds, it would be about birdwatching, and in particular birdwatchers. In 1980 Methuen published *Bill Oddie's Little Black Bird Book*. The reviewer for *British Birds* magazine called it 'the funniest book on birdwatching I have ever read'. The truth was that, at the time, there wasn't a lot of competition. *BOLBBB*, as it became unpronounceably known—may have been the first blatantly and intentionally humorous bird book, but it wasn't a piece of creative writing, nor was it full of 'bird jokes'. The point was that it was true. I simply documented what was undeniably obvious. So obvious that more than one friend or acquaintance told me—almost bitterly, I felt!—that they could have written it. My inevitably smug reply was: 'Yes, but you didn't.' Being first is sometimes more important than being best!

I am rather proud of having written *Little Black Bird Book*. Moments of satisfaction include discovering that it had become a prized import amongst birders all over the world from America to Australia. Also being told that more than one twitching husband had given it to his birding-widow wife, pleading with her: 'Read this and maybe you'll understand what makes me tick.' Whether this understanding led to acceptance, resignation or divorce I don't know. Probably all three. Most pleasing of all is that it has lasted—jargon, technology and some of the references may have changed, but the basic psychology hasn't—to the extent that it was republished in 1995, and again in 2006, and is, as far as I know, still in print, or certainly not hard to find. So if you want to read it, you can!
Yippeee!
I shall ignore that. Mind you, I did have one adverse reaction. It came from a German professor of

264

ornithology who returned his copy to the publishers with a note that read: 'I am returning this book because I was understanding that it was about blackbirds!' Presumably he was doing his thesis on *Turdus merula* (that's Latin for blackbird).

Yeah, yeah. Show-off. I don't suppose it's ever struck you that the professor might have been having a joke? 'You see, we German academics do have a sense of humour!'

I'd never thought of that.

No. Anyway, have a think about this. *Little Black Bird Book* sort of combined comedy and wildlife, and you carried on doing comedy shows (co-written with Laura) during the 1980s. At what stage did you decide to give up on the comedy entirely, and switch to wildlife?

It wasn't a conscious decision. I never thought of it that way. Though, as it happens, it had been suggested to me.

What, by somebody who didn't think you were funny?

I hope not, after working with him for so long. It was John Cleese! I suspect it was in 1989 when we did an anniversary edition of *I'm Sorry I'll Read That Again*. It was probably at the drinks party afterwards. I clearly remember John saying: 'Bill [we were on first-name terms, you know], you ought to become the David Bellamy of birds.' I don't recall him adding: 'After all, you never were funny!' I suspect that I responded fairly coyly by quipping that I could never be a David Bellamy, because I didn't have a silly enough voice. In case David B reads this, I only used the word 'silly' for comedic effect. The correct word is of course 'distinctive'. In fact, I wasn't being entirely flippant. I honestly do believe that if a presenter is to become

265

really, really famous, one of the requirements is that he or she can be easily impersonated. I don't mean just by impressionists either. It doesn't take a Rory Bremner or John Culshaw to do a recognisable David Bellamy, or David Attenborough. Roll your Rs and bellow, or tilt your head and whisper (I leave it to you to work out which is which). The previous generation of impersonators had Hans and Lottie Hass, and Armand and Michaela Denis. And it's not just wildlife presenters: Patrick Moore, easy. Magnus Pike, Barry Norman, David Frost—anyone can do any one of them. But my voice simply hasn't got what it takes. I've seen and heard 'myself' on *Dead Ringers*, and I was more like Captain Birdseye! I haven't even got a strong regional accent. There's a teeny bit of Lancastrian, perhaps, and a soupçon of Brummie, but it would take an expert to detect them. I suspect Alan Titchmarsh realises that he may have the same problem, but he's working on it. Have you noticed how his Yorkshire vowels are getting broader and broader? Or is it meant to be Lancastrian? Anyway it's 'oop north'. Maybe I'm mistaken, but I could swear he was once a cockney. He is getting more impersonatable by the week, but he'll never make it to the very top. Gardening, yes, but not wildlife. Titchmarsh the new Attenborough? I think not!

Since you mention him, do you think there will ever be a 'new Attenborough'?

Millions of people can do the voice, yes, but someone with the status, the presence, the authority, the dignity, the knowledge and the ability to convey enthusiasm and information with so much charm? Never. He is literally a historic figure. That's exactly why there will never be another like him. We are at a different stage of history now. There may be excellent presenters and great broadcasters, but they simply can't achieve the status of a worldwide icon, whose name, voice and appearance is synonymous with a whole aspect of life on earth. David is 'the' wildlife superstar. A unique pioneer. Only one person is unique and you can only pioneer something once, so no, there will never be a 'new Attenborough', any more than there will be a 'new George Best', or a 'new Joni Mitchell', or a new anybody! It's TV producers and record companies I blame. Let's appreciate people for what they can do, not who they remind us of. Every presenter, performer or artist has 'influences' and inspirations, but individualism and originality are surely the most exciting ingredients of creativity. Not just following a trend. Of course, I am not just talking about wildlife programmes, so I'd best not get all worked up about this one. Let's stick to the subject.

You mean 'you'.

That's not fair. This is a bleedin' autobiography. It's supposed to be about me, isn't it?

As long as it's interesting.

That's not for me to judge. Next question please.

OK. So *Little Black Bird Book* was your first wildlife book. Or, to put it another way, the first time you got paid for doing something about wildlife. What was your first wildlife television? How did that happen?

Of course, all through the comedy years, I kept birdwatching, and I occasionally—well, nearly always— mentioned it when we did interviews. We also incorporated my 'specialist knowledge' into *The Goodies'* scripts. I was particularly proud of my authentic choreography of the mating dance of the dodo, interpreted by Tim Brooke-Taylor and myself dressed up in dodo suits. By heck, we were wacky back in them days.

And zany. And madcap. Perhaps even surreal.

No, that was Python. No one ever called *The Goodies* surreal. It sounds too much like a compliment. We didn't appeal to the sort of people who use words like that. When Python was called 'silly' it was irony; when we were called 'silly' it was an insult.

Bill, stop it. Let it go. Back to birds, and don't let that happen again.

Sorry. As I was saying, my birdwatching hobby wasn't exactly my guilty secret. I wasn't ashamed of it. Although it should be said that it was a bit more embarrassing back then than it is now. These days, it's quite hip to be into birdwatching. There are several young rock groups who revel in it: British Sea Power dress their stage with birds. Vic Reeves and Bob Mortimer are both birders (by the way, they are both silly and surreal). Rory McGrath has now officially outed himself ornithologically, and nicked a title I sort of thought of as rightfully mine. His recent book is called *Bearded Tit*. Although it nearly backfired on him. He told me recently that when he was due to do a promotional interview on BBC Breakfast TV he was asked to refrain from saying the title of his book, because it was too rude! Rory pointed out that it was the actual name of a real bird, as well as being an irresistible and self-deprecating play on words. That is, incidentally, a very wise ploy: insult yourself, before anyone insults you. In my case, it's too late. I was called a 'bearded tit' in a Jasper Carrott sitcom many, many years ago. At least my 'character' was. I can't believe it hasn't happened since, as at least three well-known journalists practise regular Oddie-bashing.

Are you going to name them?

Oh, all right. There's Victor Lewis-Smith and A.A. Gill, neither of whom I've met, and I have no idea why I qualify for their vitriol list. And there is Jeremy Clarkson, whom I have met, and publicly been a bit critical of, so it's fair enough if he makes the occasional quip about me. In any case, 'insult banter' is one of the things that Jeremy is good at. In fact, I'd feel a bit neglected if he didn't have a go at me now and again.

You've done it again. You have gone off on a tangent. Please, just for a paragraph or two, try and stick to the point.

Which was?

I asked you what was your first wildlife job on telly, and how did you get it?

Oh yes. Actually I nearly got to it when I mentioned BBC Breakfast, but then I did go off on a tangent, didn't I?

Yes. Are you back now?

Yes.

So your first birding programme was on breakfast telly, then?

No. Or, rather, yes. But not BBC Breakfast. It was for TVAM. It was early days, and they weren't doing terribly well. They were rescued by Roland Rat, remember? 'The rat that saved a sinking ship.' For those of you too young to have seen Roland in his heyday, he wasn't a real rat. He was a puppet. Rather profane, vulgar and scurrilous, as I recall. As a rat should be. Which I shouldn't say, because typecasting animals can be very detrimental. I'm serious. Snakes, bats and spiders all suffer from poor public images they don't deserve, and they are disliked or even persecuted accordingly. Rats get the worst deal of the lot. They probably indirectly finance the whole pest control business. And electricians must benefit from all that cable gnawing. Right little money-spinners, rats. As TVAM discovered, much to their relief.

269

Bill . . .

Sorry. I'm digressing again, aren't I? Anyway, I was pre-Roland, when TVAM was still trying to uphold the worthy broadcasting values that had no doubt won them their franchise in the first place. Intelligent, dignified, socially responsible, all that kind of thing. I recall that David Frost was one of TVAM's founding figureheads, and he was busy qualifying for a knighthood, which he was eventually awarded, presumably for 'services to quality broadcasting', rather than telling old jokes, or indeed hosting *Through the Keyhole*, which, incidentally, also started on TVAM. And, as it happens, who do you think was one of the 'celebrities' on the very first show?

I can't imagine. Hey, it wasn't by any chance you, was it?

Yup.

Your house was particularly televisual then?

Yes. I suppose it was.

It wasn't chosen because you lived about half a mile from the TVAM studios, so it was convenient and cheap? Let's face it, you were on a sort of local emergency standby list for TVAM in those days.

I used to get calls at the crack of dawn. 'Bill, the archbishop hasn't turned up. How quickly can you get down here? Five minutes? Great. Thanks, mate.' 'I don't have to talk about God, do I?' 'No, no . . . talk about anything you want.'

And no doubt you talked about birds. 'Birds? Again? Oh, that's fine. Just get down here, quick.' And you did. Perhaps the offer of a more regular job was a reward for you being so often available and living so close.

Or perhaps it was because I was quite good at talking

270

about birds, and other wildlife. Give me some credit, please. Anyway, I'm afraid I don't remember the name of the charming producer who called and suggested it, but I ended up doing a regular Saturday spot called *Wild Weekends*. Frankly, it wasn't often strictly speaking terribly wild—more city farms and animal rescue centres—but it was great experience for me as a presenter. Something which I was of course doing more and more of during the 1980s.

Fax, *Saturday Banana*, that sort of thing?
Exactly.

So, because of the TVAM thing were you instantly headhunted as the next David Attenborough? Or maybe the next Johnny Morris?
No. But obviously more producers were aware that I was quite knowledgeable, especially about birds, and that I didn't have to hide behind a character, as on *The Goodies*. I was comfortable being myself.

But surely your character on *The Goodies was* yourself? You weren't really acting, were you?
Mainly over-acting I'd say, but that was the point. Our Goodies characters were sort of exaggerations of ourselves.

Tim denies that.
Well, he would, wouldn't he?

He says he hated his character. He was a pathetic wimp, and a coward, and grotesquely patriotic and . . .
. . . and very funny. Tim was as he was because Graeme and I wrote him! To be fair, he had to act more than us. Which he did brilliantly. Graeme was acting quite a bit too.

And you?
OK, I was probably acting the least. But then again, maybe that's why I've always felt comfortable being

myself on television. Instead of talking to Tim or Graeme, I began talking to the camera.

Surely, though, as a presenter you don't have to stick to a script?

Well, Tim and Graeme would say I never did stick to the script! So not much change there then. As it happens, mind you, nearly all presenting is completely scripted, especially the stuff delivered straight into the lens. What they call a PTC—a piece to camera. I don't think it's exactly a trade secret that nearly everything is on autocue. Presenters have to be able to read! Some do it better than others. Some manage to disguise the fact by blinking and shifting their eyeline from side to side. The more confident ones paraphrase some bits, rather than just read it verbatim, but it's dangerous to ad-lib too much, because there are only five or six lines on the autocue screen at any one time, so it's easy to get behind or ahead, or lose your place completely. A skilled autocue operator will be constantly aware of the presenter's style and delivery, and will control the scroll accordingly. I haven't used autocue for many years, partly because when I did rely on it (as on *Fax*) I soon discovered that I was incapable of not mucking about with the words and the timing. I couldn't even manage to do things the same way twice. I was an autocue operator's nightmare.

So, in a way, your incompetence and lack of discipline have dictated your style of presenting.

If you must put it that way, I suppose so. My defence would be that hopefully when I am talking to camera or commenting on whatever the wildlife is doing, I don't sound scripted. Because I'm not. I'd like to think it's more natural.

I think I'll give you that one.

Said he begrudgingly. But thanks. Funnily enough, I do

need to be told now and again why the people who like what I do, do like it. If you see what I mean. I know it could be attributed to my depressive nature, but I've had quite a few periods of time over the years when I really couldn't believe I was any good. Not because I didn't receive some really nice compliments, but because I myself didn't rate what I was doing, and that was because all I was doing was being myself. Maybe a bit of me felt embarrassed at the idea of thinking, 'Hey, I am really impressed with myself', or even worse, 'I'm really natural, aren't I?' But that kind of self-directed coyness was only part of it. What I really had trouble with was that it was 'too easy'! I am well aware that it is often said that being relaxed and unselfconscious on camera is one of the most difficult things to achieve. I'm sure it is, if you can't do it. But if you can, it's hard to see what all the fuss is about. I dare say that sounds appallingly arrogant, and it may well be, but believe me it can also be a very uncomfortable feeling. At times, I have felt I am a complete fake, so much so that I have questioned the validity and value of what I do. And all because I don't find it difficult! This is the downside of 'just being yourself'. I find myself thinking: 'All I'm doing is what I have done for years, except now I'm doing it on camera, for an audience of a couple of million people. What's so clever or hard about that?' It's a horribly self-centred attitude, completely discounting the fact that so many people are watching, and presumably enjoying—and maybe even admiring—what I'm doing. It's as if I am thinking: 'Ah yes, you lot may think I am doing good work, but I know better. I'm fooling you. I am a con artist. I can even fool you about my feelings. I am a better actor than you—or I?—think. I can do enthusiasm, I can do excitement, I can do shocked, I can do sad. You'll think I am being natural, but am I? Am I even being truthful? If I'm not, does that mean I am not being myself at all?'

Bill, this is getting into pretty serious stuff. Are you saying that you feign most of your emotions on the telly?

No, definitely not. I am saying that when I'm down, I feel as if I do. I am also aware that I could if I wanted to. But the giveaway—and the truth—is that I only get into such a negative mood when I am not actually making the programmes. When I am out there, with the camera crew, looking for or watching the wildlife, I never feel like that. I am not saying that on occasion I haven't had to 'reproduce' a reaction. Even doing more than one 'take' diminishes the spontaneity. There are times when I have to commentate on what the cameraman has filmed, rather than what I am actually seeing myself. I'll be honest, there have also been a few—very few—occasions when I've managed to get excited about a creature I haven't seen at all.

Bill, maybe I should stop you there. You do realise that if you are about to confess that you 'cheated' on a BBC programme, the Director-General will probably have to resign? It'll be on the front pages of every newspaper.

Great. Good publicity for the book. It's OK, this happened long ago, long before everything on television was true. I was filming up in the Spey valley in Scotland. I had never seen a pine marten. For several hours, I and the crew sat staring at an empty garden where we had been told pine martens frequently visited the bird table to dine on scraps. We saw nothing. Meanwhile, our specialist wildlife cameraman, Andy, had gone off to pick up more Scottish specialities, and GVs (general views, meaning pretty shots of lochs, mountains and forests). Whilst he was out, he got a call from a local source saying there was a 'banker' pine marten visiting a garden some way away from where we were based. The problem was we were running out of time. We had to fly back to London the next day. My producer, Stephen, had to make a decision. Should Andy go and have a bash at the distant animal, and if so, should I go with him? The first answer was yes, Andy might as well go, though there is no such thing as a 'banker' animal. Wildlife doesn't stick to a script, any more than I do. But the second answer was no. I still had scenes to finish by the hotel, and we just didn't have time to nip off on a fifty-mile excursion that might be fruitless anyway.

Cut to (as they say in the movies) the final hour before we were due to drive to Inverness airport. We were packing our cases, when Andy arrived back from his quest. It had been successful. He had got great close-ups of a pine marten scampering around on a bird table, grabbing a large jam sandwich—which is, by the way, along with peanut butter, a marten's favourite food!—and galloping away down a garden wall. Fantastic! But then again, damn! Why hadn't I gone with Andy? Because it would have been logistically impossible, that's why. 'Never mind,' said Stephen consolingly, 'you can add a voice-over saying "There's a creature round here I have never seen, but our cameraman has . . . and to prove it . . ." Then we show Andy's footage.'

What happened next I take full responsibility for. 'We could do that,' I said, 'but it would be so much better if I was actually there, looking through a kitchen window, and turning back to the camera, and getting all whispery and thrilled about seeing my first pine marten.' Stephen agreed: yes, that would have been great, but it hadn't happened, nor could it happen. At which point, I led him into the kitchen of the hotel. 'Here is a kitchen,' I said. 'There is a window.' I opened it. 'There is the back garden. There is a bird table, and there is a garden wall. The only thing there isn't is a pine marten. But we have pictures of one, close up on a bird table, by a wall in a back garden, just like this one. What's more, if we put a monitor [a small TV] outside, I can watch it from the kitchen window, and I can simulate seeing the animal. In fact, I *would* be seeing the animal. Indeed, don't show me the film yet, and I'll be seeing it for the first time.' Stephen reminded me that it wouldn't count on my British mammal list (you can't tick things seen on the telly, unless you keep a telly list). He felt uncomfortable about it, but he reluctantly agreed to perpetrate the deceit. After judicious editing, it looked totally convincing. Both I and the pine marten were clearly in the same place, looking at each other, and we both gave excellent performances. I swear no one has ever questioned the authenticity of the sequence, and it is so good it has since been repeated several times. However, I stress again that I am the guilty one, not Stephen, who still works for the BBC and therefore would not benefit from being held responsible for bismirching its impeccable reputation. It was me what did it, guvnor. Governor-General, I mean. If you really feel you must fire someone, how about Ant and Dec?

So! Pine marten-gate, eh? That scandalous deception happened on one of your BBC series, yes?
Bill Oddie Goes Wild, if I remember rightly.

Was that immediately after the TVAM gig?
Of course not. In the late 1980s and the first half of the nineties I did various wildlife orientated telly things, the more memorable or disastrous of which I have

written about in previous books, so I'm not going to do it again now, as that would weaken my case for trying to get them republished. It's worth a try. The show I was most proud to be associated with was *Bird in the Nest*, which was a week's live telly in 1994 and again in '95 and was very much the precursor of *Springwatch*. I co-presented with Peter Holden from the RSPB, and our roving reporter was Simon King. There was a companion book at the time—which may still exist somewhere—and more recently I wrote about it in the *Springwatch* book, which is definitely still purchasable in all good bookshops (and quite a few crappy ones). I will say no more, as I dare say Hodder and Stoughton are getting miffed at me plugging books that they didn't publish.

OK then, let's get back to your transformation from comedy person and kids' show host into a proper grown-up wildlife presenter. At what stage did you think: 'OK, I am now something else'? I mean that in the literal rather than the outmoded hippy sense.

I guess it would have been in the mid 1990s. By then I was not unknown to several important producers at the BBC Natural History Unit, based in Bristol. Especially following on from *Bird in The Nest*, on more than one occasion, I was told that if I had any ideas for future projects 'please let us know'. I did let them know. I presented them with several proposals. And just to prove that someone had read them, or at least received them, I was sent an equal number of rejections. I have had all sorts of things rejected over the years, not just natural history proposals, but also comedies, dramas, documentaries and panel games, so I can comment authoritatively on the matter. Rejection letters tend to be short, unenlightening and quite possibly untrue. The most honest ones just say 'No.' A more verbose version reads, 'This is not for us at this time', which is more cruel because it can be taken as a vague implication that it might be for them some other time, presumably in the future. This way you run the risk of getting your hopes up, and the TV company runs the risk of you pestering them, asking, 'Is it time yet?' To which the honest answer is: 'No, and it never will be!' The version that is probably a lie is 'We have something similar currently in production.' I really hate that one. The only smidgeon of consolation is that it must be a good idea, because they are already doing it! The shattering blow bit is that not only will that company not consider your version, but neither will any other. BBC, ITV, Channel 4: we may assume they are on different sides, but they all know one another, they all meet up and gossip—mainly in bars—and many of the individuals are constantly interchangeable. Most writers will have had the galling experience of taking a rejected proposal to a 'rival' company, only to discover that the person who turned it down has moved jobs. He won't have changed his mind. It is perfectly possible to get the same project rejected by the same person at several different companies. That is pretty distressing, but what is utterly infuriating is when you have an idea rejected, and then turn on the telly a few months later and see much the same format being made by the people who rejected your rather-too-similar-for-coincidence version.

Some might call that stealing!

Others would call it business. The company thus accused will call it 'parallel thinking', which is not only suspicious but insulting, since it implies that your idea is so obvious that every one has thought of it. You might consider suing, but you can't copyright ideas, and the

278

truth is that totally original concepts are rare indeed. What's more, the best ideas are often the most obvious. In other words, 'parallel thinking' is a proven phenomenon, and usually neither a lie nor a lame excuse. Mind you, it is still narking when it happens.

Has it happened to you often?

Fortunately, no, and I certainly don't feel I have ever been ripped off (or gripped off, as the twitchers would have it). Mind you, I might just mention that I did offer the BBC a proposal some years ago that involved live reportage of the wildlife in a rural setting. I likened it to a 'wildlife soap opera'. I called it 'Rookside'. I am not saying it bore anything but a coincidental minor resemblance to, for example, *Wild in Your Garden*, which begat *Britain Goes Wild*, which begat *Springwatch*, but I did experience a tiny tremor of pique when the BBC starting publicising their new project as a 'wildlife soap opera'. Mind you, I'd nicked that catchphrase from *Bird in the Nest*. In any case, I was in them all, and they were all successful, so who cares who thought of which ideas?

You?

No, I don't. Not really. It's just that it is nice to be appreciated, and if someone has a good idea, a bit of acknowledgement doesn't go amiss.

Do I sense another of your paranoid hobby-horses galloping towards us?

If I'm honest, yes. Though it's more of a hobby-pony. A shetland pony at that. It's just that I suppose during 'the comedy years' (as you call them) I was used to getting a writing credit, because I wrote the scripts, with Graeme or Laura, who also got a credit. What's more, no one 'interfered 'with the script, unless lines had to be cut or changed because of censorship or it was over-running. Even then we, the writers, would be

279

consulted. It was also generally assumed that the person (or people) who had written the script had also thought of the idea. This was true of most TV comedies of my era. Galton and Simpson didn't just write the dialogue for *Steptoe and Son*, they created the characters and the whole scenario. Of course, they needed great actors to bring it to life. The Goodies may not have been great actors (speak for yourself, I hear Tim and Graeme muttering), but we did provide the concept and the script, but we didn't always get the credit. It was one morning back in the late 1970s that I realised who the important people were, and who the important people thought were important!

I am talking about producers. In particular, one legendary producer: Lew Grade. I don't want to question showbiz history, but I dare say quite a few present-day producers might well wince at the notion of Lew Grade representing their kind. But boy, did he have the quintessential image of a producer! A living caricature indeed. A big man. Round bellied. Chubby. Balding. Waistcoated. Besuited. Probably had a black overcoat with an Astrakhan collar, and a Homberg hat, and always—but always—smoking an enormous cigar. Jewish, of course (that's not a comment, just a fact). He was English, but he could have stepped straight out of a Hollywood musical about showbiz. 'Lew the pro-doocer'.

He was probably more accurately described as an 'impresario', but the point was that Lew Grade had the power and the finances to put on shows, TV series and movies. Which was why we—the Goodies—were in his office, discussing the possibility of a Goodies film. It never happened, but that isn't the point of this story.

What is the point?

The point is that the first thing Lew asked us was

'Who's your producer?' At the time it was John Howard Davis. The name clearly impressed Lew, more than we did. 'John Howard Davis, eh? He produced Monty Python too, didn't he? Clever boy!' Now, I am not saying John wasn't a clever boy—he was a child actor, the original Oliver Twist no less—and he became a clever man, directing several successful shows, and serving as a Head of Comedy for a while. And yes, John had produced and directed *Python* and *The Goodies*. But he didn't think of them, and he didn't write them. Nor, of course, would he claim to have done. Nevertheless, it was clear from Lew's instant reaction and continuing statements that, as far as he was concerned, the creative force behind any project was 'the producer'. I had to bite my tongue off not to break in and protest: 'Look, no disrespect to John Howard Davis, but he is a BBC staff producer/director. I'm not even sure he gets to choose which shows he is assigned to. No doubt he could refuse if he really hated whatever he was being asked to produce, but in our and Python's case, he didn't. He does a perfectly good job as a studio director but, as it happens, the bits of *The Goodies* people tend to admire most—the filmed visual sequences—are directed by an ex-editor called Jim Franklin. John certainly didn't 'discover' or even commission *The Goodies* or *Python*, let alone have the idea or write the script.' A few years later, I would have been tempted to add, 'Any more than you, Sir Lew, invented *The Muppets*! You bought them and brought them to Britain, yes, but Jim Henson was the genius ...'

Bill, stop. Now. I'm sure it's doing you some kind of good to get this off your chest, but this has to be the most irrelevant tangent you've gone off on yet! What on earth has this bitter, paranoid diatribe

about producers got to do with you getting your first wildlife series on the telly?

Ah well, it might surprise you. If you'll let me explain.

Go ahead. Surprise me.

The lesson that meeting with Lew Grade should have taught me was that if you want to get a project done, you need to get the support of a producer. If you can allow him or her to believe that they thought of the concept rather than you, or that at least they have changed it so much that it becomes as much theirs as yours, so much the better.

That is a very cynical attitude. Also quite an insult to many people who do an entirely necessary and very difficult job.

Are you acting as my conscience? Or just being a crawler, so I don't antagonise people who employ me?

I am merely reminding you that putting on a show is a co-operative effort, in which the role of producer is absolutely crucial.

I know that now. In fact, I've known it for ages. Laura and I would never have got our shows on children's TV had it not been for Lewis Rudd at Central and Peter Murphy at HTV, but they were in charge of whole departments, they weren't *just* producers.

What do you mean by that?

I mean that when I started pitching ideas to the Natural History Unit, I didn't appreciate that things worked a little differently there. I was still in comedy scriptwriter mode. I had an idea. I wrote a 'proposal', and I delivered it straight to the top man or woman. Here it is, take it or leave it.

And they left it! In the bin.

Yes. Until . . . guess what? Until I got together with . . . a producer.

Ah, so it had finally sunk in. You had learnt a

valuable lesson.

Not really. It was a complete accident, but a very fortuitous one. I was part of a team doing a sponsored bird race round London. Raising money for charity by seeing how many species you could see or hear in a day. I was frantically scanning a reservoir with my telescope, trying to tick off a couple of new ducks, when another birdwatcher graciously invited me to look into his eyepiece, which he had already focused on exactly the birds we 'needed'. I thanked him, and immediately turned away to race back to our car, in such a tizzy that I didn't even realise we had met before. His name was Stephen Moss. A fellow birder, a part-time journalist, and a full-time television producer. Stephen well appreciated that the frenetic schedule of bird racing does not allow for relaxed conversation. There was only time to ask me one question: 'Bill, have you ever thought of doing a TV series about birding?' The rest is history.

So you owe it all to a producer?

Exactly. You didn't expect that, did you?

Well, I did actually, because I know how these things work. I also know how you work, or how you wish you could work.

How's that then?

If you had your way, you would do just about everything yourself. You'd write the script, present it, direct it, and maybe even shoot and edit it. You are a potential megalomaniac. The only thing that stops you being one is that it is physically impossible.

That is absolutely not the reason, actually. The reason is . . . it is much more fun working with other people.

And more productive?

Not always, but it can be. When it is, that's the most

satisfying thing of all: working with people who are really good at what they do.

Like Stephen Moss?

A perfect example. As soon as I had recovered from the bird race—they are seriously knackering—I met up with Stephen to compare our ideas. These days, they'd call it 'brainstorming'. I prefer to call it a chat. We agreed on just about everything. We wanted the series to deal with the skills and experiences of birdwatching, as much as with the birds themselves. The only debatable point was whether a programme should be place or subject 'led'. In other words, are the items linked by a common theme, or do we explore one particular location? We settled on the latter. At the beginning of May we did three days' filming at the RSPB reserve at Minsmere, and early in 1997, BBC2 broadcast the first episode of *Birding with Bill Oddie*.

Presumably Stephen worked at the Natural History Unit.

No. At the time he was with 'BBC Learning', the 'educational' department, based in London. I dare say our series was filed under 'outdoor leisure', or some such category, but Stephen convinced the powers that be that it would be educational enough to justify its existence. Viewers would certainly learn things. Even if it was that they *didn't* want to become a birdwatcher! The discomforts and frustrations of the hobby became an integral part of the shows. We showed it like it is, or can be—for better or worse—and the viewers liked that. One of the most popular sequences involved me being driven around a Scottish forest for five or six hours searching for a capercailzie (a huge but elusive Turkey-like bird) and seeing absolutely nothing! At the end of what was truly an excruciatingly unproductive morning, my guide—a somewhat deadpan Scottish wildlife warden—came up with an exquisitely irritating punchline: 'Well, Bill, I'm actually rather glad we didn't see anything, because that means they are safe in the forest!' I couldn't see how letting me catch a glimpse would have endangered them, but I knew what he meant.

Do you still do your programmes for BBC Learning?

No. Everything I have done since that first series has been for the Natural History Unit.

When did you switch?

I'm glad you asked me that. The first series of *Birding* had just gone out and been well received. I was in Bristol for some wildlife event. At supper, I was sitting by the then head of the unit. He introduced me to a film-maker from Canada. 'This is Bill Oddie, he's doing a series for us at the moment.' At which I truthfully interjected: 'Well, it's not actually for the Natural History Unit, it's for Learning.' He then asked me the question I was willing him to! 'Why aren't we making it?' Answer: 'Because you turned it down!'

Not long after that, Stephen and I were invited for an agreeable pub lunch by the head of the NHU, who was gracious enough to ask us if we'd mind the Bristol unit sharing the production with London. Mind? To be able to use the expertise and the archive of the NHU would be invaluable. So series two was a co-production, still British based. Series three was our European series, a concept we stretched a little by including Florida! By that time I, Stephen and our team had transferred entirely to HQ in Bristol. We have been there ever since.

How many series have you done now?

Roughly speaking, I have done a series more or less every year since that first one. Many, but not all, with

Stephen as producer. In more recent years, he has diversified, which I forgive, though I'm not sure about leaving me for Alan Titchmarsh. He also produces natural history books at a superhuman rate. Since the dawn of the twenty-first century, as well as my own series, I have had the immense pleasure of being involved in BBC2's annual live broadcasts, culminating in *Springwatch* and *Autumnwatch*. Read all about them in the official *Springwatch* book, which is alas not published by Hodder and Stoughton. There are also a few DVDs available, though in my opinion not enough. And that's about it really. Can I go now?

No, you cannot. I have several more questions.
About wildlife presenting?

Mainly, yes. Some of them only require you to give short answers, though I'm not sure you are capable of that.
I will try. Fire away.

When you first starting doing programmes for the Natural History Unit do you think some people resented you as an ex-comic muscling in on their patch, as it were?
Mmm. Probably. Nobody ever made me feel that way, but I could well understand it if they had regarded me with great suspicion, as some kind of gimmicky experiment. There were people who didn't much approve of having any visible presenter at all, let alone me. For a kick off, it makes a series harder to sell worldwide and therefore to get co-production money for, especially from the Americans, such as the Discovery Channel and National Geographic. If you ever see any wildlife TV made in the States it's almost invariably presented by a famous Hollywood actor or actress—I saw Richard Dreyfuss do rather a good one in the Galapagos. At the very least, they'll get someone

286

famous and recognisable to do the voice-over, so you spend half the programme trying to figure out who it is. Imagine the arguments at family viewing time: 'Never mind the friggin' lion being swallowed by a ninety-foot snake, is that Jennifer Aniston or Goldie Hawn doing the commentary?' Any visible presenter can present a problem. Unless it's Attenborough, the universal authoritative icon, or a 'character' like the late Steve Irwin, on whom you will get no further comment from me. There certainly were film-makers and producers who felt strongly that any human presence in a wildlife film distracts from and dilutes the 'purity' of the genre. There still are. I can understand that. Surely, though, one of the brilliant things about wildlife as a subject is that it can be presented—in the widest sense of the word—in so many different ways.

Of course you are not the only one. Ex-comic gone serious, I mean.

Exactly. Mike Palin, Terry Jones, Tony Robinson, Stephen Fry, Bill Bailey. Not a bad club to belong to! But of course as well as comedy, the other thing that we all have in common is that we are all rather well educated. MAs and B.Sc's abound. I don't think any of us deserves to be called a gimmick! We know what we're on about.

Well, that covers that one. Not a short answer, and maybe a teeny bit defensive, but OK. Actually it leads me to a pretty inevitable question. Do you prefer being involved in comedy or wildlife?

Well, obviously, first of all, I'm going to say that I have been fortunate enough to have enjoyed careers in both. I'm certainly not going to say I prefer comedy, because that would suggest I'm hankering after a past that can be no more, which would be sad. I might also add that I've been involved in the right things at the right age. Madcap knockabout comedy is a younger man's game. It hurts! Nowadays, it would probably kill me. Presenting nature is a far more dignified and appropriate activity for a man of a certain age, or indeed older. If I must make insidious comparisons ...

Which you must.

I would have to say that I definitely prefer the *people* who are involved with wildlife to those in the world of showbiz. As the song says, 'There's no people like show people'—is that good or bad?—'They smile when they are low.' How wise is that? I am all for 'putting on a happy face', but if it is only a mask, it'll end in tears. Is that profound or facile?

A bit of both.

Ah well, yes, you see, that's my answer to 'which do you prefer.' I enjoy a bit of both. There is one very important thing that comedy and wildlife series have in common. They are both television. I think of a wildlife programme as a show. The viewers are an audience. If they are not entertained, they will switch off. The definition of 'entertainment' may vary. The audience may be amused, thrilled, moved, impressed, fascinated, informed, even educated, but the one thing they mustn't be is bored. That is a thought I always have in my head when I'm working on a sequence: 'This could be boring. Whatever the subject is, it could be fascinating, but it could be boring.' To pinch a phrase from the world of comedy: 'It's the way you tell 'em.' That refers to jokes, and it is very true. It also applies to drama: 'It's the way you act it.' In the case of wildlife, it is the way you present it.

However, I don't mean it's all down to the presenter. There may not even be a presenter. With a wildlife show it may be the way it's filmed; it's most definitely the way it's edited, and the way the soundtrack is used;

and—perhaps above all—it's the way the story is told, in pictures or in words. The latter may well be the responsibility of the presenter, i.e., me. The first requirement of my job is to engage the audience. In that sense, I am doing a performance, and some of the criteria are much the same as in acting, be it comedy or drama. You must make the audience understand and listen to what you're saying. Quite literally. No mumbling, don't go too fast, or too slowly, don't use words they won't understand, avoid esoteric jargon, help them focus on what you want them to see or hear, and convey your enthusiasm, and any other emotions you are feeling. Timing is vital, so space your comments and information. Above all, the audience must believe you, and believe in you.

Blimey. That lot sounds like a drama coach's notes on how to play Hamlet.

Maybe, but it applies just as much to presenting as acting. Which doesn't mean of course that presenting is acting. It is not pretending (except in the cases I have confessed to in this book!). Unlike acting, the cardinal rule is 'be yourself'. But just make sure yourself isn't boring!

Bill, I don't want to lead you into a contentious area . . .

But . . .

but what you've been going on about sort of implies that you think some presenters are boring.

Not just presenters, the whole presentation. I thought I'd explained that clearly enough. Obviously I am failing to live up to my own standards.

No, it's my fault. I wasn't concentrating.

That's my fault too. I lost your attention.

Maybe, but you've got it back now. Especially if you will honestly answer my next question. Are

there things that you dislike or even hate about other wildlife programmes?

Wow. No names ... but ... OK, what do I hate? Actually 'hate' is far too strong a word. Let me be a little more oblique. There are things that I personally try to avoid in my series, mainly because they are clichés. Predictable music for example. I know a fair number of viewers don't like music at all on wildlife programmes, and I can understand that, if only because nature itself often provides a far better soundtrack. My rule tends to be that if there are natural sounds available, don't cover them with music.

But Bill, you always have music on your shows.

That's true, but here's my excuse and my argument. Firstly, it's not always my decision.

Buck passing, eh?

It could be the director or the editor's choice. I may have been overruled, or I may have concluded that it's not so intrusive that it's worth arguing about! Or indeed I may have agreed that the music has enhanced the mood or the atmosphere, just as good movie music can. I would also claim that if you replay one of my programmes and dissect the sound track ...

How sad would that be?!

... most of the music is over the 'linking' bits. The travelling shots (my car rattling through the countryside, or me walking, which is more environmentally friendly). Or over the GVs (the scenics). If at all possible, we use 'local' music. For example, no Scottish glen would be quite complete without the distant skirl of the pipes.

A cliché if ever I heard one.

OK, but some things become clichés because they are appropriate. My favourite travelling music was during my American series—*Bill Oddie Back in the USA*—

290

because that allowed us to use all those great 'on the road' type songs. Chuck Berry, Canned Heat, lots of bluegrass and blues. Those who have read this far will be well aware how obsessed I am with music! So that's my excuse. For me, music used intentionally and meaningfully can enhance the wildlife experience.

But some of the clichés you are not so fond of?
Some are so corny they should be avoided. I'm sure you know what I mean. As soon as a bird soars to a certain height, it changes gear down into slow motion, and in comes the 'flying' music. In the old days, it was usually flutes and harps. Then they invented synthesisers, and it became synthetic 'ambient' music—New Age waffle. In recent years, there is often the addition of a female wordless vocal. I'll swear there is a generation of viewers who believe that some species flap at about two beats a minute, and call like Enya.

Other rarely avoided clichés include the inevitable 'spring is here' and 'the flowers are opening in slow motion' music (often similar to the 'birds in flight' tunes); the mournful 'winter is coming' music, and of course the ominous low-pitched chords that precede the entrance of any predator. Musical equivalents of *jeux de mots—jeux de musique?*—are deemed almost obligatory to accompany and distract from the usually decidedly unromantic coupling that animals and birds go in for. I can't object to that—I'm sure we've done it more than once (which is more than can usually be said for the wildlife)—but I do think it's a shame to opt for the soppy rather than the raunchy. I mean come on, if you want proper rutting music let's have a really obscene Prince track, or how about the climax of 'Je t'Aime'?

Is there a French theme developing here?
No. The French don't do wildlife. Except on menus.

291

Any more clichés?
That's French too.
So it is. Anyway . . .
Storyline and commentary clichés. There are hundreds of them. Mind you, I have to partially accuse the creatures. We who make wildlife programmes go on about showing 'interesting behaviour'. Of course what we really mean in most cases is 'misbehaviour'. Animals and birds fighting, fucking or eating one another. The standard storyline is in itself a cliché, because nature isn't terribly inventive or imaginative when it comes to the basic circle of life. Whether it is hedgehogs, hummingbirds or hymenoptera (ants, bees, wasps, etc), a year in the life has much the same ingredients, and so therefore do many of their movies. Start in winter. Photogenic snow and ice. It appears bleak and empty, BUT there is life. Cut to creature, either hibernating or struggling to survive. BUT there are signs of spring. Cut to spring arriving. Our creature (they are always 'ours') perks up, and possibly fills up on newly available food. BUT love is in the air. He or she sets off to find a mate. BUT 'our' male has a rival. Rival males fight, maybe to the death. BUT our hero survives. The female joins in or admires some kind of mating dance (display) and then allows the winner to fertilise her. She produces eggs or babies. All is going well, BUT a predator pounces and eats some of the offspring. BUT others are protected by the plucky parents and survive. BUT soon the leaves will turn to gold. Autumn, a time of plenty, and lots of lovely scenics. BUT our creature has work to do. The weather may still be fine BUT winter is coming. Cut to snow again. And thus it has always been, and always will be, and frankly would we have it any other way?

I have provided and spoken the 'script' for countless

films with essentially this storyline. It is inevitable. What's more, it is dramatically satisfying. The ideal plot. Nature is a very competent playwright. She knows the rules: a good story must have a beginning, a middle and an end. You could call it a cliché, but it is also a winning formula. It is also what happens. It is true.

So what are you whingeing about?

Well, some wildlife commentaries are awfully . . . bland. Is that the word? I call them BUT scripts. You listen the next time there's a wildlife film on. Count the 'BUTS'! The truth is they were probably written by the director, or a researcher, or maybe the editor. Someone whose main job is not writing.

So you write all your own scripts?

Well, yes. Or rewrite the ones I'm given. I sometimes keep some parts.

How magnanimous of you!

It's not ego. It really isn't. It's just that I may be a presenter and a voice-over, but for most of my life I have mainly been a writer. I'm not the only one. The usual suspects: Mike Palin, Terry Jones et al. You look at the credits: it says 'presented and written by'. That makes sense.

Look, I hear what you're saying, and I understand that it's important to you, and not entirely because you are a megalomaniac, but I am sure there are some people who can't stand *your* commentaries, no matter how much time and effort you have put into searching for the *mot juste*, or honing your metaphors, or whatever it is you writers pride yourselves on. I'm willing to bet there are viewers who wish they could cut out the commentary and the music, and just watch and hear the wildlife.

Fair enough. Let's face it, that is exactly what I enjoy doing myself when I'm out there for real.

So, why are you on the shows at all? What's the point of you presenting? What are you trying to do?

That's a bit aggressive for an alter ego.

I'm not an alter ego, I am a devil's advocate. I am giving you a chance to explain your 'mission', if you have one.

Well, I do actually. I'm not sure I'd call it a mission, but there are things I'm trying to do. First and foremost I am trying to create (or help create) an entertaining TV show. Have I already said that?

Yes.

Well, I've just said it again.

You also said you keep telling yourself, 'This could be boring.'

So?

It is. Tell me something new. I want to know what you are trying to do for the viewers as well as just entertaining them.

OK. Well, you may remember I did a couple of series called *How to Watch Wildlife*. A decent if dull title, but the shows did exactly what it said on the tin. I told people where to go, what to look out for, how to identify it, all that sort of stuff, but I hope it did more than that. I wanted to call it 'How to *Enjoy* Wildlife'.

Why didn't you?

They wouldn't let me. Anyway, what I try to do in my programmes is not only to demonstrate the mechanics, the techniques, as it were, but also to convey the experience, the emotions. If I can put over the fact that *I'm* fascinated and having fun, then hopefully viewers will think, 'I wouldn't mind having a bit of that myself.' To which I reply: 'Well, you can. Keep watching, because I won't just tell you where to go and what to look for, I'll try and teach you how to look, how to appreciate, how to feel even. In other words, how to enjoy wildlife as much as I do. Possibly even more!' I hope that doesn't sound patronising or pretentious.

No. It could sound a bit 'worthy', but hell, just because I work for the devil, why do I have to be so ungracious and mean to you? Spreading enjoyment sounds a thoroughly laudable aim.

Blimey. Thanks. Let me tell you something that will make you laugh.

Now you're getting cocky.

A journalist (don't know who, but I applaud him) once defined the difference between my and David Attenborough's style of wildlife programmes. He said: 'It's as if Attenborough's are *Playboy* "centrefolds", and Oddie's are "readers' wives"!

That is funny. And true.

I totally agree. Mind you, you have to have seen 'that kind of magazine', as it were. For those who haven't—is there anyone?—I'd put it this way: Attenborough shows you things you can never see or have, I show you things you can. Either way, the outcome is hopefully enjoyment. Of course, the other big difference is that his series have enormous budgets, mine don't.

In other words, you are cheap.

So was that crack. And clichéd. I preferred you when you were being nice.

Tell you what, I've allowed you to get awfully serious about programme making for quite some time now.

I appreciate it.

OK, but I reckon it's time to soften the mood a little. Some more light-hearted questions. Have you ever had a near-death experience?

In pursuit of wildlife, you mean? Only one that I was

aware of at the time. I suspect Laura and I may have been in mortal danger on our honeymoon. I took her with me filming in Papua New Guinea.

Cheapskate.

It was very memorable.

I dare say it was. In those days there were headhunters and cannibals, weren't there?

Oh yes. We didn't get eaten or have our heads shrunk, but I think we may have come pretty close to being murdered.

You think?

We'll never know the whole truth, but if you want to know more ...

Don't tell me, you've written about it in—which book?

Follow That Bird. It could be republished any minute. However, I have never written about the time I nearly drowned.

Now's your chance.

I wasn't literally filming that day, but I had been. In the Seychelles, in the Indian Ocean. Again I was with Laura. I owed her a second honeymoon (I still do!). We were having a couple of days on the very aptly named Bird Island. Literally millions of birds nest there—mainly terns. However, it wasn't birds I was in pursuit of, it was marine life. The Seychelles were the first place I tried snorkelling, and it remains the only place where I have actually enjoyed it, or indeed managed to float rather than choke and flounder. But I did nearly drown— despite the fact that I'd set out to explore a fantastic coral reef in no more than two or three feet of water. I do not dive. I have a great aversion to being submerged. If I get out of my depth, even by a few inches, I panic. Neither would I knowingly ever take a risk. OK, I had chosen not to wear flippers that day, but

296

that was because the water was so shallow I could walk back if my feeble attempts at the breaststroke let me down, which they would if I had to swim more than ten yards! It takes a lot to get me into the sea, but close-up views of tropical coral reef life are among the things that can lure me. So there I was, alternating between treading water and floating on the surface, utterly captivated by fish that looked as if they had been painted by a modern artist (they are called 'Picasso trigger fish'!), plus shoals of tiddlers that light up like neon, the occasional octopus, and corals of every shape and colour. It is one of the ace Natural History clichés to call underwater 'another world', but it surely is. What's more, on Bird Island it wasn't creatures of the deep, it was creatures of the shallows.

I was loving being one of them, until I suddenly realised that I could no longer see the reef below me. In fact, I couldn't see anything at all below me. Just seawater. I wasn't just out of my depth, I was entering the abyss. I didn't panic immediately. I managed to turn round and try to swim back towards the shore. Then I panicked. The sea was totally placid, but there was a current pulling at me as strongly as a tug-of-war team. It wasn't actually sweeping me further out, but it was preventing me getting in towards safety. I tried all my other strokes: doggy paddle, splashing around, and finally sinking. I was also choking from the water gushing down my snorkel. I ripped off my mask, and began yelling and waving frantically during the few seconds I could take a breath or stay afloat. Through my half-open, salt-stinging, spray-spattered eyes I could just about make out two figures on the beach, lying under a sunshade. They were apparently fast asleep. I yelled louder. Loud enough to wake one of them. A bloke. He seemed to be looking in my direction. I waved at him. He waved back! I know it's an old gag, but I swear it's true. Then he shouted out 'Hi!' and waved again as one would do to a friend, rather than at a drowning man. It was almost as if he knew me. The feeling was mutual, but at that moment I was convinced we would never meet again, whoever he was. At the same time, I had two horrible thoughts. One was that if he did know who I was, he would be assuming I was just fooling around, acting the giddy goat, as an ex-Goody was supposed to do. The second thought was, 'I am going to drown.' Fortunately, the continuation of that thought was to decide to shout it out loud several times, 'I am drowning! I am not joking! Drowning!'

Thank the Lord—or my theatrical experience—for clear diction and good voice projection. I may not have had acting lessons, but I sure can make myself heard! The man got the message, raced into the surf, and swam strongly and rapidly in my direction. Before rescuing me, he greeted me by name: 'Bill! How are you doing?' A question which I answered only after he had grabbed me in a reassuringly authentic life-saving grip, and towed me back to the shore. 'I'm better now, thanks!' I assured him. We did indeed know each other. 'Bill! Fancy seeing you here!' 'Freddie! Blimey! And Jane!' A slender blonde uncurled herself from under the sunshade, and greeted me cheerily, possibly totally unaware that her man had just saved my life. I soon told her. Later I told Laura, and everyone else on the island. And I have been telling people ever since.

You were a twit to go snorkelling without flippers. I know, and I was dumb to be so entranced by the fishes that I didn't realise I'd drifted out beyond the reef. As it happens, apparently it is a 'circular' current on Bird Island, so if I had relaxed and lain on my back, it would simply have carried me round and round the shoreline, and I suppose I could have waved as I floated past the hotel, and somebody would have rowed or swam out and got me. BUT (and this is an entirely justified BUT) that someone wouldn't have been Freddie, from Rod, Jane and Freddie, the hosts of *Rainbow*! The only thing that could have topped that was if I'd been rescued by Zippy and Bungle!

I'm rather glad I asked you that question. And—I might as well admit it—I'm rather glad you survived.

That's one of the sweetest things you've ever said to me.

I mean it, I may seem a little abrasive sometimes, a bit sarcastic maybe, as if I don't really take you very seriously, or maybe don't respect what you do, but I don't mind saying that, over the last fifteen or so years, I reckon you have done a pretty decent job.

Thank you. What about the fifty or so years before that?

There was some good stuff—successful, popular and all that—but let's face it, what you were doing then wasn't so—how can put this?—valuable? useful? important? You know what I mean.

I think I do, but I also think you are wrong. The comedy years—as you insist on calling them—may not have been so overtly worthwhile or something, but actually I am very proud of having been involved in a fair number of things that entertained quite a lot of people. Making people laugh is a pretty useful service, I reckon. It can be quite important too. Believe me, it is one of the best definitions of 'job satisfaction' if somebody tells me that a show I've been involved in has affected their life –for the better, of course!

Perhaps listening to *I'm Sorry I'll Read That Again* got them through the stress of exams. Maybe watching *The Goodies* was the only time in the week the whole family got together. I have had people come up to me in record shops and say my show (now long gone) on Jazz FM introduced them to music they'd never heard before and now love. That's really good to hear.

And I dare say people have told you that it was you that got them into birds and other wildlife, right?

Yes, it has happened. Very kind of you to mention it, though I suspect you're only trying to get me off comedy and music and back to nature.

You know me so well. Five years ago, you were awarded some kind of medal, weren't you?

I wondered when that was going to come up.

An OBE. You are Bill Oddie OBE! Weren't OBEs a running joke on *I'm Sorry I'll Read That Again*?

Yes. And on *The Goodies*.

And haven't you always been quite scathing about the Queen's honours?

I have been quite scathing about the Queen's all sorts of things actually.

You are not what people would call a royalist, are you?

I suppose not.

You are more what people would call an anti-royalist?

I suppose so. At least, a non-royalist. Where is this leading?

Bill, knowing you as well as I do, what I can't help asking is: Why on earth did they give you an OBE? And why on earth did you accept it?

The official reason was 'For Services to Conservation'.

Do you think you deserved it? No offence

intended, but I wouldn't call you a conservationist.
Neither would I.

So you didn't deserve the OBE?
That's not for me to say, is it? But it does lead me on to
your second question: why did I accept it? I presume
you are implying, 'considering I am not a royalist'.

**Sort of, yes. Plus, frankly, I had you down as
exactly the sort of person who would reject a gong,
because it would suit your anti-establishment
image.**
Fair enough. I thought I was that kind of person too.
However, I happen to know that the so-called Queen's
honours list isn't entirely the personal choice of the
Queen. How could it be? She's had a sociable life, and
she's travelled a bit, but she can't know everybody.

**Maybe she ropes in a few other royals and they get
to nominate a few of their favourites.**
In which case, I'd like to think Prince Charles and
maybe one or two of those young princes might have
put in a good word for me. And I once met Princess
Anne at the Chelsea Flower Show, in the Wildlife
Trust's garden, and she didn't ignore me. I can't
remember what she said, though. Something like 'Nice
garden', I expect. I do remember what Princess Diana
said to me at a big charity do. She stopped right by
me, looked me up and down and said: 'I see you've
dressed up for the occasion!'

Had you?
By my standards I had. I had a clean T-shirt, at the very
least. I gave her a 'cheeky madam!' type look, and we
both laughed. Well, we both smiled. It wasn't exactly a
Will Carling relationship, but it was sweet. Of course
the fact that I had been seen in public bantering with
Diana certainly wouldn't have helped get me on the
honours list. No doubt Prince Philip had me struck off

immediately. That's probably why it didn't happen till relatively recently. Forgive and forget sort of thing.

Bill, would you please just answer one bloody question simply and clearly? Why did you accept an OBE?

Because I know that support for my nomination would have come from people I know, and maybe have worked with, and whose approval I would genuinely be honoured to receive. I know this is how the process works, because on more than one occasion I myself have been asked to write a letter of 'recommendation' for someone who has been nominated. So I have to assume that several of what you might call my peer group (which by the way doesn't include any peers!) 'voted' for me, as it were. I decided that to then turn down the award would be ungracious and indeed ungrateful, if not slightly insulting. Added to which, several members of my family fancied a day at the Palace.

Was that fun?

Actually yes, it was a lot of fun. I was only allowed three guests. Kate (my eldest) volunteered to miss out on the treat, and I dare say was glad of the opportunity not to go! She is more susceptible to the pressure of her principles, and I don't think she'd mind me saying that a day with the royals is not really her thing. Added to which, she has plenty of 'famous' friends from the TV and movie world and, let's face it, celebrity spotting is one of the reasons to go to a gong-giving day. Bonnie was certainly up for that. So were Laura and Rosie. With them it's 'anything for a laugh!' As it turned out, the celebrity spotting part was a bit of an anticlimax. It takes several days to get through all the presentations so, though everybody knows the full list of recipients, you don't know who you're going to get on your day.

We were hoping that David Beckham would be top of the bill, but he was a couple of days later.

So who was the most famous celeb on your day?

Me. How disappointing was that to my lot! And to me, actually.

Had you—as Princess Di would put it—dressed for the occasion?

I certainly had. Though, contrary to popular belief, you don't have to. I can't imagine that anyone would voluntarily choose to wear the garb of ridicule and torture that is 'top hat and tails'. It sounds so frivolous and flighty, doesn't it? 'Top hat' conjures up magicians and white rabbits, and Fred Astaire, whilst 'tails' sound like what you'd wear at a fancy dress party where you come as your favourite animal. If only! I would happily have worn a ring-tailed lemur's fine appendage, or a fox's brush. Though had I sported the latter, I dare say a proportion of those present might have instinctively yelled 'Tally-ho!' and pursued me with dogs.

Who do you mean?

No names! Of people, or dogs.

So you didn't wear top hat and tails.

Very few people did. Like I said, anyone on the list is sent a cheery little letter some weeks before the event, which says quite clearly that 'formal attire is not obligatory'. How cool is that?

Aren't there any other sartorial stipulations? Such as 'smart casual', or 'no jeans or leather jackets', or 'you will not be admitted if you are barefoot or topless'?

Nope. It doesn't even mention suits and ties! As it happens, though, I did buy a dark suit especially for the occasion. I don't look forward to wearing it again, because it will be at a funeral. I never wear a tie, because it gives me severe claustrophobia of the throat. On the only occasions I have worn one it has been only a matter of minutes before I have had to loosen it. I look like Frank Sinatra after a rough night!

'It's quarter to three, there's no one in the palace'! Get it?

Very good, but of course far from the case. There were thousands of 'guests' in the main hall, and hundreds of us gathering in an anteroom, waiting to be briefed by a very tall shiny gentleman called, I believe, a royal equerry. I'm sure there are lots of jokes and aprocryphal stories thereto attached, but I'll leave those to Graham Norton. First, we were divided up into MBEs, CBEs and OBEs. We didn't actually have to put our hands up, but I'm sure many of us were clocking which group people we'd been chatting to were joining, and there was quite a bit of muttering about which BE was most prestigious.

I think number one is a C (commander), number two O (officer) and number three M (member). They're all quite good of course. The BE bit isn't so good, as it stands for British Empire.

Which is perhaps reason enough to turn it down?

I've been through that one. I didn't, OK? As we shuffled around into our teams, I was glad I hadn't. I was beginning to appreciate that this was a fantastic 'people experience'. There were lots of what I'll call 'ordinary' people. People who do things that are easy to define. It may be their job, or charity work, but they are good at what they do, some of them outstandingly so. What's more, what they do is also good for other people. They are providing a service, they bring care, comfort, hope, and—yes —even pleasure. That's why sports and showbiz celebrities deserve this kind of 'official' recognition. It is surely *not* because their activities contribute to the national economy—which is an argument I have heard mooted in the past. It is because they have, in the broadest sense of the word, entertained millions of people, and thereby made a considerable contribution to many, many lives. I am not, of course, saying that that is *why* singers sing, actors act and sports personalities play whatever they play, but they still deserve recognition and indeed gratitude. However, there were also many people in that room whose altruism is far from 'accidental', who are simply dedicated to helping others and, in doing so, help us all.

In other words, they 'benefit society'.

Exactly. Medical research, human rights, social work, charity work, and so on, all represented by ordinary people who are stars in their own right, but who need no audience to applaud what they do.

I'd call them, by any standards, pretty extra-ordinary people.

So would I.

So, why do you call them 'ordinary'?

Well, I suppose because, in my opinion, they are living in and benefiting the real world. I understand what they are doing. Anyone can. But there was another type of person in that room. I am not sure what to label them (and any label may well be judged unfair) but I wouldn't call them 'ordinary'. I don't understand what they do. I don't understand the world they live in. That's probably at the root of why I feel uneasy at the very idea of royalty, and aristocracy, privilege, the gentry, posh people. How could a lad from Rochdale feel any other way?!

So you felt you sort of didn't belong?

Not with 'them', no. They were mainly men and some of them stood and walked with what I suspect was a military bearing. I presume they were being honoured for military activities. Others were being rewarded for

services to 'government', 'business' and 'industry', none
of which I can ever believe is free from some element
of dodginess. There were also people who presumably
were long-serving members of the royal household.
Chief corgi walker, or polisher of the Queen's horse
brasses, that sort of thing. Call me totally prejudiced if
you like. . .

You are **totally prejudiced.**

I know, but there was a divide in that room. We used
to call it a division of class, but we don't use that word
any more, do we?

But it still exists, doesn't it?

Of course it does. It was definitely 'us' and 'them'.
Anyway, I lurked in the back row, like a naughty
schoolboy whispering in class, but the reassuring fact
was that I was by no means the only one. I suspected
all of 'us' would have been in the back row if it were
possible. There was a kind of nervousness in the air, but
it stemmed from a feeling of 'what on earth am I doing
here?!' Several people said exactly that as we were
herded into queues, and very slowly began shuffling
towards the door that presumably led to the main hall,
the audience . . .

. . . and her!

The first surprise as we emerged into the wings, as it
were, was that the music, which I and others had
assumed was being piped from CDs, was actually being
played by a live band. A small giggly group of us had
been conjecturing that maybe the Queen used these
interminable ceremonies to catch up on the 'latest
releases'. Maybe HMV send over a selection of the sort
of stuff they think she might like.

Such as?

I have no idea, though Her Majesty was once quoted
as saying she always leapt to her feet at the first bars of

Abba's 'Dancing Queen', because 'One loves to dance and it is about one!'

Not true, apparently, but a nice thought.

Yes, but now we realised that it wasn't a recorded soundtrack at all. At the back, above the packed auditorium, was a balcony full of musicians. And it wasn't a polite orchestra playing favourites from Classic FM, it was a rollicking ensemble driven by a solid rhythm section of drums, bass and electric guitar, with blaring brass and swinging saxes. They were dressed in ceremonial military uniforms. At the time, I assumed this was because it was 'the band of the Queen's Own something or others' regiment', but looking back, I wonder if it was meant to be a tribute to the golden years of British trad jazz, when bands were in the habit of dressing up in costumes. Dick Charlesworth's City Gents wore dark suits and bowler hats, Acker Bilk's lot had stripey waistcoats and again bowlers, and I'm sure I remember quite a few who went in for the military look, though I'm blowed if I can remember their names. Presumably they wanted to look like New Orleans marching bands, or maybe they'd gone for a Sergeant Pepper look.

Bill, I'm sure you'd love to think the music was laid on specially for you, but it seems more likely that the repertoire was chosen by Her Majesty.

In which case, she is clearly a big fan of Hollywood musicals. The equerry's briefing had already been accompanied by the distant strains of *The Sound of Music*, and as our queue edged ever closer to the Queen's podium (it wasn't a proper throne) we were being regaled with selections from *South Pacific*. I kid you not, I stepped forward to receive my OBE to the tune of 'There Is Nothing Like a Dame!'

Do you think she was getting you mixed up with

Tim Brooke-Taylor? Anyway, the next question is what anyone who has been introduced to the Queen will inevitably be asked by the next people they meet . . .

I know the one: 'What did she say? What did she say? What did she say?' It is in triplicate, because it was asked by Laura, Rosie and Bonnie, almost perfectly synchronised.

So what *did* she say?

You don't expect me to answer immediately, do you? You have to relish these moments, you know.

Did she know who you were? Did she recognise you?

I don't think so. Which was a bit of a relief, because I really wouldn't have blamed her if she'd said: 'Oh, it's you, is it? The ex-Goody. You lot kept having a go at me and my family, didn't you? I only used to watch it for that Tim Brooke-Taylor. He was more our class. Double-barrelled name, went to Winchester College. I know he was only acting when he pretended to fancy me, but I'll tell you, I wouldn't have kicked him out of bed! I mean, given a choice, Prince Philip or TBT, who would you shag? But you, you scruffy little oik, I only gave you an OBE to see if you'd take it. What a bleedin' little hypocrite you are. OBE, OBE—joke, joke. But now it's "Oh, thank you, ma'am. I am so honoured." Yeah, sure. Well, I'm not giving it to you. Better still, take it, and give it to Tim. Oh, and tell him "Nothing Like a Dame" was specially for him. Now buzz off. I always preferred *Python* anyway!'

Finished the stand-up routine, have you? What did she really say?

Actually, I don't think she did recognise me. There is an equerry who stands by her, and he whispers in her ear. Presumably he said something like 'He does wildlife television', because, when he called me forward, she said: 'It must be a nice job making television programmes about something you enjoy.' It was more of a statement than a question, but I was presumptuous enough to respond. I was just beginning to say, 'Yes, Ma'am, it's great. I suppose your equivalent would be doing TV shows about corgis, or horses'— which I thought was a nice chatty line—when the equerry gave me a stern look that clearly said: 'No talking. That's it. Go!' At which point, I committed a breach of etiquette that is probably punishable by life imprisonment in the Tower of London. I turned my back on Her Majesty!

Surely the equerry told you not to do that during your briefing?

Several times. 'Just say, "Thank you, Mam" (not "marm") and, whatever you do, back away from her.' I didn't mean to do it. Honest I didn't. It's just the natural movement after someone has given you something. You say thanks, turn, and walk away. Who the dickens walks backwards? And indeed why? Surely Her Majesty is not offended by the sight of a clothed backside? Indeed, if you were allowed to wear real 'tails'—like maybe a bunny's—it would be a laugh for her.

Yeah, and I bet she could do with a chuckle after two hours of handing over medals to people she doesn't know, accompanied by songs by Andrew Lloyd Webber.

Or maybe she gets possessed by an irresistible urge to goose an unguarded male rump. Specially if you got confused, turned away and bowed. 'OK then, matey, you're asking for it.' Pinch! I bet Diana would have done that, had she ever become Queen. Anyway, no sooner had I turned away, than I realised my crime, and I executed a spin turn that Fred Astaire would have been proud of. I almost wished I *had* worn top hat and tails. And maybe it was my imagination, but I could swear I heard the band strike up that very tune as I exited the hall. 'I'm putting on my top hat ...'

Sounds like a fun day out for all the family.
It was. And hey, Your Majesty, if you are reading this ... only joshing.

So, is it worth having an OBE?
Do you mean are there any 'perks'? Does it 'open any doors', as it were? None whatsoever. It didn't even help me get decent seats at a Prince concert (despite the royal reference).

Have you ever worn it?
Once. At the BBC Natural History Unit's Christmas Party. It had a 1920s theme. I went as a striking worker (the general strike, I mean) wearing a cloth cap, collarless 'grandad' shirt, hobnail boots, and my medal. I said it was a political statement, but actually it was anything to avoid wearing a suit and tie. All the other blokes wore full evening dress, and—even more disappointingly—not one of the girls wore a headband or one of those sexy short flapper dresses with fringes round the hem. There was also a grave absence of Charlestons.

Bill, I am going to play devil's advocate again. There may be people who will be offended by how facetious you are about the honours list, and what it means to be awarded something like an OBE.
My response to that is twofold. My facetiousness—as you call it—is in no way directed at the brilliant people who are 'honoured' every year. However, there are aspects of the whole palaver that I don't feel terribly reverential about, and I am sure I am not alone in that. 'Cash for honours', 'old-boy networks', outmoded ceremony, privilege and snobbery, all that sort of thing.

310

But listen, if you want me to wind this up on a serious note . . .

Go ahead.

If my trip to the palace had been scheduled for a couple of weeks later, I would not have gone. I undoubtedly would not have accepted the OBE, and I would have publicised the reason why.

So what happened two weeks later?

Blair and Bush invaded Iraq.

7

And finally . . .

Bill, we are getting towards the end.

I wish you'd stop saying things like that.

I only mean the end of the book.

I know that, but you have the air of one who is about to ask me 'looking back' type questions.

Well, you are no spring chicken.

No, but I am organic and free range, and I've lasted quite well, and I hope to be clucking around for a little longer. I like what Jane Fonda said in her autobiography. When she turned sixty she regarded it as the start of the next phase in her life. Not necessarily the last!

Surely I can ask you to look back on your life so far without making you feel you are uttering your last words on earth?

It might depend on the questions. Carry on then.

Well, you know the kind of songs you are supposed to sing when you get to 'this stage in life'? Like 'Non, Je ne Regrette Rien', and 'I Did It My Way'?

311

Yes.

Well, how do they apply to you? Do you have any regrets, and did you do it your way?

At this point in time—and I probably have to face the fact that it is not very likely to change that much in whatever future I have left (thanks for reminding me)—the answer to both those questions would be yes. Yes, I have lots of regrets, and yes, I did do it my way. Which is one of the regrets, because my way wasn't always so good. I have to say, I think those are two of the crassest songs ever written. Both are incredibly arrogant, utterly self-centred, and frankly stupid. Nobody, surely, can get through life without there being a few things they wished had turned out differently? And what kind of an excuse is it to say, 'I know I was a complete bastard, but at least I was a bastard in a different way from all the other bastards'? Both those songs sound like guilt talking. Methinks they do protest too much.

I only asked. I'd still like to know the answer.

I told you, 'Moi, j'ai beaucoup de regrets.'

So what are they? What do you wish you had done, but you didn't?

The first one won't surprise you. I wish I had learnt to swim when I was a kid. I was good at most other sports, so my housemaster assumed I could swim, and put me in the relay team. I kept trying to tell them I couldn't swim, but they wouldn't believe me, until I took over the last leg three yards in the lead, and sank! Mind you, let's look on the bright side: if I had been a decent swimmer I wouldn't have been rescued in the Seychelles by Freddie from *Rainbow*!

Any other things you wish you'd done at school?

I should say so, most of them involving—or rather not involving—girls. I was a very late starter, but I made up

312

for it eventually. The thing I really regret is that I didn't learn to read or write music. It's not that I am not musical. I am very musical, I'd be dumb to deny it. I've written hundreds of songs, and sung them, and I can muck about on several instruments, but staves and 'dots' mean nothing to me. They say it's easier to learn when you are a kid, but then I know lots of people who were put off by pedantic music teachers.

But what if you'd had a good teacher?

Actually, I'm not sure it would have made any difference. In 2006 I did a programme for the BBC in a series called *Play It Again*. It should have been called 'Play it for the First Time', because the idea was that a celebrity (isn't it always?) learnt to play an instrument that they hadn't tried before. Jo Brand learnt the organ, and Aled Jones the drums. I chose electric guitar. My teacher was very patient and, as it happens, very attractive too, but I remained almost totally immune to being taught the correct guitar techniques. But that experience did teach me something about myself. I finally had to accept that I am sort of unteachable. I don't know whether it's impatience or misplaced confidence, but I have to do it myself, or not at all. The same applied to sport. I was naturally a fair tennis player, but I had a lousy backhand. People kept urging me to have a few coaching sessions, but I just couldn't do it. For years I ran round anything on my backhand, and took it on the forehand instead. I had a vicious forehand!

Do you still play the electric guitar?

Yes, I do. I had the pleasure of interviewing Mark Knopfler, and Dave Davies of the Kinks, both of whom were self-taught. Their advice was: 'Just play. Listen to records and play along, and play with mates, especially if they are better than you. Only play what you enjoy.'

That's when it struck me that that's what my attitude has been to more or less anything throughout my life. I only do things I can enjoy without having to take lessons, study or practise. It's not that I am lazy. I work almost obsessionally on the things I get fun out of. I play the guitar nearly every day. But I do it my way!

Badly.

Who cares? No one's listening except me! To me it doesn't sound too bad.

Next regret please.

Well, it's not unconnected with my inability to be 'tutored'. I am utterly inept when it comes to current Information Technology.

In other words, you are crap with computers.

I wouldn't know. I haven't got one!

Blimey. Don't you even use e-mail?

No, but that's partly self-preservation. I used to be inundated with viewers' letters after a show like *Springwatch*. I simply couldn't cope. Now, though, everyone sends e-mails, so I never get them, which—much as I love the viewers—I am quite glad about. The big problem is not that I ever feel an urgent need for a computer, it is that my incompetence sometimes makes me feel desperately inadequate, as a human being. This would be almost comic, if it weren't for the fact that, if I am in a depressive state, my sense of being 'left out', or unable to communicate, can become really quite overwhelming.

So why don't you just learn how to use a computer? Take lessons.

What? Like I did for the guitar?

OK, teach yourself. It's not difficult.

I dare say it isn't, but I can manage with my word processor, so I've never got round to a proper computer, and once I'm feeling confident again, I don't care!

Is this something you've only had problems with in recent years—since computers, as it were?

No. I used to feel totally intimidated by Graeme Garden's typing! I wrote my parts of the scripts in scrawly longhand. He typed his parts immaculately. If he wanted me to change something, it was no problem to scribble out some new lines, but I used to feel terrible about asking him to re-type stuff. It looked so neat, it seemed sort of 'set in stone'. Graeme had to reassure me that he really didn't mind typing it again, so if I had suggestions, speak up! Of course, these days writing partners just bung e-mails at one another. Another reason for giving up comedy!

So, let me get this straight, you regret not being able to use a computer?

Sometimes. And if I don't get round to it, I suspect I will regret it even more in the future. What do you think?

I think you're being pathetic! Any other things you wish you knew about, or that make you feel inadequate?

There are lots. I am very good at making myself feel totally ignorant. A visit to the accountant does it within minutes. I haven't a clue what they are on about. Politics, physics, cars (I'm quite proud of that one), most of history, and supposedly great literature. I hardly ever read proper books.

Didn't you study English Lit at Cambridge?

Yup. That's probably why I don't read any more. Pedantic tutors. Great at killing enthusiasm for just about anything.

Bill, I have one more cliché for you: 'It's never too late!'

It will be one day.

You know what I mean.

I do, and I agree actually. I dubbed 2007 'the year of the guitar' and 'the year of the video camera', because I started filming wildlife myself. 'Bill's Wild Wobblycam'. There could be a series in it? 2008 so far has been 'the year of the autobiography'. Maybe 2009 will be 'the year of the computer'.

That's a much healthier attitude! Talking about the future . . . have you still got ambitions? Things you want to do before . . .

. . . before I go?

Or before you are no longer capable of doing them.

Oh yes, that's a much nicer way of putting it. Not! I'm sure I have already said that the main thing I'd like to stick around for is to watch and enjoy—no, revel in— the progress of my daughters and my grandchildren. They are all capable of doing special things, in fact most of them already have. Kate was a terrific actress, and is now on the way to being an equally terrific writer and director. Bonnie is a fantastic dancer ('street', not ballet!), dance teacher and choreographer. Rosie is a singer-songwriter with her own totally distinctive style (and you can't say that about many girl singer-songwriters these days!). Lyle, my grandson, is also clearly destined to be a musician, he can play anything with strings and can already emote a vocal like most singers never will. Ella and Gracie are only five and six, but they are very special. I know every father and grandad says stuff like that, but you wait and see. I just hope I'll be watching with you. Actually, one of my ambitions—or perhaps daft fantasies—is to see the whole lot of them involved in the same elaborate production. Rosie could turn out to be the catalyst. She has a sort of multi-media attitude to creativity. Rosie Oddie and the Odd Squad is the name of her band, but her vision is that 'the Squad' produces not only music, but also art, video, DJ-ing, the lot. So come on you guys: Kate writes the script and directs. Rosie does the music, featuring Lyle and the girls, and Bonnie choreographs. Laura should do publicity and promotion. I'll sit back, enjoy it, and claim a share of the royalties. So I won't have to work in my old age.

Do you want to retire then?

No way. Seriously and absolutely not. Fortunately, in a sense, I have nothing to retire from. Or rather, there aren't any rules that say I **have** to retire.

The BBC could stop employing you.

Indeed.

People could stop enjoying what you do.

Of course.

You might just run out of energy and enthusiasm.

I did. For nearly two months early in 2008. I didn't like it. I don't want it to happen again.

But it might.

For heaven's sake! It's usually *you* telling *me* not to be negative.

Ah, but I am also you. So which is the real Bill Oddie? You or me?

You mean me or you? Both. Either. I don't know. It's often easier for me to say what something isn't than what it is. For example, if you asked me what's my favourite kind of music . . .

What's your favourite kind of music?

. . . I'd say all sorts. Rock, soul, some country, some folk, some 'world music', but not all of it. I can tell you my most un-favourite, though.

What?

Opera. As it happens, I have met some delightful opera singers, but I can't bear the sound they make. But then, to use the biggest and truest cliché of them all—that's a matter of taste. Knowing what or who you are as a person is more a matter of judgement. And even then, who is the judge?

Religious people would say 'God'.

I would say 'other people'.

Wouldn't you also say 'yourself'? Self-knowledge has always been pretty highly rated throughout history. Didn't Shakespeare say: 'Know thyself'? Or was it 'To thine own self be true'?

He said both, I think. That's one of the few good things I did learn from reading English Literature at uni. In fact, most of my life, I have rather prided myself on being self-aware. I have always thought, and indeed said, that I know myself pretty well. It was only when I turned sixty, and had my first depression, that I realised I don't! Writing this book has confirmed it. I know a lot more about what's happened to me, but I have probably never been less sure about who I am.

But I dare say you know what you are not?

I am not dishonest. I do not avoid the truth about myself, or other people. I am not what I suspect a lot of people—'the public'—think I am.

What do you think they think, then?

That I am mostly cheery and happy-go-lucky. (I am not.) That I live in the country. (I have read that I live in Norfolk! I don't.) That I hate cities. (I live in London and love it.) That I drink real ale. (I don't drink beer at all.) That I am a huge jazz fan. (Not any more!) That Kate Humble and I don't get on. We do!

OK, OK. With respect to Kate—and even you— none of those are exactly meaningful misconceptions. Tell me something more important. Something you are not, that really matters.

OK. It isn't up to me to judge whether or not this

318

matters, but I am NOT an 'expert' on the environment.
I am not totally ignorant, but it is certainly not my
'specialist subject'. If you asked me now to clearly
elucidate on the issues of global warming, the
greenhouse effect, ozone levels, climate change, GM
crops, sustainability, carbon footprints, and the scientific
evidence concerning the state of the world and the
future of mankind, I would be pushed to do it. I am
neither scientist nor sage. I am not even what I'd call an
active conservationist. I have served on various
committees, and my name is on the notepaper of
many of the 'usual' wildlife organisations. I am also
happy to be a figurehead for fund-raising campaigns,
and for the work of groups I support such as The
League Against Cruel Sports, or Friends of the Earth. I
did go through a period where I seriously questioned
the value of 'lending my name' to a cause, but I was
assured that having a celebrity on board made all the
difference between getting media coverage and not.
This is true—which one might consider a rather sad
comment on the state of things—and it's not a major
chore for me to say 'yes' and send a photo, so I often
do. It's hardly worth an OBE, though!

**Expert or not, would you not agree that you have
helped get more people interested in wildlife?**
I said I was not an expert on the 'environment'. That's
not the same as wildlife. I am quite expert on that,
especially birds!

**Sorry. So has your 'expertise' got other people
interested?**
I hope so. I also hope that I am right in believing that if
people enjoy something they will want to protect and
preserve it. Enjoyment of wildlife leads to conservation.

So you are a conservationist?
In so far as I think wildlife is important, yes, of course.

Why is wildlife important?

I really hate that question.

I know. You once said that it was the question that journalists always ask if they haven't bothered to do any research before an interview. You actually vowed that if anyone asked you it again, you wouldn't answer.

Correct. Instead I respond with questions of my own. Why is music important? Why is entertainment, or art, or sport, or anything important? The answer is quite simple: because all these things contribute to 'the quality of life'. Life is important. I'm not going to go on about it. I've said it often enough. So has Attenborough. So have many wiser and more eloquent people than I, and there is plenty of evidence that a large percentage of human beings agree. Added to which, the state of 'nature' is the state of the earth. Where we live. It's not just about wildlife, it's about our life. You know, I really had no intention of coming on all preachy like this.

I believe you. After all, it's not as if you are saying anything we don't all know. And it's not as if anything you say is going to make any difference, is it? Or anything you do. Or anything any of us do. The truth is, we're buggered, aren't we?

I know that if the natural world is buggered, then so are we.

It is, so we are. Am I right?

I don't know. Why should I know? I told you, I am not an expert.

You are a human being, though.

Yes. That is one thing I do know. I also know that whatever is going to happen to the world is up to human beings. Not God. Not even nature. Us. Actually no, that's wrong. It's not us. Not 'ordinary people', like you and me. Not even the 'us' that I was with at

Buckingham Palace. It's up to the people in charge. Not the people getting the gongs, those giving them.

Do you mean the Queen?

Of course not, though it wouldn't do any harm for any of the world's monarchs to vow to save the planet. I am really talking about the people with power. Royalty, presidents—especially *the* President—prime ministers, governments, military leaders, religious leaders, the Pope, leaders of industry and multinational businesses. There are relatively few people in the world who affect and dictate the way millions and millions of the rest of us live, or die. It's up to them. We can each do what we can, and say what we think, but ultimately our future is in their hands.

And do you believe that they will do the right thing? Do you think they all know what the right thing is?

What do you think?

I think no wonder you get depressed. Bill, I don't mind you getting all serious on me, but you realise this is a real bummer. Not the jolly sort of thing you say on *Springwatch* at all.

I wouldn't be allowed. Mustn't mention politics, or name names. But our survival depends on politicians, and individuals, and they do have names. There is no such thing as 'they'. I really mean that. We often use the expression, usually about something we are cross about. 'They are digging up the road again.' 'They have raised income tax.' I use it about the BBC: 'They won't let me say that.' Who are 'they'? It's a person, or people. We know who they are. Or we can find out. If we don't, how can we know who to complain to, or to blame, or even to thank? 'They' don't exist. 'They' is lazy thinking. 'They' is avoiding confrontation.

'They' aren't meant to end like this.

What aren't?

Autobiographies. Can't you say something a bit cheerier to finish off with?

I'm sorry. I didn't mean to get all heavy. A positive ending, that's what they'd like.

'They' being?

The publishers. My editors, Rowena, Helen and Steve. And probably most of my readers, but I don't know all their names. Right then. Here goes. It's a wonderful world. Well, the good bits are! Human beings are capable of wonderful things. Alas, they are also capable of ruining everything. However, I am not saying there is no hope. I am not saying don't bother to feed the birds, or to lag the loft, or to recycle your bottles, or to turn your lights off. I am saying join the Wildlife Trusts, or the RSPB, or anything! I am saying use your vote to support green policies. I am saying protest. I am saying speak out and act on what you believe in. I am not saying give up. I am saying do what you can. But I am not saying it just to you and me, I am saying it to those who have the power.

But are they listening? To you, or anyone else?

That I do not know. One thing I am pretty sure of . . .

What's that?

They haven't read this book!

Bill Oddie
I July 2008

Picture Acknowledgements

Most of the pictures are from the author's collection.

Additional sources: BBC Photo Library, Nigel Bean/ naturepl.com, Dale Cherry, Friedman-Abeles NY, Granada TV, ITV/Rex Features, News International, Ben Osborne/ naturepl.com, Gavin Smith/Camera Press, Richard H. Smith/ Dominic Photography, Southern TV, Sunday Mercury, Thames Television, James Veysey/Camera Press. Every reasonable effort has been made to trace copyright holders, but if there are any errors or omissions, Hodder & Stoughton will be pleased to insert the appropriate acknowledgement in any subsequent edition.